Krishna in Mahabharatham

notionpress.com

Krishna in Mahabharatham

Aravamudan Krishnan

notionpress.com

Notion Press

Old No. 38, New No. 6

McNichols Road, Chetpet

Chennai - 600 031

First Published by Notion Press 2015

ISBN: 978-93-52061-35-8

All names, situations, background and content are purely the imagination of the author. There is no connection to any living or departed beings, or present or past events.

Preface

In the year 2013, I published the book 'Mahabharathathil Krishnan' in Tamil. This book is its English version. The aim is to reach a vast number of readers.

Mahabharatham is one of the great epics of India, written in Sanskrit by Sage Vyasa. Krishna plays an important role in Mahabharatham. It is very difficult to identify who is the hero of Mahabharatham. However, Krishna's role is very crucial in that epic and there would be no Mahabharatham without him. Mahabharatham is essentially a story depicting the rivalry between Pandavas and Kauravas who were first cousins. Pandavas led by Yudhishtra were virtuous, whereas Kauravas led by Duryodana were symbols of evil. Pandavas were compelled to undergo a very long and arduous forest life, after treacherously getting cheated by the wily Kauravas. They faced many dangerous ordeals having been deprived of their own kingdom. They tried to get back the lost kingdom in the legitimate way but failed due to the stubborn and unjustifiable opposition of Kauravas. War became inevitable between the two. Ultimately Kauravas were totally eliminated and Pandavas succeeded. Krishna was an ally of Pandavas throughout.

If Pandavas had emerged out of their exile successfully and had also won the war, it was entirely due to Krishna's direct and indirect assistance throughout, which had restored the glory to Pandavas.

Kauravas had the physical support of the invincible grandfather Bhishma, the formidable teacher Drona, the most valiant ally Karna and hosts of several other great warriors. It would have been impossible for Pandavas to kill them all and register victory, if Krishna had not been associated with them. Bhishma, Drona, Karna, Duryodana and others had to be killed despite their enormous power and skill. Krishna had been identified as the principal architect of vanquishing them all one after another. It was, however, noteworthy that Krishna never touched a weapon in the war. Krishna's role in the entire Mahabharatham has been the subject matter of criticisms. But, a correct reading of the original text in a dispassionate manner and a very strict interpretation of the sequences would reveal that Krishna had acted strictly adhering to established codes of Dharma and warfare. The object of this book is to understand Krishna's role in Mahabharatham truly and in the proper perspective. Krishna was the direct incarnation of Lord Narayana on earth as a man and Lord Narayana would never play a questionable role.

In Mahabharatham, Srimad Bhagawad Gita forms an integral part. It is Bhagawan Krishna's gospel to remove the darkness of Arjuna but its message is for the entire mankind Srimad Bhagawad Gita is a jewel whose glitter shines not only in India but all over the world as it carries several translations. This book contains that subject matter presented as simply as possible.

I commend this book to the readers for their correct understanding of its contents.

A.KRISHNAN

Old 72, New 15, Luz Avenue, 5th Street,

Mylapore, Chennai 600004

29th May 2015.

Ph. No 24992998, 9444022998.

Contents

1. Krishna's Birth

"For protecting the noble people,
And to destroy the evil-doers,
For establishing righteousness (Dharma) firmly,
I incarnate in the earth from one era (Yuga) to another."

This was Lord Krishna's divine voice.

Incarnation as Krishna by SRIMAN NARAYANA, the Most Supreme God was to fulfill the above objectives.

Towards the end of the last Dwapara Yuga, Goddess Earth took the form of a cow and made a prayer to Lord Brahma. Goddess Earth pleaded that She was unable to bear the heavy burden on her caused by innumerable evil-doers and she appealed to Lord Brahma seeking mercy and deliverance from that unbearable burden. Lord Brahma consoled her by revealing that SRIMAN NARAYANA would be born in earth and destroy all the evil elements oppressing it.

Jayan and Vijayan, the two guards of SRIMAN NARAYANA were cursed to be born as Hiranyakshakan and Hiranyakasipu, the cruel Rakshsasas who were dreaded for their innumerable atrocities tormenting the three worlds and SRIMAN NARAYANA took incarnation as VARAHA and NARASIMHA respectively to get rid of them. Ravana and Kumbakarna were the next two cruel Rakshasas, who were killed by SRIMAN NARAYANA who was born as Rama. The third pair was Sisupala and Danthavakra. They were also symbols of evils. SRIMAN NARAYANA was then born as Krishna for killing them. But, Krishna had the broader perspective of reducing the entire burden oppressing the earth due to the several cruelties of the entire community of Rakshasas.

We shall see in this book in detail as to how Krishna carried out all the three principles as enunciated by him.

The story of Krishna is quite long. It is full of great wonders. It contains several astonishing and amazing episodes. SRIMAD BHAGAWATHAM has several stories about Krishna, describing his childish pranks and of his several unimaginable deeds as a toddler, as a child and as a boy. He had played a very large and important part in the wonderful epic MAHABHARATHAM, by assisting the five Pandava brothers in several incredible ways securing for them many victories in tough situations in the manner only he could have done. Even though the aim of this book is to depict Krishna's role in MAHABHARATHAM, it would also be essential to know about the role he had played in SRIMAD BHAGAWATHAM in appropriate situations.

Krishna's birth was itself a great event, but shrouded in unbelievable mystery. The story of his growth was full of his strange happenings, which were awesome and mystical, daring and exhilarating. Though born as any other child from a mother's womb after due period of pregnancy, he showed his divine form to his father and mother very briefly. His way of life right from his birth was full of divine features. The mystery surrounding his birth started even as he appeared on earth, his mother delivering him. His divine perspectives were manifest, even during the days he was sucking the mother's milk, when he was kept in the toddler's cradle. Is it possible to describe in full splendor all his apparently playful acts, but the products of divinity? Can they be counted? Once the great Nammalwar, was immersed in meditation, reflecting in his inner vision, the childish playful acts of Lord Krishna and his concentration was so deep and penetrating that he did not open his eyes for six months! We shall, in this book, try to study the episodes in Mahabharatham, describing how he exhibited his divine qualities in getting his objectives fulfilled, though he did them all as a man.

Devaki was Kamsan's sister. Kamsan was known for his cruelties and he was a dreaded demon. But, he had poured his love and affection on his sister Devaki. After the marriage ceremony of Devaki and Vasudeva was very well celebrated, Kamsan had himself started driving the chariot for taking the married couple to the bride-groom's place. At that time, a voice from the sky was heard disclosing, "Kamsa! The son to be born to Devaki, on her eighth pregnancy would kill you." Kamsan's affection turned into extreme anger. Devaki and Vasudeva were kept in jail immediately.

The secret behind Krishna's birth, as Lord Vishnu's incarnation, was divulged in this context. The fact revealed was that the son to be born on Devaki's eighth pregnancy would kill Kamsan. That message was worded very intelligently. It did not specify that Devaki's eighth son would kill Kamsan. Balarama was born after he grew in Devaki's womb, as her seventh child. But he was shifted to the womb of Rohini, another wife of Vasudeva and so Balarama was born to Rohini. This secret was not known to anyone, including Kamsan. Krishna was born to Devaki, when she conceived him as her eighth child. But Krishna was Devaki's seventh child, and actually born to her, if counted correctly.

Sriman Narayana took the decision to be born to Devaki and Vasudeva as Krishna. His immediate aim was to kill Kamsan. But before Kamsan was killed there were several Rakshasas also killed by Krishna. There were several cruel Rakshasas annihilated by Krishna after Kamsan was killed.

The first six sons born to Devaki were killed by Kamsan mercilessly, immediately after they were born. Devaki became pregnant on the seventh occasion. The seventh child also would have met with the same fate at the hands of Kamsan. Krishna's mysterious strategy started working to save the seventh child. That was for Sriman Narayana to take birth as Devaki's seventh child. Actually Adishesa, Sriman Narayana's divine snake bed, as Sriman Narayana's another manifestation, was to be born to Devaki. He was to grow as Krishna's elder brother and be Krishna's close companion in all his pursuits.

Sriman Narayana summoned Mayadevi (Goddess Durga) and disclosed to Her His grand plan. Rohini was Vasudeva's another wife, living in Nandagopan's palace in Gokulam. The fetus in Devaki's womb, as Devaki's seventh child, was to be transferred to Rohini's womb. Sriman Narayana would be born to Rohini as her son to be known as such to the world. That child was Balarama.

The fetus in Devaki's womb had suddenly disappeared. Everyone believed that Devaki had suffered an abortion. But, the fact was something else, not known to anyone.

The plan drawn by Lord Narayana was taking its course. Krishna was to appear in Devaki's womb as her eighth child. Yasoda, wife of Nandagopan, would also be pregnant at the same time. Mayadevi was to be born to Yasoda as her female child at the same time in Gokulam as Devaki would deliver Krishna, in the jail. Vasudeva would be carrying the just born Krishna to place him by Yasoda's side, who would be unconscious and bring her female child to Devaki as her eighth child. Mayadevi would escape from Kamsan. Krishna was to grow in all grandeur in Gokulam as Nandagopan's son.

As soon as Sriman Narayana was preparing Himself to enter into Devaki's womb, with Vasudeva as His father, there were some awesome features in Vasudeva's body. Vasudeva was shining like Sun and was lustrous like Moon. With Sriman Narayana deciding to be born as a man and with Devaki conceiving Him, Lord Brahma and Lord Siva accompanied by all gods in Heaven reached the jail in which Devaki was kept imprisoned. They began to worship Sriman Narayana. Their prayer, which finds a place in Srimad Bhagawatham, is an outstanding one, unparalleled in beauty. They end their prayer by acknowledging that Sriman Narayana would soon incarnate as a man in Earth and annihilate all those Rakshasas who were oppressing the noble people resorting to unrighteousness by their cruel deeds and they were expressing their gratitude to Sriman Narayana. Devaki thus got herself placed in an exalted status as soon as Krishna entered into her womb. The dark dungeon in which she was kept became a Heaven with all gods appearing there. Devaki also shined like Sun. With Sriman Narayana in her womb, she was resplendent like a burning fire.

Kamsan went to see Devaki in the prison after coming to know that she was pregnant carrying her eighth child. As Sriman Narayana was in her womb, she was looking exceedingly bright in a scintillating manner. The natural smile in her face, caused by the divine grace added to the glow in her whole body, never before seen by anyone. Kamsan realized that Sriman Narayana was growing in her womb and was going to be born soon. He got frightened that he might be killed even at that moment by the baby in her womb, though not born yet. He even thought that he would rather kill Devaki at once before her child was born. But, he did not want to be responsible for causing death to a woman. As soon as he returned to his palace, he saw Sriman Narayana everywhere because of hallucination, in his seat, in the hall, in his bed, in his food and in his drink. He saw Him in his eyes

Krishna was born in the month of Avani (Sravana), on Ashtami Thithi (Eighth day of Moon's growing phase), in Rohini as his birth star. That was the most auspicious time. All those significant happenings, which were to be found in several seasons only, were seen to have synchronized all at the same time then. Rohini star was ascendant in the sky above. All the planets and stars were shining with tremendous luster, offering the most beautiful sight, as though celebrating the event specially. All the four directions in the sky, though they were passing through the rainy season, looked as though that it was the spring season and looked clear, bright and serene. All the cities and villages throughout the earth exhibited a vivid show as though they were in a mood of celebration. Rivers recorded a steady flow of clear water, a spectacular sight to see. Plenty of lotus flowers blossomed in water tanks with great delight. All the trees in the forests showed their respective varieties of flowers, in different colours, spreading themselves thickly in the branches. Bees and birds were humming sweetly, spreading their enchanting music. The wind blew pleasantly. The sacred Homa fires raised by the Brahmins rose up auspiciously, signifying the mental happiness of all the people and their inner feelings of distress caused by Rakshasas turned out to be one of consolation that good says were ahead of them. The Heaven was full of mirth of music and dances. Sages and saints spread flowers everywhere. Lord Vishnu emerged from the womb of Devaki exactly in the midnight. Devaki shined like the full moon, full of glory. Lord Vishnu appeared before Vasudeva and Devaki with His four hands, Sacred Chakra, Sacred Conch, Sacred Mace, with the bright Kaustuba gem in His Chest, bright ear rings in His ears, the yellowish silk garment in His waist and His body resplendent in blue colour like the rainy clouds. Lord Vishnu blessed Vasudeva and Devaki with His extraordinary manifestation, a vision which yogis, saints and sages always long for.

The just born Krishna had to be taken to Gokulam and left there. Yasoda's child, the female child just born to her had to be brought to the prison by Vasudeva. There was a very strong heavy downpour of rain outside, now a change brought about by the Lord. Lightnings and thunders were menacing. Vasudeva and Devaki were still tied strongly by heavy iron chains. The doors of the jails were firmly and strongly locked. Many guards were very brisk in their duties, by walking back and forth vigilantly. But, is it possible to describe the mystery created by Krishna? The chains binding the arms of Vasudeva and Devaki were thrown down, the locks opening automatically. Vasudeva and Devaki were struck with wonder. They saw Lord Vishnu appearing before them in full splendor. Vasudeva was the first to start his heart-rending prayers to Lord Vishnu. That is a brilliant passage in Srimad Bhagawatham. He ended up his prayers by expressing his fear that Kamsan might appear immediately. He prayed to Lord to turn at once into a normal human child, after hiding His divine figure. Devaki also, after seeing with her eyes the brilliance of Lord, started offering her prayers, with great exhilaration. That again is another wonderful passage in Srimad Bhagawatham. She also prayed to Lord Vishnu to change into a normal human child, before Kamsan appeared suddenly in the jail.

For facilitating the child's comfort and protection, a basket with a soft bed and canopy appeared suddenly. The locks everywhere were thrown open automatically. The huge iron doors of the prison cells were flung open. The guards were also thrown into deep slumber, losing their consciousness. Adishesa spread his hoods to be an umbrella to protect the child against rain waters. Yamuna River in floods opened up to provide a safe passage for Vasudeva to cross the river and reach the other bank. All in Gokulam were lying unconscious. Yasoda had no sensation that she had delivered a girl child. Vasudeva left Krishna by her side and took away the girl child. He returned to Mathura and entered into the jail cell. Then all the reverse processes took place and status quo ante was restored. The jail doors were locked again. The locks were all there as before. The guard woke up. Thus, Krishna's mysterious deeds started right from the time of his birth.

Devaki Krishna born in the prison was growing up as Yasoda Krishna in Gokulam.

"On one night, the son born to one woman was growing as the son of another woman, secretly."

Krishna's birth has not been dealt with elaborately in Mahabharatham. However, in this book, it is essential to know, to start with, about the appearance of Krishna on earth.

Krishna's deeds as a child were many, incredible and enchanting. They are to be enjoyed by us by going through Srimad Bhagawatham.

2. Krishna Meets Pandavas — Draupadi's Swayamvaram

Kunthi was Krishna's paternal aunt, as she was the sister of Vasudeva, Krishna's father. The five Pandavas, the sons of Kunthi were therefore Krishna's 'athaans' (meaning aunt's sons), the first cousins, considered as a fond relationship. Krishna had always shown due affection to all the five Pandava brothers, the result of blood relationship. Yudhishtra (Dharmaputra) was the image of straight-forwardness. (Dharma-Righteousness). Dharma was like his breath. His entire thoughts and deeds were shaped by the principles of Dharma. He was like another form of Truth. His four brothers, Bheema, Arjuna, Nakula and Sahadeva were also ingrained in various virtuous qualities. They were not so much devoted to adhering to the principles of Dharma alone to the extent Yudhishtra did. But, they were found to obey to Yudhishtra always. It was no wonder that Krishna had placed his affection on Pandava bothers. A good person will normally be seen aligned with other good persons. It was Krishna's closeness with Pandavas that had led Pandavas to emerge with glory in several ways; enabled them to wriggle out of several challenges successfully; to tackle courageously several difficulties confronting them and to secure victories in wars which they had to fight. However, it was towards Draupadi, Pandava's wife that Krishna showed greater attachment. Draupadi was an ardent and sincere devotee of Krishna, on Whom she placed unswerving faith. Pandavas were no doubt aware of Krishna's divinity. They used to pray to Him now and then, when they were caught in intriguing situations, but it was not as though that they had Krishna dominating their thoughts always. However, for Draupadi Krishna was her God. Krishna was Supreme Soul for her. She had absolute faith on Krishna, to whom she had surrendered. Her surrender to Krishna was so total that it became Krishna's responsibility to protect her visibly or invisibly. There was a strange similarity between the two. Draupadi was also known by name 'Krishna'. Krishna is a Sanskrit name meaning 'black in colour'. Lord Krishna was black in complexion. Draupadi was also black in complexion. Though they both were black in complexion they were enchanting in appearance, unmatched in beauty. We shall see in this book all those episodes in which Krishna performed several rare deeds, rescuing Pandavas and Draupadi, in particular.

Krishna saw Pandava brothers at the time when Draupadi's Swayamvaram took place. It may also be said that Krishna appeared there in order to put an end to a great conflict like situation.

When Pandavas were still very young, they had a miraculous escape along with their mother Kunthi from the palace made of inflammable lac concealed intelligently in it, which was set fire, in accordance with the murderous plot planned by the Kauravas led by Duryodana. They crossed many hurdles and got over tremendous challenges to their safety and ultimately reached a village, in which they were living incognito. It was Duryodana's evil plan to burn alive Pandavas and their mother and to get rid of them once and for all. That plan had the blessings of Dhritharashtra, Kaurava's sinister father. They were able to escape alive only because of the counter plan which Vidura, Pandavas' trustworthy uncle, for their sake, had made. However, Dhritharashtra, Duryodana, his brothers, Karna and all others believed that Pandavas and Kunthi had succumbed, got burnt and were reduced to ashes and they felt very much relieved. The whole world was not aware of what had happened really. There was none even to guess that Pandavas would have escaped alive with their mother. Krishna, however, was certain that Pandavas and their mother were alive.

Draupadi was the daughter of Drupada, King of Panchala. Drupada was a magnificent king and he was greatly valiant. Draupadi had, in fact, appeared from the fire of Homa performed by Drupada. She was, therefore, not grown in the womb of a mother. She was wonderfully beautiful admired by the whole world for her elegance. Though black in complexion, she was like a gem full of natural brilliance.

There were many princes vying to win the hands of Draupadi and King Drupada thought fit to arrange for a Swayamvaram for Draupadi to choose her bridegroom. A mighty challenge had to be met by the one, who deserved to be her husband. That prince should be the top expert in using his hands and eyes with precision and in his minute brain power in such a way that his overall expertise as a valiant personality was put into test for his dexterity to emerge victorious. There was a majestic bow kept in Drupada's grand hall, which had to be lifted first and then stringed. Five arrows made of a special metal had to be set in that bow, one after another. They had to be aimed to pierce through a small aperture in a wheel rotating above. The rotating wheel and the aperture in it were not to be seen by looking at them above straight. Instead their images in plate containing oil, just vertically exactly below should alone be seen with eyes focused below. What a challenge! If Drupada came out with such an unimaginable test for a bridegroom to marry his daughter Draupadi, her eminence as a girl of enormous beauty, personal traits and accomplishments could be understood. (There was a hint that Drupada was aware that Arjuna was alive and he believed that Arjuna would appear and that he would alone emerge victorious in the test or that the test was so devised in such a way that Arjuna alone would be the winner, precluding all other contenders).

The news of Draupadi's Swayamvaram reached the ears of Pandavas. As they were confined to a single village for a long time and had their activities curtailed, they were looking for an opportunity to get mixed with people. News of Draupadi's Swayamvaram had enthused them, but they had no intention to participate in it. They did not abandon their guise as Brahmins and so went to Drupada's capital taking care not to reveal their true identity.

There was countless number of people attending Swayamvaram. Among them, there was considerable number of prominent persons. All the hundred sons of Dhritharashtra, led by Duryodana, the eldest, had assembled in great excitement. Karna was the most significant participant. Sisupala, Jarasandha, Salya were known for their enormous physical strength and valour and they were there with great anxiety and expectation. As Pandavas had not chosen to reveal themselves as those with the royal background, they were found mixing with the ordinary people in the vast crowd which had assembled.

The competition started. Many princes had to hang down their heads in utter shame for having failed. Many kings and princes were unable even to lift the heavy bow. Their performances were miserable and disappointing. Sisupala, Jarasandha and Salya, though succeeded in lifting the bow and stringing it, were unable to aim the arrows accurately. Karna was reputed as the most talented archer among those who had assembled. He lifted the bow. He also stringed it. Draupadi, however, had hatred towards him. She uttered a few unpleasant words which meant that she would not accept Karna and her words were heard by Karna. Karna felt disgusted on hearing them. As destiny played its part, Karna had to abandon his effort and walk out.

There was none to succeed and so there was an uproar. All started jeering at Draupadi that she was bound to remain a virgin throughout her life and would never be married.

Arjuna, who was in the midst of several other Brahmin spectators, stepped towards the arena. On seeing him, many fellow Brahmins started expressing their reactions. Some said that it would be below the dignity of the Brahmin community to take active direct part in a Swayamvaram to compete. There were some others who remarked boastfully that if a Brahmin did, in fact, succeed, that would prove that there was no challenge which a Brahmin could not meet and record success. There were some who expressed, "Let us see a Brahmin achieving what princes could not. We would look into the repercussions thereafter". There were some who said with pride, " His personality, body structure, appearance, majestic movement, overbearing look, dignity, all these definitely indicate that he is going to succeed."

Krishna and Balarama were two outstanding personalities in the midst of spectators. Their presence was not meant to take direct part in Swayamvaram. There would always be a divine angle in whatever Krishna did. The subsequent happenings would reveal the purpose for which Krishna and Balarama registered their presence there.

Arjuna still in the guise of a Brahmin and without disclosing his identity enquired of Drishtadyumna, "Is a Brahmin permitted to try?" Drishtadyumna was also known for his supreme valour and he was Draupadi's brother.

"There is no bar on anyone to take part in the competition. The participant should be hailing from a respectable family. That is enough. I will not retrace from this assurance. I affirm to you."

Sisupala, Jarasandha, Salya, Karna, Duryodana and others like them, though they had failed in their attempts, got irritated that a Brahmin had shown audacity. Krishna saw and was sure that it was Arjuna who had appeared and shared his joy with Balarama.

Arjuna meditated upon Lord Narayana for a while and then moved towards the great bow. He lifted it and set the string. With no fuss, with no hesitation and with no sign of diffidence, he took the five arrows and sent them one by one to pierce through the aperture in the rotating wheel above, but by concentrating on the image in the oil kept in a plate below. Arjuna had succeeded effortlessly. Draupadi, with great delight, garlanded Arjuna who was still in the guise of a Brahmin.

All those in the main hall and all the spectators had no hint that the 'Brahmin' who had succeeded in Swayamvaram was Arjuna. So far as they were all concerned, all Pandava brothers had perished in the devastating fire in Varanavata. But, there was one exception and that was Krishna, who had come to witness the event specially. It was not at all Krishna's intention to also be a contender for handling the bow. He, in fact, did not ask anyone from his fellow Yadavas also to compete. As for Krishna himself, the purpose of his visit was not just to be a spectator. For Krishna, who was Lord Narayana, it was certain that Arjuna would not fail to take part in Swayamvaram. Though the palace in Varanavata was set on fire and Pandavas were compelled to stay in it on account of the intriguing plot drawn by Kauravas, it would not have been impossible for Krishna to anticipate that Pandavas might not have been burnt but escaped unhurt and Krishna had felt always that way in his inner conscience. However, no proper opportunity arose for him to locate where exactly they were hiding themselves. So far as Krishna was concerned, his visit to Panchala was definitely on the expectation that Vijaya (Arjuna) would be met there. Moreover, Krishna undertook a great responsibility to resolve a mighty issue which had developed there.

For Karna, Salya, Sisupala, Jarasandha, Duryodana and other princes, the event of Draupadi garlanding a Brahmin caused in them a terrible shock and consternation and they felt greatly ashamed of their own failure. Their impudent argument was that Draupadi ought not to have wed an impoverished Brahmin instead of a prince. That led to skirmishes first and then resulted in the outbreak of a war. Arjuna, still as a Brahmin, took a leading part in the war and he crushed Karna inflicting on the latter a humiliating defeat. Bheema, also in the attire of Brahmin, fought against Salya and others and their opponents had to face utter defeat. Krishna could easily recognize Arjuna and Bheema but still kept that secret to himself, excepting for exchanging his delight with Balarama, remarking, "Look! The one who is seen revolving fast like a speeding wheel in the fight is Arjuna only." Pointing towards the other who had vanquished the powerful Salya, Krishna happily commented, "Look! That Brahmin appearing as though he is possessing the strength of many elephants for throwing out Salya and flinging the latter on earth is Bheema only."

Krishna felt that the further prolongation of war might result in untoward complications. He was keen that, in that particular environment, it would not be wise to reveal the true identity of Arjuna and Bheema and that would not be the opportune moment for the truth to come out. Before the situation could become uncontrollable, Krishna intervened and declared loudly, "It is not contrary to principles of justice for Draupadi to marry a Brahmin. There was no ban on a Brahmin for participating in the competition." He thus sought to bring about peace. He managed to prevent a great calamity overtaking Panchala, by his dexterous handling of the tense atmosphere.

In the battlefield, which was facing such a severe storm, it was Krishna's far-sightedness, which prevented further unpleasantness and possible disaster. For Arjuna and Bheema, who were still appearing as Brahmins that was not the opportune time to reveal their true identity. Krishna was conscious of the fact that in case the battles had prolonged, success would certainly be for Arjuna and Bheema. But, before events were allowed to happen as predestined, premature disclosure of truth would complicate matters. There were other three Pandava brothers and there was their mother Kunthi. Krishna could foresee how Draupadi's future would turn out to be. That had to be allowed to happen in a due manner. Arjuna and Bheema must first reach their village along with Draupadi and both of them must continue to be recognized as Brahmins.

Arjuna took Draupadi along with him to meet his mother and brothers. Krishna, in order to get confirmed that whom he saw as Brahmins were in fact Arjuna and Bheema, followed them secretly and reached their village. He saw Kunthi, all the five brothers and Draupadi. Balarama also entered into the hut and offered his respects to his aunt Kunthi. Yudhishtra and his four brothers were surprised to find Krishna and Balarama there.

When Yudhishtra asked them, "How did you come to know that we are here and more particularly that we are still alive", Krishna replied very wisely and aptly, "The place where a fire is kept cannot be hidden. The fire, by virtue of its inherent nature, will betray itself." Krishna should have kept in mind Arjuna's and Bheema's tremendous valour and their irrepressible qualities when he used the metaphor of 'fire'.

Krishna and Balarama left after taking leave of them.

Drupada came to know that Pandavas were all alive and only they have been seen in the guise of Brahmins. Though Arjuna had won Swayamvaram and so became entitled to wed Draupadi, events were such that she had to be the wife of all the five brothers. Draupadi gave her full consent for that proposition.

The marriage ceremony took place on a grand scale. After their marriage, Pandavas and Draupadi along with Kunthi were living in Drupada's palace.

For Dhritharashtra, Duryodana and his brothers, Bhishma, Drona, Karna and others, the news that Pandavas were alive reached them through the well intentioned Vidura. They also came to now that even though Arjuna had succeeded in Swayamvaram and Draupadi had garlanded him, she had married all the five brothers with full consent and that they were living happily with Drupada in his mansion.

For Dhritharashtra, the first shock was that all Pandavas were still alive. His second shock was that the five brothers were remaining united and having Draupadi as their common wife. His third shock was that Drupada, a powerful king and his son Drishtadyumna of very great valour were of full support to Pandavas and that they were all living together.

Dhritharashtra realized that Pandavas were in a far more superior position of strength compared to his own sons. Though Bhishma, Drona and Karna were always associated with him and his sons, he felt clearly that despite their full united support, his own overall strength would not be a match to Pandavas. He was firm in his opinion that with Drupada having been aligned with Pandavas, they were unassailable.

They all held consultations in Hastinapura. There was a suggestion that Pandavas were to be invited back to Hastinapura and half of the kingdom was to be offered to them. Duryodana, Duchhasana and Karna were opposed to that idea vehemently. Bhishma and Drona were in full support of the proposal to entrust Pandavas with half of the kingdom. Dhritharashtra was of the view that maintenance of peace with Pandavas would be the wisest act to do. He desired to send Vidura to Panchala, convey to Pandavas their intention and persuade them to return to Hastinapura at once.

Vidura arrived at Drupada's capital and explained everything in the correct perspective. Yudhishtra and his four brothers had a suspicion that in Dritharashtra's proposal there might be some hidden bait to cause harm to them.

Krishna happened to be with them at that time. Pandavas felt that Krishna's views were necessary and so they made a request to him.

Krishna was always aware of what were going to happen in times to come, what, how and when! He told them, "You may accept the invitation and return to Hastinapura. You may also accept half the kingdom offered to you. But, you must seek Drupada's consent first."

Krishna was Lord Almighty! Krishna, God he was, was able to feel that the stage for the next course of events was getting ready. But, Krishna, as a man, advised Pandavas to seek the counsel of the elderly and respectable Drupada on that important matter.

Drupada gave his consent for Pandavas to accept the proposal brought in by Vidura. Pandavas, after returning to Hastinapura, accepted Dritharashtra's proposal offering them half the kingdom. However, the territory offered to them was barren like a desert. They still accepted it. They were bent on converting that barren land into a rich cultivable, fertile and prosperous area. Krishna brought experts from Dwaraka in order to plan for prosperity and execute it properly and quickly. Krishna had warned Pandavas not to depend on anyone from Hastinapura to help them. Accordingly, due to the assistance provided by Krishna, Kandarvaprastha, a beautiful capital city took shape. Yudhishtra, as its king, along with his four brothers, grew that area as a prosperous territory and its marvelous growth was such that others were envious of its uniqueness. Kandarvaprastha was eventually renamed as Indraprastha, in honour of Indra, who had a major role to play in the construction of the city. Under Yudhishtra's upright and righteous rule, people were all happy and contented.

3. Subhadra's Marriage with Arjuna

A great festival was taking place in Dwaraka. Krishna had brought Arjuna to Dwaraka, as the latter was visiting many holy places on pilgrimage. The city was decorated beautifully and it presented a lovely spectacle. There were celebrations everywhere. All the people were immersed in immense joy due to the recreational extravaganza. They were also enthusiastic to have Arjuna in their midst.

Arjuna and Krishna were walking merrily in the roads of Dwaraka, which was celebrating the festival on a grand scale. They saw Subhadra passing through at that time. Subhadra was the younger sister of Balarama and Krishna. Vasudeva was her father. Subhadra was a highly beautiful girl. She was found wearing exquisite ornaments and attractive garments and she was looking like Goddess of Beauty, in the company of her girlfriends. Arjuna, the moment he saw her as the image of beauty, was enchanted by her and he fell in love to her. Goddess of Love had pervaded in him. Krishna noticed Arjuna having fixed both his eyes on Subhadra, without blink, out of extreme feelings of love and spoke to him, with broad smiles,

"Arjuna! You are now on pilgrimage, mostly visiting holy places known for their sanctity of sacred water resources! How is it that you are now under the spell of passion? She is my sister. Her name is Subhadra. My father is extremely fond of her. If you have lost yourself to her, struck by love, I shall talk to my father."

Arjuna replied, "She, the daughter of Vasudeva is the sister of Va(a)sudeva! Is there anyone who will not be enticed by her beauty? I shall indeed be fortunate to marry her. Tell me how I can attain her. I am prepared to do whatever is needed in order to have her as mine."

Krishna told him "For those girls born in royal families, Swayamvaram is the process normally resorted for selecting a suitable bridegroom. But, I doubt whether, in the case of Subhadra, that method will work. It is not possible to peep into her mind and to know what her mental aspirations are or what her expectations are. Those, who are familiar with scriptures, are of the view that it would be admirable for princes known for their valour to kidnap beautiful girls forcibly and marry them. Arjuna! You, therefore, carry away my sister. Who knows what will be her preference, if Swayamvaram is arranged for her?"

Balarama, in fact, desired to offer Subhadra to Duryodana in marriage. Krishna was aware of that. Krishna felt that in case Swayamvaram was to take place that would lead to complications.

Arjuna and Krishnan thought fit to consult with Yudhishtra first. A suitable messenger was sent secretly to Yudhishtra and they got the consent.

Arjuna came to know that Subhadra, for participating in the festival, would be proceeding to Raivathika hills. As he had succeeded in obtaining Yudhishtra's consent, he, after consulting with Krishna, drew a plan to kidnap Subhadra.

He collected weapons and swords and kept them with him. He also covered his entire body by spreading thick leather made shields. He got into Krishna's gold chariot. Subhadra had completed her prayers in Raivathika hills. She bowed to Brahmins respectfully. After properly circumambulating deities, she started to return to Dwaraka. Arjuna, under the full spell of love towards Subhadra, approached her, and after lifting her up, placed her on the chariot. Subhadra was very ecstatic, as she knew that it was Arjuna carrying her away and she too loved very much to marry him. She, therefore, was in Arjuna's company with great enthusiasm and they were driving fast towards Indraprastha.

Yadava heroes were all shocked. They, in thousands, took weapons on their hands and they began to chase Arjuna in order to attack him. When Balarama was apprised of these developments, he began to consult with Yadavas. He also blamed them saying, "What were you doing? Krishna is seen remaining silent. You should not get enraged before getting Krishna's views first. Let him express his view. You carry out whatever his desire is."

Balarama then spoke to Krishna, "Krishna! You are not uttering a word. What are you looking at, remaining silent? Krishna! Arjuna was given a warm reception, by honouring your words. He was also treated with respect. That mean fellow does not deserve our courtesies. Will one throw away and break the plate on which he was served with rich dishes as feast? A person, born in a noble family, although he may be desirous of selecting a girl for marrying her, should not behave in this outrageous manner. He ought not to have betrayed his hosts. He has put us into shame. He has insulted you. He is now inviting death to himself, by kidnapping Subhadra. He has kicked my head down with his feet. How can I tolerate it? I shall alone, single-handed, in my rage, take upon myself the task of vanquishing all princes and kings on earth. I shall not tolerate the grave misdeed of Arjuna."

All Yadavas shouted in support of Balarama. Krishna, however, began to utter these words, which were just and with good intentions.

"Arjuna has, in fact, supported our family by his deed. He never considered us as vain onlookers. Pandavas are also doubtful whether a Swayamvaram would end up with an auspicious note. Is it desirable to give away a girl cheaply in the name of Swayamvaram? Is she a commodity for sale in a shop? Arjuna has decided to carry away Subhadra forcibly. Scriptures permit that. This manner of marriage is proper. Subhadra is a girl full of several accomplishments. Arjuna is also an outstanding prince. He is the son of Kunthi. He belongs to Bharatha dynasty. There is none in the world comparable to him. He is capable of defeating Indra even. His chariot is known for its unparalleled glory. The horses in his possession are those which were gifted by me to him. It will be proper for us to seek peace with him and invite him. If he were to engage us in war, he will reach Indraprastha after crushing us into defeat and that would do grave damage to our fame. There is no insult to us if we get along with him in peace."

Krishna's words were accepted by Balarama and Yadavas. The marriage of Arjuna with Subhadra took place on a grand scale, Krishna playing a splendid role in the marriage ceremony.

4.1. Rajasuya Yagam

Mayan happened to be very closely known to Arjuna. "I was saved by you. In token of my gratitude to you, I should offer something priceless, which no one else would even imagine to do. In the same way Viswakarma is for Devas (Gods), I am the foremost architect for Asuras (Rakshasas). Please give me an opportunity" That was Mayan's plea to Arjuna.

Mayan would have been burnt to ashes in a devastating fire which raged in a fearsome forest. He was saved by Arjuna, in accompaniment with Krishna.

Arjuna told him, "You are the one who has been saved by me. It will not be proper for me to expect any help from you." As Mayan was repeatedly insisting, Arjuna expressed, "You do something of benefit to Krishna. Whatever you do for the sake of Krishna would tantamount to showing your gratitude to me." Arjuna thus diverted Mayan towards Krishna.

Krishna was the guardian for the whole Earth. He was the protector of all the people in the world. He never aspired for anything to himself. However, he had determined on one important matter and spoke to Mayan, "Oh! The Greatest among Architects! You are extremely desirous of fulfilling my desire. I want you to plan and construct a new and magnificent palace and a hall, which will create the greatest happiness to Yudhishtra. That hall should be of an outstanding elegance. That should be hailed as the best, the like of which no one should have seen in the whole world. If someone enters into it, he should not have seen anything better than it. That structure should be a combination of all the exquisite concepts of buildings known to Gods, Asuras, and men. That should be the forerunner for any other building to come up."

Krishna had decided on creating a huge royal palace for Yudhishtra, including a Raja Sabha (Royal Court), with an outstanding and elegant appearance, never before seen. Krishna was Lord Almighty and he could foresee what were to happen in the future. Or, perhaps He wanted to set the tone for the events to start happening as already ordained by Him. But, he could not reveal them to anyone. He planned for such a mansion to come up, which would be the first act to set for all important events to happen one after another thereafter, culminating ultimately in his own mission, for having incarnated on Earth, getting fulfilled. Krishna had an especial affection towards Pandavas. Whatever was done by him for the sake of Dharmaputra (Yudhishtra) the eldest, that would mean equal enjoyment and benefit for all the five brothers.

Mayan had that request made to Krishna, because of Arjuna's inducement. However, Krishna, keeping the future in mind, did not prefer to seek any favour for himself. He had the welfare of Pandavas in his mind and with Dharmaputra eventually ascending as the Emperor, he wanted a huge incomparable palace, including the most elegant Raja Sabha to be constructed for the latter.

Mayan was exceedingly pleased to hear Krishna's proposal. He drew a wonderful plan immediately and showed it to Krishna and Arjuna. Mayan had conceived how that palace for Dharmaputra should look like.

Krishna and Arjuna took Mayan to Dharmaputra. Krishna expressed his desire to return to Dwaraka. Krishna, whom the world worshiped, also known as Kesava with his broad attractive eyes proceeded to Dwaraka, to be with his father.

Mayan had completed the entire construction, devoting his entire undiverted attention. No one would have seen a structure like that even in Deva Loka (Heaven) or on earth. One would need extraordinary skill if he was called upon to describe it adequately and fully. Dharmaputra was extremely happy on seeing it, as were his brothers and wife.

Celestial Sage Narada paid a visit to meet Dharmaputra. He was extended a grand reception, consistent with his high divine status. Dharmaputra took Sage Narada around the newly constructed palace and hall and mentioned very proudly, "You, capable of moving with the speed of mind, would have seen several Raja Sabhas everywhere, including Lord Brahma's and Lord Indra's. Have you seen one comparable to what is here, or superior to it?"

Sage Narada replied, "I have not seen anything comparable to this. But, I can describe to you Brahma Sabha and Indra Sabha." So saying, he gave an elaborate description of those divine Sabhas.

Sage Narada, subsequently, suggested, "Oh! Dharmaputra! Raja Suya Yaga is a highly commendable ritual. Only an emperor ruling the entire earth will be able to perform it. Several impediments will occur to prevent its successful completion. All kings of other States are to be conquered and some of them may also have to be killed. That may lead even to the earth's destruction. You think over deeply and decide what is to be done." Sage Narada thus put into Dharmaputra's mind the idea of performing Raja Suya Yaga.

Dharmaputra had developed a great desire to perform Raja Suya Yagam. His brothers and ministers were also supporting that move. However, Dharmaputra was keen to first obtain Krishna's consent for the proposal. He was absolutely right in his decision to seek Krishna's approval on the matter of such a high importance. He, in fact, started to meditate within himself, on these lines.

'Krishna is the foremost among all persons in this world. Even Gods would not have known about his greatness fully. He possesses all capabilities comprehensively. He is also of mighty physical strength. He had chosen to appear in this world, only due to his own choice. There is nothing that he does not know or is not aware of. There is nothing beyond his reach for accomplishment. There is nothing which he cannot bear upon himself.'

With his thoughts running on those lines, he sent a messenger to Dwaraka, with an invitation to Krishna to visit Indraprastha.

(Although Dharmaputra had a keen desire to embark upon that most difficult task of performing Raja Suya Yaga, he did not wish to venture into it without first meeting and consulting with Krishna. The several words of advice given by Krishna were of utmost importance. Apart from offering several words of counsel, he took a significant and important part in conducting the Yaga and completing it. If his initial suggestions had been ignored, Raja Suya Yaga would not have even commenced. Even if commenced, it could not have been completed successfully. Let us see how.)

When Dharmaputra's messenger saw Krishna and told the latter, 'Dharmaputra is keen to meet you,' Krishna replied to him, 'I too desire to meet Dharmaputra.' He then proceeded to Indraprastha.

Dharmaputra, at first, received Krishna and bowed to him respectfully. Though Krishna preferred to conduct himself as Dharmaputra's brother, the latter offered his respects to Krishna as he would do to his father. Bheema also paid his respects with all humility. Krishna called on Kunthi, his dear aunt and made kind enquiries as customary. He was talking to his bosom friend Arjuna with great ecstasy. Nakula and Sahadeva treated Krishna as their own mentor. Pandava brothers, after extending to Krishna all due courtesies, which were normally shown to Lord Almighty, offered to Krishna an exalted seat. When Dharmaputra was satisfied that Krishna had taken adequate rest, he spoke to Krishna,

"Achutha! I am desirous of performing Raja Suya Yaga. But, that cannot be achieved by only wishing to do it. Mere wish will not do. You know fully how that has to be undertaken and conducted. One, who possesses all virtuous qualities, is shown unreserved respect by all and is the supreme head of all the kings of all States, is alone considered worthy of performing that Yaga. But, your words of advice would only be the proper guide for me in this crucial matter. Some around me, who are my consultants, do not prefer to point out my deficiencies, on account of their close intimacy with me. Some, who would see it as an opportunity to further their own personal interests, would tell me flattering words, hiding their true intentions. Some would hold the view that what would do good to themselves, would also be beneficial to all others. Those around us are usually of these categories. You are the only person, who transcends all these divers tendencies. You are the only person who has full control on yourself, devoid of anger and low senses. You are the only one who is in a position to tell me, what shall actually result in the welfare of the whole world."

These were the wonderful words coming out of Dharmaputra, who was immersed in devotion to Krishna and who was always righteous minded. It was no wonder that Dharmaputra spoke like that. These words not only described Dharmaputra's highly noble qualities but also reflected on Krishna's unique greatness. Krishna would never be carried away by flattery of others. He never entertained short term mean-minded thoughts in himself. He never wished to encourage silly and immature approaches to any matter. Instead of looking narrowly at Dharmaputra's sole benefits, he would rather aim at rewarding the whole world with due benefits and his approaches would always be broad-based. Dharmaputra's words were on this background.

Krishna spoke to Dharmaputra in great detail.

"Oh! King belonging to Bharatha Dynasty! You indeed possess all great qualities and you indeed show admirable tendencies meant to exalt you in the eyes of others. They are in great abundance in you. You certainly deserve to perform Raja Suya Yaga. You are in complete knowledge of all the relevant matters. I am left with very little words to tell you. Those kings of various States, now living and about whom we are all aware of, are of inferior caliber, compared to those who have all been killed mercilessly by Parasurama, son of Sage Jamadhagni. Oh! Eminent King! King of this Earth! The kings now left with us on this earth are all found to have their own age long traditions to observe and are also found to draw for themselves their own tenets too. You are aware of them. All kings consider themselves as descendants of either Puru dynasty or Ikshvaku dynasty. There are now one hundred separate races of kings. They have no doubt derived eminence due to their origin. Their numbers have increased. Their standards have also enhanced. and they are spread in different directions. The kings now on this earth have sought to inherit what their forefathers had left for them and to enjoy them. There is one Jarasandha, who has conquered all the kings and had subjugated them. He has appropriated to himself all the riches and precious belongings of the kings under his control and he claims to be their sole master. His authority and domination have spread throughout the center of this land. He has disunited all the kings, who are now divided and separated. Oh! Maharaja! Only that king who is mighty, who has established himself as the master of all other kings with limitless authority and who has his hegemony prevailing all over the earth, deserves to be the Emperor and the undisputed ruler. Oh! King! The mightily valourous Sisupala has succeeded in obtaining Jarasandha's patronage and has become the Supreme Commander of the latter's army. Bhogadatta, the king of Kurusha State, an expert in deceptive techniques is subservient to

Jarasandha, like a disciple. There are other two powerful kings, who have become Jarasandha's slaves. Many and many kings have surrendered to Jarasandha. Bhogadatta, who was very intimate with your father, is now prostrating before Jarasandha, and is lying at the latter's feet. But, he is internally friendly to you. Purujit, son of your maternal uncle and is the torch-bearer of Kunthi race, is alone close to you. Those around Jarasandha are vast in number. Kamsa had married Jarasandha's daughters. Kamsa has been killed by me. Jarasandha is, therefore, opposed to me bitterly. He even attacked us. But, we were unable to conquer him. On our own, we have decided to keep far aloof from him and we are now living in Dwaraka. Oh! King of Bharatha Dynasty! You alone are worthy of becoming the Emperor. You have to bring into your midst all the kings of various States. Raja Suya Yaga cannot be performed unless and until Jarasandha is killed. He has kept under his custody all the kings in his capital city Girivraja. Jarasandha has secured boons from Lord Siva, after performing several Yagas and observing severe penances. He has, therefore, become formidable and there is none to defeat him. Maharaja! If you are to conduct Raja Suya Yaga successfully, Jarasandha has to be killed first and all the kings under his custody should be got released. This is my view. You better take a decision after a great deal of analysis. You please let me know what you wish to do."

Krishna's splendid acumen, knowledge, wisdom and his range of acquaintance with the affairs of the world were those to be acknowledged as wonderful. If Raja Suya Yaga was to be taken up and completed successfully, Dharmaputra should first install himself as the Emperor, as the undisputed single leader for all the kings. He must bring under his control all the kings of all the States in this land. But many kings had already been enslaved by Jarasandha and kept as his captives. When Dharmaputra had sought Krishna's advice, Krishna should lay stress on the actual state prevailing then. Krishna had accepted that Dharmaputra was worthy of performing Raja Suya Yaga. But, the big stumbling block was Jarasandha, who was mightily powerful and formidable and who could not be conquered. Krishna had thereby hinted that the time had come for the elimination of Jarasandha.

Krishna had already succeeded in bringing into being that magnificent palace including the stunningly beautiful hall (Raja Sabha), full of unimaginable and innovative characteristics, designs and architectural marvels far superior even to a similar structure in Heaven (Deva Loka). He had Sage Narada visit Indraprastha and sowed the idea of performing Raja Suya Yaga in Dharmaputra's mind. There were many more to happen in future. Let us have a look at them one after another.

Krishna was able to present the true picture of the conditions prevailing in all the States and about their rulers. If Dharmaputra was to perform Raja Suya Yaga, he had to bring under his control all those kings and be the master of all the States. He would be in a position to take adequate steps to conquer them, only after he had the full knowledge of their actual status. Krishna was thus of assistance to Dharmaputra for the latter to get apprised suitably. Dharmaputra had assumed correctly that a prior consultation with Krishna would be absolutely necessary. He told Krishna,

"You are outstanding in wisdom. No one else would have expressed to me, what all you have done. There is no one in this world to tell me very clearly and without the slightest doubt whatever about the implications of Raja Suya Yaga. Every State has a king no doubt. But, no one has so far installed himself as the Emperor. It is an uphill task to reach that highest status. Desires and aspirations of men are many. They are of varied kinds. Men's expectations are as vast as Earth is. However, peace of mind is the only one outlook which gives me full satisfaction. I shall not attain greatness by performing Raja Suya Yaga. I am very apprehensive after coming to know about Jarasandha's invincible valour, about his formidable strength and about his ruthlessness. After knowing that even you have reservations about opposing him, I cannot dare to call myself as a man of needed strength. I am still debating within myself whether Jarasandha could be killed either by you or by Balarama or by Bheema or by Arjuna."

Dharmaputra thus revealed his lack of courage for performing Raja Suya Yaga. Bheema, after listening to Dharmaputra, came forward to offer his views. He said, "Krishna has brain power. I have physical power. Arjuna has winning power. We three, standing united, shall get rid of Jarasandha like the spreading fire of Yaga."

Arjuna was also emphatic that Jarasandha should be eliminated.

Krishna offered these pertinent remarks, "No one can predict when he will meet with his death. Or it can happen in the night; it can happen in the day time. There is no guarantee that one will escape death only by avoiding taking part in a war."

(We should read Srimad Bhagwath Gita for detailed expositions of Krishna on this subject.)

"By drawing a proper plan with the application of clear and sharp brain, by avoiding to get caught in the web of destiny, by serious endeavours, one can achieve success. Those, who are wise, should fight against enemies. Those opponents may be persons of enormous strength. They may have under their control a well- trained army. But, still success can be registered against them, if a well thought out plan is drawn, by using the brain power and by resorting to strategic methods. Entry into the enemy's camp has to be made first secretly. If, in proper time and in a proper manner, the enemy is attacked, we shall not be disappointed."

4.2. Death of Jarasandha

As Dharmaputra requested Krishna to narrate the story of Jarasandha, Krishna told him,

"There was a king called Bhrahadratha. He was ruling Makara kingdom. There was no one comparable to him in any war. He had two wives. But, he had no son. Once, a sage called Chanda Kousika was in deep meditation under a tree. Brahadratha, accompanied by his two wives, extended very devoted service to that sage, and the sage was immensely pleased. The sage offered to bless the king with a boon. The king prayed, 'I want a son.' When the sage began to meditate, a mango fruit fell on his lap. The sage handed over that fruit to the king, and the latter passed it on to his wives. The two queens cut that fruit into two and each ate one half. They became pregnant eventually. However, when delivery took place, each queen had half of a child. Each half had one eye, one hand, one leg, half belly, half face, half body and thus was exactly half of a full baby. Out of fear, both the queens threw away the two pieces of one baby. They were lying on a road in a corner. At that time, a Rakshasi by name Jara took on her arms both the pieces of that baby. She joined both the pieces together. That became a prince of remarkable valour. The sound emanating from him had the effect of spreading waves of shock throughout the kingdom. Jara entrusted that son with Brahadratha, who was immensely happy. He also named his son as 'Jarasandha' meaning 'united by Jara'. As his son was growing, Sage Chanda Kousika visited the king and said,

'This boy's beauty, physical strength and courage are stable and permanent. He will acquire all greatness. No one will possess as much capabilities as he has. His enemies will all be extinguished. Even the astras of Gods will have no effect on him. All the kings on Earth will be oppressed by him. He will draw into himself the might of all other kings. The whole earth will be under his control.'

"Brahadratha handed over the rulership of the kingdom to Jarasandha, after a few years. Jarasandha, who got crowned as the king is now ruling with great pride that he cannot be conquered by any."

"He has captured so far eighty six kings of other States and kept them under his custody. Once he completes the tally of one hundred kings by capturing them, he will offer them all as sacrifices to Lord Siva and please Him."

"Jarasandha has married the two daughters of Kamsa. He is antagonistic to me as I had killed Kamsa."

"This is the proper time to kill Jarasandha. He cannot be defeated in a war. But, I have a plan to finish him. Bheema has the needed strength. Arjuna has the skill to save both of us. We three, like the three sacred fires facilitating the completion of three Yagas, would put an end to Jarasandha's life. He is full of arrogance. He will offer to fight against us three, on one to one basis. Bheema alone has the strength needed to destroy him. You have full faith on Bheema's strength as well as on me and send Bheema and Arjuna along with me."

Bheema and Arjuna became extremely happy on hearing Krishna's words. Dharmaputra spoke to Krishna,

"Achyutha! Oh! Destroyer of Enemies! You are the guardian of us Pandavas! We are all dependent on you. What all you have uttered are brilliant in wisdom. You never appear before anyone whose face is never looked at by Goddess Lakshmi. I am always ready to abide by your commands. I have come to the conclusion that Jarasandha is deemed to be dead already. I also consider that all the kings kept under his custody stand released. Further, I derive full mental joy that Raja Suya Yaga stands completed successfully. Oh! Guardian of the World! You please take up such measures as are needed for carrying out the task, with great diligence. I cannot live at all without your support. There is nothing which cannot be conquered with Krishna and Arjuna undertaking by joining their hands together. Bheema is outstanding in strength as he is in beauty. He is highly resourceful. When he is with you both, what is there which cannot be accomplished! Water flows where there is a deep cavity! You are the top most expert in statesmanship, for fulfilling the royal expectations. You are capable of completing all tasks."

Dharmaputra continued, "Anything can be won, under Krishna's leadership. He has outstanding wisdom. He has full knowledge of the intricacies of royal issues, by handling them cleverly. His fame is well spread in the world. He should be asked to take up the leadership for any task to be undertaken, before the first step is made. Only Krishna knows in what way a venture is required to be undertaken and what strategies are to drawn up for its fulfillment. Let his brain power, physical strength and achievement motivation act together."

Krishna, Bheema and Arjuna started their journey to the capital of Magadha Desam.

They wore the dresses of Snaathaka Brahmins. Their appearances as Snaathaka Brahmins were astonishing. That was a clear enough message of the impending death of Jarasandha.

The three reached Girivraja, the capital city of Magadha Desam. They avoided entering into the city, through the regular gateway and chose instead a narrow lane to gain entry. (It is customary to skip the regular gateway for entering into the enemy territory). They entered into the city, by walking along a narrow lane in a hill called Chaithyaka, which was a place of worship, established by Brahadratha, father of Jarasandha. They also smashed the peak of Chaithyaka hill. Many Brahmins belonging to Girivraja witnessed those inauspicious events happening before their eyes. They met Jarasandha conveying those messages.

As Krishna, Bheema and Arjuna were wearing the garments of Snaathaka Brahmins, they did not carry any weapons with them. Their arms were like weapons. Many shops were open. Lots of garlands made of flowers and hanging in the shops were for sale. They were wearing some of those garlands. They reached Jarasandha's palace. Again, by avoiding entering into it through the main door, they climbed up the compound wall and jumped into Jarasandha's palace.

(These steps were in accordance with the plan developed by Krishna beforehand).

As they looked like persons hailing from highly illustrious races, they went straight to Jarasandha. Jarasandha also extended to them due courtesies, by offering them welcome. Krishna told Jarasandha, “These two with me are observing some vows. They are, therefore, resorting to (Mauna) silence. They will not talk anything until this midnight. They will converse with you thereafter.”

Jarasandha requested them to stay in their Yaga Sala (Hall of Rituals) that night.

Krishna, Bheema and Arjuna went to meet Jarasandha at the midnight. Jarasandha gave them permission to meet him and adhered to the tradition of honouring the guests, who were Brahmins, despite the midnight at that time.

Krishna, by way of greeting Jarasandha said, “Let you attain the Holy Heaven with no strains on your part.” Bheema and Arjuna looked at each other cryptically when they heard those words of Krishna.

Jarasandha offered them seats. It was not as though Jarasandha did not feel suspicious of them. He told them, “Brahmins, while observing the vow of Snaathaka, would not were garlands in their necks and would not apply fragrant sandal paste on their bodies. Though your appearances are of Brahmins, symptoms of royal background are visible in you. Please tell me truthfully who you are. Truth is like an ornament for kings (Rulers). Why did you enter into my city after smashing into pieces Chaithyaka Hill peak, instead of passing through the main gate? The wrath of the King is of no threat for you. Brahmins are experts in the choice of their words. Your deeds are found to be contrary to your outward appearances. What exactly is your objective?”

On hearing this, Krishna, who possessed a great mental equilibrium and who was skillful in his words, replied with great composure and in a majestic tone, "Oh! King! You deem us as Snaathaka Brahmins actually. Brahmins, Kshatriyas (Royals) and Vysias (Trading Community) these three segments of people are permitted to resort to the vows of Snaathaka. They have their own special characteristics, as also those common for all. A Royal (Kshatriya), possessing some special characteristics is seen enjoying some admirable privileges. We are wearing garlands made of flowers. We have applied sandal paste on our bodies. Such persons will acquire some rich rewards and benefits for themselves. For those born in the royal race, strength in their own arms is a natural phenomenon. Conversing skills are also found in them. But, they will not be outrageous. Lord Brahma, the Creator, has conferred on the arms of kings, His own strength. If you are desirous of testing it, you will have an occasion just this night. A wise man will never move into his enemy's place, by passing through the latter's main gate. Only friendly persons adopt the regular straight path. Having entered into the enemy's place, we shall not accept any courtesies shown to us by him, unless our objective is fulfilled."

Jarasandha told Krishna, "I have done no harm to you. I am free from any guilt so far as you are concerned. Why are treating me as your enemy? You are at fault in talking to me in this fashion."

Krishna replied, "An outstanding King, an incomparable King, has taken a determination to uphold the righteous principles of the royal races. We are here as your enemies, on his command to us. You have kept under your custody many kings of this world. Having done so, you claim, 'I have done no harm.' How can one king torture other kings? Having taken them into your custody, you are planning to offer them as sacrifices to Lord Rudra. Your sin may extend to reach us also. We are those adhering to Dharma (Righteousness). We have capabilities to ensure that righteousness prevails and is strictly adhered to. We have not come across instances of human beings offered as sacrifices in Yagas. Why should you offer kings as sacrifices for Lord Sankara? One reaps the result of his actions, depending on their nature and the time of their occurrences. We are here to help those kings, who have been captured by you and tortured by you. We have come here to kill you."

Krishna continued, "Oh! King! You are so arrogant that according to you, there is no one equal to you in valour. That is due to your mental fallacy. You are so envious of your powers that you do not recognize anyone else as either superior to you or equal to you. We are quite capable of opposing you. Your valour is quite within our own to meet. In fact, we are not Brahmins at all. I am Hrishikesh (Krishna). These two are Pandavas. Oh! King of Magadha Desam! We call upon you to fight us. You may choose to fight on one to one basis, on a continuous stretch. You better release all the kings presently under your custody. Or else, you will reach the sky of Yama."

Jarasandha spoke, "I have not imprisoned any king so far, without first fighting against him and defeating him. Is there anyone in my custody now, who has not been defeated by me? I am ready to fight. Shall we fight on the basis of one army against the other's, or on one to one basis straight? I shall accept the challenge and fight."

Krishna asked, "You fight against one of us. Whom do you wish to fight against?"

Jarasandha dismissed the idea of fighting against Krishna as he considered the latter as worthy of being ignored because Krishna belonged to weak Yadava community. He rejected Arjuna because according to him, the latter looked like a weak lad. Bheema was of enormous physical strength. He was also known for extraordinary valour in the utilisation of mace. Jarasandha, therefore, desired to fight against Bheema, on account of the latter's enormous strength and expertise in using the mace as weapon, a matter of ego.

Jarasandha and Bheema began the fight, using maces as their weapons. Both were experts in war. Jarasandha was unable to extricate himself from the firm grip of Bheema. Bheema felt that the proper time had come for putting an end to Jarasandha's life. He, therefore, looked at Krishna meaningfully and Krishna told him, "This Jarasandha is destined to be killed by you only. You, therefore, kill him immediately."

Bheema lifted Jarasandha over his head and swirled the latter rotating one hundred times. He then put Jarasandha's body under both his legs, with the body's back on the floor. Bheema began to break it. Krishna took one dry grass (Dharbha) and tore it into two, using that as the signal for Bheema to do likewise with Jarasandha's body. Bheema took under his grip both the legs of Jarasandha and tore the latter's body vertically into two, from head to feet. Though Jarasandha's body had been split into two identical portions, they rejoined together immediately into one full body and Jarasandha was back to life as before. Fighting between them was resumed. Krishna again took another dry grass and split that into vertically into two parts. But, this time, he placed the two equal parts in such a way that the bottom portion of one part aligned with the top portion of the other part, not making it a whole one. Bheema understood the significance of Krishna's signal. Bheema tore Jarasandha's body into two, kept the head part of Jarasandha's body with the leg portion of the other half. The two portions of Jarasandha's body did not join again and he was dead. His corpse was lying on the floor. Jarasandha's life ended pathetically.

Krishna got into the chariot and took with him Bheema and Arjuna in order to release all the kings kept in imprisonment by Jarasandha.

The kings, who were set free from the prison, began to praise Krishna. They said, "Oh! The Great Hero! Son of Devaki! This sort of virtuous deed on your part is not a wonder at all! You have saved us all, who were sinking in the deep lake called Jarasandha, with the assistance of Bheema and Arjuna. Oh! Lord Maha Vishnu! The most celebrated gem of Yadava Community! We have been saved by you at the time when we are blessed with an auspicious period. Your fame has grown enormously. Oh! Gem among Men! We bow to you with our head worshipping your feet! You please command us as to what requires to be done by us. We shall carry them out, however tough they may be. Why? You may deem that they have been successfully completed."

Krishna told them, "Dharmaputra is keen to perform Raja Suya Yaga. That king has tremendous affinity in adhering to the principles of Dharma (Righteousness).

He craves to establish the honour and dignity of the race of the kings. Knowing from me that this is the outlook of Dharmaputra, you should all come forward to assist him in his endeavor."

All the kings endorsed by assuring, "We shall do so."

Sahadeva, son of Jarasandha, paid his respects to Krishna by bowing to the latter. Krishna made him the king of Maghada Desam.

Krishna accompanied by Bheema and Arjuna returned to Indraprastha. He announced proudly to Dharmaputra, "Bheema has killed the most powerful Jarasandha. All the kings captivated by Jarasandha and kept in Girivraja have been freed."

Dharmaputra reverently worshipped Krishna and embraced Bheema and Arjuna.

Krishna after taking leave of Pandavas returned to Dwaraka,

The killing of Jarasandha is an important episode in Mahabharatham. Krishna had to plan in a subtle but bold manner the strategies to kill him. He carried it out in a precise manner and at the most appropriate time.

Krishna could have himself killed Jarasandha. But, he did not prefer to do so directly. If he had been telling that he had been defeated by Jarasandha that was part of his actual plan, which had greater significances. It was not possible to engage Jarasandha in a war, by amassing a huge army for attacking him. The boon secured by him had given him protection against such an attack with a view to kill him. He was born with two equal half pieces of body, but was joined together by chance to become a giant Rakshasa. He was so immensely powerful that he defeated many kings of several States and held them captive. No army was capable of defeating him. Although he was perpetrating many cruelties on others, he, at the same time, was also seen adhering to some commendable principles. Having known about them in a judicious manner, Krishna had prepared a clever plan, with no loopholes in order to conquer him. Krishna utilized Mayan's services for establishing a huge mansion with rare architectural designs and wonderful structures for Dharmaputra. Sage Narada was brought into picture for inculcating in Dharmaputra an innate desire for performing Raja Suya Yaga. Raja Suya Yaga was meant not merely for installing Dharmaputra as the Emperor. Jarasandha was to be eliminated first. Then ego issues born out of jealousy were to be arisen, on completion of Raja Suya Yaga. Pandavas had to undergo forest life. War had to be fought between Kauravas and Pandavas. The huge burden on Earth had to be destroyed, paving the way for fruition of the purpose for which Lord Vishnu had incarnated as Krishna. Raja Suya Yaga was the first foundation for all those to happen later on. Raja Suya Yaga might have conferred a great glory on Dharmaputra. Krishna had to annihilate the mighty Jarasandha and Sisupala, who were indulging in unbearable atrocities. In Jarasandha's death, Krishna had registered twin objectives. The other achievement was that eighty six kings were brought under Dharmaputra's tutelage on their own volition. There would have been no better righteous path for Dharmaputra to crown himself as the Emperor.

Krishna took advantage of Jarasandha's adherence to some virtuous principles, in order to eliminate him, his own strengths turning against him strangely. One of Jarasandha's principles was that he showed due respect to Brahmins. Another one was that he would accept to fight on one to one basis if invited to meet a challenge. Because Krishna knew that Jarasandha would not fail to show respect to Brahmins, he took along with him Bheema and Arjuna disguised as Brahmins. Krishna accomplished what he aimed at, by the clever use of his brain power, which could not be done by deployment of an army. A question might arise as to whether it was proper to disguise as a Brahmin, in a fraudulent manner. Krishna had himself clarified to Jarasandha that Kshatriyas (Royal descendants) and Vysias (Traders) were permitted to adopt vow as Snaathaka Brahmins. Again, for vanquishing Jarasandha, the only means available was to challenge him on one to one fight. Krishna, in a righteous way, offered to Jarasandha that the latter could have either himself or Bheema or Arjuna to fight against. Jarasandha, who was proud of his own strength, would not come forward to fight against another one of questionable strength and Krishna, with that as his strategy, asked Bheema to go along with him to Girivraja. Krishna was absolutely certain that only Bheema had the strength to kill Jarasandha and he had the divine message that Bheema alone would kill Jarasandha. The only method would be to tear his body into two pieces. They should not be allowed to lay in a way that that they would rejoin together. Krishna gave clever signals to Bheema to prevent that from happening. Krishna's overall strategy thus succeeded. He saw to it that a great burden oppressing Earth was destroyed. Eighty six kings accepted Dharmaputra as the Emperor voluntarily. There was no obstacle for Dharmaputra in performing Raja Suya Yaga. Sisupala was the next to be got rid of. Krishna's next aim was that. Let us now look into that part of the story.

4.3. Sisupala Killed

There was great prosperity everywhere under Dharmaputra's rule. The people, in great happiness, were immersed in joyous activities. The desire of Dharmaputra for taking steps to perform Raja Suya Yaga was getting intensified. Bheema, Arjuna, Nakula and Sahadeva, the four Pandava brothers, took adventurous expeditions in the four different directions and were amassing success after success. All the kings of different States in Bharat Varsha did not hesitate to accept Dharmaputra as their Emperor. Krishna who knew about what all were happening and what would be happening made a visit to Indraprastha from Dwaraka.

Sage Vyasa describes Krishna in this context,

"Krishna knew everything. All are within his knowledge. He is the most ancient. He is the soul of Vedas. He is unconquerable. Only people with transcendental knowledge can understand him. He is the foremost of all living beings spread all over the world. He is the origin of everything. He is the Creator. He is the one destroying everything at the time of deluge."

In short, Krishna is placed before us as Lord Sriman Narayana.

The most important event of putting an end to Jarasandha had taken place, paving the way for Raja Suya

Yaga. The kings kept under his custody were got released. They all had accepted Dharmaputra as the emperor. Pandava brothers, by undertaking various adventurous expeditions in all the four directions, had brought the kings of all the States, to accept Dharmaputra as their paramount leader. Krishna, known as Kesava also, had been in the background of all these achievements.

As soon as Krishna entered into the city of Indraprastha, it began to shine brilliantly like a place engulfed in darkness getting illuminated by Sun's rays. Dharmaputra, accompanied by his brothers, sages, ministers and other prominent persons, accorded to Krishna a hearty welcome and he addressed Krishna,

"Krishna! It is because of you that this whole earth has come under my hegemony. All the treasures heaped here have become mine due to your grace. You please accord me permission to undertake the performance of Raja Suya Yaga. For one to conduct it properly, along with you and in the company of my brothers, you should guide us. Govinda! I request you to accept the first prominent qualifying ritual (Diksha) before the commencement of Yaga. When you have Yaga performed duly, I shall be rid of all sins and become pure and clean. If you permit us, my brothers and I shall also adore ourselves with the qualifying rituals (Dikshas). We are eager to be benefitted by the most virtuous Yaga."

Krishna after praising Dharmaputra for his virtuous qualities, said,

"Oh! Best among Kings! You deserve to be honoured with the title of Emperor! Raja Suya Yaga will accordingly be performed. When you complete it successfully and when you attain the benefit of that Yaga, we shall all rejoice that we have achieved a great victory. My thought has always been your prosperity. That indeed is my outlook. You please command me as to what role I should undertake in the performance of Yaga. I shall be bound by your order."

Dharmaputra told Krishna, "Krishna! That you have come over here in response to our wishes is itself a sure indication that my effort will bear fruit. My job will certainly be carried out successfully."

Arrangements for performing Raja Suya Yaga had commenced. Pandavas, with great enthusiasm and immense vigour plunged into action to make Yaga a grand success.

As an important step, Dharmaputra asked Nakula to visit Hastinapura for inviting Bhishma, Drona, Dhritharashtra, Kripa and Duryodana brothers. They all arrived at Indraprastham for attending the ceremony. Many kings from different States all over had also assembled in great numbers in Indraprastham. Dharmaputra was in immense joy. He also distributed various tasks for several individuals. Krishna was entrusted with the sacred duty of according due welcome to Brahmins, for washing their feet reverently as customary and to look after their comforts. Actually, Krishna had himself volunteered for that engagement. Krishna, who was in fact Lord Vishnu, had expressed His wish to take up that sacred duty, believing that He would stand fully benefitted by duly honouring Brahmins that way.

The most crucial moment for commencement of Raja Suya Yaga was round the corner. Dharmaputra requested all the invitees to occupy their respective seats earmarked for them with due care. He turned his face towards Krishna. Krishna's face was resplendent like the glow of Sun. Krishna was the Guardian of Universe (Janardhana). He was the storehouse of all energies sustaining the Universe. Sages, Saints and enlightened persons too had not known about His true manifestation. He was the source of origin for all living beings and non-living objects. He will not allow all those who have surrendered to Him to remain helpless. He had no beginning; He had no end. He was the One destroying all His enemies. He was the One who had conquered anger (Krotha) and petty desires (Kama). He was the refuge for those caught in catastrophe. He was the One who was not influenced by the three passages of time, namely, past, present and future. His graces are countless. Dharmaputra, by way of honouring Him, offered the noblest seat, a seat which was never occupied by any one before, to Krishna, Who was shining like Sun.

(Krishna is thus described and even more poignantly in Mahabharatham. It was Krishna who made Raja Suya Yaga possible of getting performed. He was going to take a very important role in that Yaga. There were protests and oppositions against him. Krishna had eliminated them all. Let us proceed.)

Argyam (Honour by way of pouring water in the palms reverentially) was about to be offered to the most distinguished guest, as the first ritual. Dharmaputra made an appeal to Bhishma in that regard. Bhishma was the eldest for the race of Pandavas. Bhishma was also an enlightened personality. Dharmaputra's action in making his appeal to

Bhishma was the wisest and the most desirable step. He addressed Bhishma,

"Oh! The First among Kauravas! Son of Santhanu! Revered Bhishma! Oh! Grandfather! You please let me know and let me hear from you as to who that first person is to be and guide me as to how I should proceed."

Bhishma made a thorough appraisal with his superior wisdom and came to the conclusion that only Krishna deserved to be the first, among all in the world, to receive that honour and that only Krishna deserved to be chosen for that first reverential worship and that was the result of his wholehearted opinion. He proclaimed in the assembly,

"Like Sun, who, with its own natural glow, shines in the midst of the stars and planets, Krishna has graced us with his presence here and has distinguished himself before us, because of his brilliant resplendence, superior valour, immense power and unmatched stature in the midst of several Kings, Rulers and Experts who have assembled here. He is like Sun in the territory in darkness without sunshine; he is like the Wind in a territory which is devoid of circulation of air. He is here spreading glow in this venue of Yaga and is plunging us to great rejoice and bliss."

Sahadeva, who was permitted and prompted by the elderly Bhishma, walked towards Krishna and in order to offer to the latter the first honour, Sahadeva, reached the vicinity of Krishna. Krishna was also mentally prepared to accept that offer. All the kings in the assembly looked at one another's face, exchanging meaningful message of unanimity and were glad to endorse the suggestion to honour Krishna. However, Sisupala alone could not bear with the choice of Krishna to accept the first honour. He began to talk abusively about Bhishma and Dharmaputra, in the presence of those eminent persons in the assembly and also started to condemn and deride Krishna. He said,

"Oh! Descendent of Kuru! In this assembly of eminent and famous rulers, who have graced us by their august presence, this man, born as a Yadava, does not deserve to be chosen for this royal honour. He may be admired by Pandavas as great and revered by them. But, their action to exalt Krishna to be adored in this way is not symbolic of their own greatness. Oh! Pandavas! You are still only youths! You do not understand what righteousness (Dharma) means. Righteousness has many delicate implications. It has several minute dimensions. Bhishma, who is after all the son of a river, is deficient in wisdom. He has, therefore, ignored the guidelines prescribed in the holy texts in this regard."

"Oh! Bhishma! If a man like you, possessing virtuous qualities and observing laudable traditions, is to conduct himself in such a way that only opportunistic benefits are sought, he is fit to be condemned by those who are wise and who are choosing to be straightforward with integrity. This man is born as a Yadava. He is not a king. How is he eligible to be treated with respect by all those assembled here who are kings?"

"Oh! Dharmaputra! If elderliness on account of age is the criterion, Vasudeva (Krishna's father) is here satisfying that qualification. How is it proper for him to offer respects to his own son? If you want to choose one who is interested in your welfare and who is also closely associated with you, Drupada is here. If you want to choose a great Teacher

(Acharya) Drona is here. If your outlook is for one who is competent to help you in performing this Yaga, Vyasa has graced you with his presence here. That most eminent one among the mankind, who has also the great distinction of not meeting with death, until and unless he himself volunteers to embrace it, that Bhishma has come over here. Why then have you chosen Krishna? Aswaththama, Duryodana and Kripa are here. Karna, the disciple of Parasurama is here. If you had already made up your mind to honour Krishna, you need not have sent invitations to all the kings."

"We have not been offering monetary tributes to Dharmaputra out of fear, or for seeking personal gains, or because of love for him, or with a view to appease him. As he adopts righteousness and is desirous of adorning himself as the Emperor of Earth, we have honoured him by offering the tributes of wealth to him. He is now insulting us. The word 'Dharma' in his name has been earned by him not because of legitimacy! This wretched fellow has slaughtered the eminent Jarasandha in an unrighteous manner. Dharma (Righteousness) has deserted Dharmaputra! On account of his silliness, Krishna is being honoured specially. Oh! Janardhana! These forlorn Pandavas, who have been left as orphans, on account of the fear engulfing them, have behaved meanly and you should have guided them properly and come forward to reject their offer. Why have you accepted this honour, which you do not deserve? You should have rejected outright this honour, offered to you by these mean- minded persons. Like a dog licking happily the ghee spilled on the ground, you are accepting the offer which you do not deserve. It is not as though that their deed is meant to show disrespect to the kings. On the other hand, Pandavas have insulted you. For you, who is not a king, like the wife of one who is impotent, like a rare spectacle appearing before a blind man, this honour to you is a sheer waste. It is now evident as to what sort of person Dharmaputra is, what sort of person Bhishma is and what sort of person Krishna is. Those, who have assembled here, have also revealed their true identity."

After bursting out, Sisupala walked out of the assembly hall. There were some kings too following him.

Dharmaputra tried to reach Sisupala and spoke in a conciliatory tone, also in an appealing way,

"Do not insult Bhishma by accusing him that he was ignorant of the principles of Dharma (Righteousness). Many kings, who are elders in age, have endorsed the proposal to honour Krishna. You must also accept that. Bhishma has full knowledge of everything about Krishna. You have not understood about Krishna to the extent he is aware of."

Bhishma now began to address the gathering,

"Krishna happens to be the eldest of all in this world and is the first among us because of his unparalleled stature. It is not proper to talk to the one softly and in a conciliatory way, who refuses to accept the offer being made to honour him. He, who is the leader of Kshatriyas (Rulers) in combats, having conquered over a Kshatriya and brought him under his tutelage, but still bestowed freedom after releasing him, becomes Guru to the latter."

"There is none in midst of our kings assembled here, who has not been conquered by Krishna, by valour. Krishna is the greatest hero, who is the mightiest in valour and is of undiminished glory. He is to be honoured not only by us, but by all in the three worlds. All important Kshatriyas have been defeated by Krishna, sometime or the other. This vast borderless universe is in stability because of Him. We actually worship Him, who, amidst us, is unequalled and is the most ancient. We have none else to worship. I have bowed to several elders, full of mature wisdom and they have all spoken to me about Krishna's great qualities and superior virtues and about his wonderful capabilities. I have heard from persons depicting the most intelligent Krishna's many astonishing deeds since his birth and praising him enormously. Oh! Sisupala! If we are worshipping Krishna, it is not due to our immature perception, not because we seek gains from him or rewards from him. All those on earth devoted to him who have faith in Lord Almighty, are worshipping him."

(It was no wonder that Bhishma had the inner knowledge that Krishna was actually Lord Narayana. All the activities of Krishna as a child had in fact portrayed him as Supreme God. Even as a baby, he had killed Rakshasi and Rakshasas. As a boy, he had vanquished giant Rakshasas and defeated notorious and powerful kings. Krishna had displayed not only his supreme valour and prowess, but had also shown his great acumen and cleverness. His deeds were full of astounding sagacity. Bhishma, with those divine attributes of Krishna in his mind, had pronounced indirectly that Krishna was Lord Almighty).

Bhishma continued to expound more on Krishna's greatness.

"If we have come forward to extend to Krishna the first honour, that is due to his fame, due to his wonderful valourous deeds, due to his several victories recorded by him. When we were examining whom to select for the first honour of Argya and other salutations, we have not failed to take account the accomplishments of even the youngest. There are, in fact, in this assembly, persons who have achievements to their credit, who have skills and wisdom, enhancing their standing. But, above them all, we have considered carefully and chosen 'Hari' as fit to be honoured first. (It is significant to note that Bhishma refers to Krishna as Hari. Hari is Lord Vishnu.)

Among Brahmins, he possesses superior wisdom; among Kshatriyas, he possesses the most distinguished valour and he is supreme; among Vysias, he possesses wealth and riches of various kinds; among those in the fourth category, he is considered as the eldest, deserving to be honoured. There are two reasons for our worshipping Govinda. He has wonderful expertise in Vedas and all the auxiliaries of Vedas. He is outstanding in valour. Is there anyone in this world superior to Kesava in dignity? Generosity, knowledge, intelligence, wisdom, expertise in Vedas, courage, modesty, success, experience, cleverness, humility, beauty, firmness, mental perfection and equilibrium and abundant prosperity are all those which have enshrined permanently in Achyutha. Therefore, you have to offer the first honour to such an outstanding Krishna, who possesses several unmatched qualifications, who is like our preceptor, like our father, like our teacher, and who deserves to be worshipped. Hrishikesa is one who is capable of helping you in completing this great Yaga. He is worshipped because he is our Preceptor, Snaathaka, King, Friend and Achyutha."

(Bhishma refers to Krishna as Achyutha, Govinda, Kesava, and Hrishikesa)

"Krishna is the most ancient source of the universe. The universe will get dissolved ultimately in him. All moving and non-moving objects have all emanated from him. Krishna was the minutest Prakruthi (Cause - the original source) before the creation process started. He is the Creator. He is Permanent. He is beyond the reach of all living beings. He is, therefore, Achyutha. He is entitled to be worshipped in the most eminent manner. Sun, Moon, Stars, Planets and Directions have all been cast stable in their respective positions, by him and are linked to him. Intellect, Senses, Primary Elements, Ether, Fire, Water, Earth, Air, the four categories of lives have all Krishna as their intrinsic support. Like Agni Hotra which is the most important segment of Veda, like Gayathri among Mantras (Hymns), like a King among the mankind, like the Ocean for the rivers, like Moon among the constellation of stars, like Sun among several resplendent luminaries for all the worlds, like Meru among mountains, like Garuda among the birds, the renowned Kesava is the most important guardian for all the three worlds and for Gods in Heaven too. For whatever period of time this great universe has spread upwards, downwards and laterally and to whatever extent it has grown, only Krishna is their face (Entry Point).

This Sisupala is an ordinary boy. He has not understood Krishna and how great Krishna is. That is why he has been commenting adversely on Krishna at all places and at all times. Persons who have brilliant brains see where Dharma (Righteousness) and high value characteristics prevail. Whether they are young or advanced in age or are reputed, none of them fails to regard Krishna as worthy of their worship. No one else fails to worship Krishna. If Sisupala considers that Krishna is not to be honoured, let him conduct himself in the same way as a person commits a crime"

Bhishma's long address was one which was absolutely scintillating. His observations were as clear as Veda's portrayal of Lord Narayana.

On the conclusion of Bhishma's talk, Sahadeva began to address very excitedly. "If there is anyone in this assembly objecting to Krishna getting honoured, I shall place my foot on his head."

No one came forward to challenge. Celestial Sage Narada was also present in the assembly and he declared, "If there is anyone not willing to honour Krishna, he is as bad as dead, though alive. We should have no communication with him."

Sahadeva walked towards Krishna and completed the act of honouring Krishna first, in the prescribed manner.

Sisupala's anger became uncontrollable. He shouted, "When I am here as the leader of a powerful army, why are you silent? I am going to attack Pandavas and Yadavas."

Sisupala uttered some words to a few kings and asked them to revolt. In response, they also said, "You cannot consider that we too have agreed for the honour extended to Krishna."

Sisupala and a few kings were getting ready to walk out. Krishna realised that they had in fact prepared the ground to wage a war. Dharmaputra, getting worried, spoke to Bhishma, "Many kings seem to have got enraged. What shall we do now? Yaga must take place. No one should be affected in any way."

Bhishma told him, "Dharmaputra! Do not get alarmed. A dog cannot kill a lion. What I have done is for our advantage and is in line with noble principles. These persons are antagonistic to Krishna, in the same manner as the barking dogs are trying to wake up a sleeping lion. Krishna is now like that lion which is sleeping. Thinking that Krishna has not reached the state of being fully awake, Sisupala is endeavouring to convert his fellow kings as lions. This Sisupala has no brains. He, gathering with his other kings, is desirous of marching into the Sky of Death (Abode of Yama) propelled by Krishna, who is the Soul of this Universe. Krishna wishes to absorb to himself the enormous powers and potentialities which are in Sisupala's possession. (Bhishma was aware of what Sisupala was capable of. Sisupala was not of an ordinary caliber. If he had the audacity to challenge Krishna, he must have certainly carried with him that much of strength and courage. Was it not true that Lord Vishnu had taken incarnation as Krishna with a view to kill Sisupala?) Improprieties and mischievous tendencies have begun to mislead Sisupala and his associate kings. Dharmaputra! Madhava is the Creator! He is the one who exterminates all the four lives in the three worlds."

On hearing these words of Bhishma, Sisupala had reached the vortex of anger. He began to abuse Bhishma using unpleasant words. He also poured blasphemous words on Krishna. He was referring to Krishna's various daring deeds since the latter's childhood days, to Krishna's playful but enrapturing activities with all segments of people in Gokulam, to his valourous exploits, to his intellectual brilliance, to his clever strategies, but in a derisive manner by way of ridiculing Krishna and commented disrespectfully on Krishna satirically wondering in what way Krishna was great and in what way they all had portrayed him in superlative terms! He accused Krishna for having engineered Jarasandha's death unjustifiably. He condemned that Krishna's killing of Kamsa was full of blames. For him, Krishna's unique feat of lifting up Govardana Mountain and holding it in his arm for seven consecutive days was not at all a laudable achievement and that Govardana Mountain was after all an insignificant ant hill! He hurled several such abuses on Krishna. Bheema was unable to control himself on listening to Sisupala's malicious outburst. Bheema caught hold of Sisupala's arms. Bhishma pacified Bheema and he began to narrate the story of Sisupala.

"When this Sisupala was born, he was seen possessing three eyes and four arms. When he cried immediately after birth, it resembled the donkey's bray. His father and mother were shocked over the newly born baby's unusual and dangerous features. There were several bad omens all around. They had decided to abandon the child. At that time, a voice was heard from an unseen source in the upper region of the sky (Asareere). It said, 'Oh! King! The son born to you will be very fortunate in his life and will have enormous strength. You do not, therefore, have any apprehensions about him. You nurture him without any inhibitions. He will not meet with death at your hands. This is not the destined time for his death. But, the one who is going to kill him at a later stage is already born, with weapon in his possession.'

On listening to these terrifying words, the fond mother out of pity for the child queried the unseen source of words from the sky, "I bow to you by folding both my hands reverently. Who is the one destined to kill my son? Is he a celestial god or anyone else?"

The voice from the sky replied, "If, as soon as this child is placed on the lap of such a person and the child's extra arms get detached like the five hoods of a serpent and fall on the ground, and the child's third eye vanishes on looking at that person, only that special person will be your son's killer."

Several kings of other States thronged to have a look at this child, after coming to know of its unusual features. King of Chedi (Sisupala's father) received them with due honour. He also kept the baby on the lap of each king. In that way, one thousand kings were tested. But, nothing happened to the child and it continued to remain with no change taking place. Krishna and Balarama also visited that place. King of Chedi's wife happened to be the paternal aunt of Krishna and Balarama. She, after extending due courtesies to them placed the child in Krishna's lap. What a wonder! The child's extra arms got detached and fell on the ground. Its third eye also vanished.

On seeing this significant event, the queen became very apprehensive. She was struck with great grief. She begged Krishna and prayed for a boon, "Oh! Superior Warrior with Mighty Arms! You please grant me a boon. You are the one who relieves the distress of those in grief and grants refuge to those oppressed by fear."

Krishna told the queen, who was his aunt, "Great Lady! Do not be panicky! Do not be fearful of me. Aunt! What is the boon you want me to grant to you? What do you want me to do? Whether I am capable of granting or not, please ask me. I shall abide by what you ask me to do."

The queen, who was Krishna's aunt, made a sincere plea, "Oh! Most Valourous! Gem of Yadava Community! You shall excuse, for my sake, whatever crimes Sisupala perpetrates on you. Oh! My Protector! That is the boon I seek."

Krishna told his aunt, "I shall excuse him if he commits up to one hundred crimes against me, which are otherwise quite fit to cause the death punishment for him. Do not be sad."

(Krishna's words meant that if Sisupala were to go beyond one hundred crimes, the latter would be killed by him.)

Bhishma narrated this story to Bheema. He continued, "If Sisupala is preparing for a war now, it is not due to his own desire. Krishna, the Lord of this Universe, is actually behind this move, kindling it to happen. Sisupala is near to his death. He is after all a tiny portion of Krishna's energy. Krishna is going to withdraw that energy and absorb it within himself."

Sisupala began to abuse Bhishma hurling very harsh words. He, thereafter, challenged Krishna, saying,

"I call upon you for a war. I shall fight until I kill you and Pandavas. Pandavas too are to face extermination. They are to be killed because, without honouring the other kings, they have worshipped you first, although you do not belong to a royal family. They have been bowing to you since their boyhood days, because they regarded you as fit for that. You are unfit for that great honour. You are a slave yourself. You are loathsome. You are not a king. You are here, to be killed by me."

Then, Krishna began to address in a steady manner all the kings and Pandavas in the assembly,

"Oh! Kings! This Sisupala is one with a cruel heart. He is our enemy. He has caused several atrocities to our Yadava community. Although born to a woman from Yadava Community, he has always been antagonistic to us, tarnishing us incessantly. He is the son of my aunt. But, at the time when we were far away, he tried to set fire to Dwaraka. Boja King Ugrasena was engaged in entertainment in a mountainous area then. Still Sisupala massacred Yadavas and kept many in shackles. He stole away the horse, when my father was making preparations for performing Aswa Meda Yaga and his intention was to abort the sacred ritual. He kidnapped the wife of Babu, a Yadava King. This sinner, bent on torturing the wives of others kidnapped them forcibly. With a view to cause me difficulties, he joined hands with Jarasandha. He has perpetrated several crimes against Yadavas by dubious means. By way of respect to my aunt, I have been tolerating hitherto all his atrocities. Now, fortunately for me, his intolerable irritations to us are taking place right in your presence. You have come to know of all the pernicious deeds of this Sisupala against me. All his crimes had been taking place behind my back. Now, in this assembly for what he has committed unjustifiably and arrogantly out of ego and pride, he is fit to be killed by me. I shall not excuse him now for what all he has denigrated me. This fool tried to usurp Rukmini, my wife, only in order to hasten his departure to the gate of death."

On hearing these words of Krishna, all the kings shouted at Sisupala and admonished him. However, Sisupala did not relent. Laughing derisively, he spoke,

"Krishna! Are you not ashamed to talk about Rukmini in this assembly of kings? Rukmini should have become my wife. Will there be one, other than you, who will come forward to mention in the assembly of kings, that his wife had been previously proposed to somebody else? Krishna! Whether you will pardon or not pardon, whether you will talk in a friendly manner or show anger, what can you do to me?"

Krishna had crossed the boundaries of patience. By his divine mental exercise, he summoned His Holy Wheel (Chakra). Holy Chakra had reached Krishna's hand. He pronounced these words loudly,

"Oh! Kings of Earth! You hear me why I have so far been excusing him. By way of respect to his mother who had pleaded with me, I have been tolerating him for the crimes perpetrated by him against me one hundred times. That was the boon which his mother had sought from me, and which I had granted. He has gone above the count of hundred crimes. I shall now kill him in your presence."

Krishna, the Leader of Yadavas, who vanquished his enemies, in anger, aimed His Holy Chakra at Sisupala, severing Sisupala's head from neck. It was as though a peak of mountain was thrown down. There was a huge noise like that of thunder. Sisupala was dead. A brilliant ball of light emanated from his body. It moved towards Krishna and merged with Him.

All the kings saw that rare wonder happening. Rains began to pour down from the sky, which was, however, cloudless. Thunders were fearsome. Earth was shaken. Sages were greeting Krishna.

An important event, signifying the birth of Krishna, as Lord Vishnu's incarnation, had taken place

Slaying of Sisupala is one of the most important events in Mahabharatha. Jaya and Vijaya, the cursed guards in Sri Vaikunta, were born as Sisupala and Dantha Vakra in Krutha Yuga. Krishna's aim, in his incarnation, was to kill Sisupala and Dantha Vakra and many more powerful Rakshasas, thereby reducing the earth's huge burden.

Raja Suya Yaga was performed on a grand scale. When Krishna was preparing to return to Dwaraka, Dharmaputra told these words, with great gratification, "Govinda! With your grace, I have performed this great Raja Suya Yaga in a noteworthy manner. I feel immensely pleased. Kings ruling the States on this earth come under my suzerainty. They have paid huge tributes of riches to me, which are inestimable. How will I agree for you to return to Dwaraka, leaving me alone here? Without you with me, my heart will not at all enjoy happiness."

Krishna met Kunthi to take leave of her. He said, "Aunt! Your sons have attained the high status of respectable and powerful rulers. They have amassed wealth of enormous proportions, which are immeasurable. They have registered several huge victories. Let you remain rejoicing over them. I leave for Dwaraka, with your permission."

Krishna took leave of Draupadi and Subhadra also.

5.1. Draupadi Protected

Pandavas lost everything in the gamble, falling as victims to the treachery of Kauravas. Draupadi was also lost by them. Duchhasana drew Draupadi forcibly and brought her in the assembly hall. He was Duryodana's younger brother. If there was any competition between these two brothers for assessing the most atrocious qualities possessed by them, the judgement would end up in utter confusion. Karna's role in exposing Pandavas to unthinkable shame was also extraordinary. He told Duchhasana uttering these harsh words abusing Pandavas,

"All belongings of Pandavas have been won by Sakuni. Draupadi has also become our slave. You remove all the clothes of Pandavas as also those of Draupadi."

Pandavas, out of sheer despair and wretchedness removed their clothes on their own accord. Duchhasana, with no trace of remorse or compassion towards a woman, out of sheer vindictiveness and with no sense of shame and uncontrollable aggressiveness, caught hold of Draupadi's sari covering her and began to remove her sari forcibly. Draupadi was miserably shaken and utterly perplexed. She cried for help. The five Pandava brothers were aghast and speechless. They did not have the temerity to come forward to step in to stop the treacherous act of exposing Draupadi to face the most shameful onslaught. Draupadi was drowning in the sea of grief. She was struck with the utmost fear that there was none to help her. She was totally helpless and she threw both her hands up. She was a woman and her meager physical feminine power could not resist the masculine energy of that devilish Duchhasana. But, she had a stroke of fortuitous revelation in her. A long time ago, Sage Vasishta Maharishi had counseled her that if she meditated upon Lord Hari while facing the utmost danger to her, she would be protected and she remembered that at that critical moment. She was fortunate to have seen Krishna, that Lord Hari, face to face, a God walking before her many times. But, Krishna was not there before her where that tragedy was overtaking her. Draupadi had her eyes closed. She, meditating upon Krishna, had the vision of Krishna appearing before inner eyes. She prayed and submitted that she was surrendering to Krishna.

"Oh Lord! You are one seen permanently in Sun's Mandala (Circumference)! Narayana! Lotus-eyed! Adorned with the aesthetic peacock's feathers! Decorated with Makara Earrings (Makara is a rare sea creature) Wearing the shining crown! With your personality shining like gold! Holding holy conch, holy wheel, and holy mace in your arms! The resident of Dwaraka! Govinda! With your eyes resembling the lotus! I surrender to you! Please protect me. Achutha! Govinda! Loka Natha! Lakshmi's Consort! Destroyer of Grief! Janardhana! Krishna! Greatly Enlightened Lord! Creator of Universe! Protector of the World! Protect me, surrendering to you."

Draupadi, with these words of utmost sincere prayers and tears flowing from her eyes, surrendered unquestionably to Lord Narayana in the form of Krishna.

Duchhasana, with unmitigated aggression was trying to disrobe Draupadi by pulling her sari out and strip her. But, Krishna's grace had prevailed. No sooner than Duchhasana untied one sari, another one from an unknown source had covered her completely. As Duchhasana managed to pull out the second sari, the third one appeared from nowhere! No harm could be done to Draupadi's modesty. Many and many saris were there covering her in the quickest sequence. There were innumerable saris in different colours and some pure white. Saris were in hundreds and the heap of saris was huge. Duchhasana, unable to bear the physical strain and totally exhausted gave up his obnoxious attempt; fell down in a helpless condition. All those in the assembly hall were wonder struck and were blaming Duchhasana.

(Krishna gave protection to Draupadi, though he was in the unreachable far away Dwaraka. Draupadi's five husbands, who were known for their enormous physical strength, did nothing to intervene and save her. Draupadi had no personal physical strength in herself. Her memory of Lord Hari had dawned on her suddenly, in the right time. She offered the utmost sincere prayers to Krishna. 'Please protect me! There is no one else, to save me.' These were the words of her surrender. Krishna, visible ordinarily, was not present in that assembly hall at that crucial time. But, His grace hastened to reach Draupadi and saved her).

5.2. Krishna's Vow

The defeat sustained by Pandavas in the gamble not only deprived them of all their possessions, everything, but also rendered them as slaves of Kauravas. They were sent on exile to live in the forest for twelve years, and for one more year in such a way that they remained incognito, not recognized at all, with the penalty stipulation that if, during the thirteenth year any one of them was spotted, they would again be forced to remain in exile for another twelve years plus that extra one year.

Krishna had not known about these developments. He would be explaining the reason for it.

Krishna, on coming to know that Pandavas were living in the forest, proceeded to the dense forest for meeting them. His heart was burning in extreme anger. He spoke to them expressing his great grief.

"This earth is going to drink the bloods of Duryodana, Karna, Sakuni, Duchhasana and others responsible for what has happened to Pandavas. We shall, after killing them, and also slaying those around them and the kings supporting them, install Dharmaputra in the throne. The gamblers are to be annihilated. Only that would be the permanent act of Dharma (Righteousness)"

Arjuna pacified Krishna. He began to narrate all the wonderful and brilliant deeds of Krishna, one after another, which were awesome too. After hearing them, Krishna replied to Arjuna,

"Arjuna! I am very closely associated with you; you are closely associated with me. Those, who are united with me, are also united with you. Those, who are united with you, are also united with me. The one, who hates you and is inimical to you, also hates me and is inimical to me. One, who moving along with you always and is in agreement with you, also moves along with me and is in agreement with me. Oh! Arjuna! You are there, irrepressible! You are Nara! I am Narayana! We both, as Nara and Narayana, appeared on earth long ago as saints, with a view to achieve a great purpose. Partha! You are in me! I am in you! You are the most outstanding one born in the race of Bharatha. Anything between us, which may be different, will not be cognizable to others."

(These words of Krishna are from Him as Lord Narayana. Each word is very significant. The intimate friendship between Krishna and Arjuna is the most remarkable phenomenon in Mahabharatham and is the backbone of Mahabharatham. Their friendship was the most powerful one, unassailable.)

Draupadi, who was with them, began to address Krishna. Having been deprived of all the possessions and after escaping from the invasion on her modesty, with then undergoing exile in the forest, Draupadi was meeting Krishna for the first time. In the same way a baby, long separated from its mother, would burst with uncontrollable tears, Draupadi, seeking Krishna's protection, started crying. However, the mental balance had not deserted her. She, praying to Krishna as Lord Narayana, ever ready to rescue those surrendering to Him, made this plea.

"Sage Vyasa and other great elders identify you as Prajapathi, the Creator. You are the Creator of all the worlds. You are Lord Vishnu! You are Yagna! You are also the one performing Yagna. Yagnas are being performed only in order to reach you and to please you. Saints admire you as the one who protects all, tolerating all the faults and you are Satyam (Truth). You are the one emerging from Yagna called Satyam (Truth); you are Brahma, Siva and Indra. You are with them all and all your activities, in their company, are like child's play for you! Deva Loka (The Heaven) is immanent in your Holy Head and the earth is spread under your Holy Feet. All the worlds are contained within your Holy Stomach. Only you are Omnipresent...!"

Draupadi prayed to Krishna on these lines and she did more. She continued,

"Krishna! Having been invigorated out of my devotion to you, I shall now pour out to you all my miseries. All celestials are you and the entire mankind is you. You are Supreme Almighty. Krishna! How was I, the wife of Pandavas, the sister of Drishtadyumna, your friend, dragged to the assembly hall? I was, at that time, in my monthly period. I was wearing a single garment. I was trembling. I was crying, in the presence of several kings in the assembly hall. The cruel sons of Dhritharashtra were jeering at me."

"At that time, Pandavas, Panchalas, Vrishnis and Yadavas were all assembled in the hall. But, none of them had the courage to denounce the act of treating me as a slave. Oh! Krishna! Am I not the daughter-in-law of Bhishma and Dhritharashtra? Yet, despite all my high credentials, I was made a slave. I accuse Pandavas, who are immensely powerful, and who are invincible in any war, for the reason that they remained silent when I, their legitimately married wife, a woman of renown, was dealt with cruelly by Kauravas. Bheema's valour is condemnable! Arjuna's valour, who is proud of possessing the invincible Gandiva Bow, too is condemnable. No one saw them as possessing any valour. This world has an eternal standard of justice. A man however degenerated he may be, must spring up to protect his wife, legitimately married by him. One, who protects his own wife, also protects his progeny. By protecting the progeny, he protects himself. That is because a progeny is in fact a reproduction of one's own self. Pandavas have not shirked their responsibility of protecting others. But, they had deserted me, when I was crying for protection."

Draupadi, after speaking in this manner, told Krishna clearly,

"I am born in a highly noble race. My appearance on this earth was itself very unique, supremely remarkable and unprecedented. I am the fond wife of Pandavas. Krishna! Among all women, I am the most esteemed. I show great affinity to my husbands. Though I carry with me all these praiseworthy credentials, I have been dragged forcibly, with my hair pulled as a rope, in the very presence of Pandavas. Each Pandava is known to be at par with Indra."

After uttering these words, Draupadi covered her face in great grief and wept. She continued, "Krishna! I need your protection which I deserve. There are four reasons for it; our blood relationship: the dignity which I carry: our friendship: your lordship.

(Blood relationship—being the wife of Krishna's aunts' sons

Dignity—having emerged from Holy Yaga Fire and not born from the womb of any woman.

Friendship—due to her devotion to Krishna.

Lordship—Krishna is Lord Narayana's manifestation and so is Paramathma)

After hearing the words of Draupadi, Krishna made this declaration, in the presence of all.

"Oh! Draupadi! Those against whom you are having indignation and anger will leave their respective wives weeping for them, in the same way you are now shedding tears; those women will find their husbands lying on the ground, with their lives lost, on account of the sharp arrows discharged by Arjuna piercing their bodies, resulting in flood of blood flowing out. Do not be sad. Whatever I can I do with my power, will all go to help Pandavas and for their sake. I say this in the name of Satyam (Truth). You will rule as Queen. The sky may fall on Earth; Himalayas Mountain may explode into pieces; Earth may crack to powder; ocean may get dried; my words will not go waste."

This is a very important episode in Mahabharatham. This brings out the vow of Krishna, which tells us in advance of the end of Kauravas and about the ultimate glory attained by Draupadi by becoming the Queen meaning thereby that her husband ascended the throne as Emperor, surrounded by his lovely brothers.

'There is another important unsaid aspect which may be noticed in this episode. Draupadi had not at all mentioned to Krishna that she had been saved from the attempt to disrobe her only by the divine grace (Krishna's). Krishna too had not said that he had, in fact, saved her. Draupadi did not acknowledge to say, 'Krishna! I surrendered to you. You had saved me.' Krishna also did not reply to say, 'Did I not rescue you on that occasion', by way of reminding her. It is not clear why Mahabharatham had remained silent in this regard.

Krishna spoke to Dharmaputra,

"Oh! King! I might have prevented those acts of injustice against you, if I had been in Dwaraka at that time. Even if Dhritharashtra had not sent me an invitation, I would have gone over to participate in the game of gambling played by you. I would have prevented you from playing, for the reason that gambling results in many undesirable consequences. Acquaintance with women, gambling, hunting and drinking habit are the four evils which arise out of cruel desires. People lose all their wealth due to indulgence in these four evils. Wise persons do avoid gambling particularly. I would have prevented Dhritharashtra by words of good counsel. If he had failed to abide by my good words of advice, I would have resorted to the use of force at my command to compel him to desist. If he had attempted to attack me seeking the assistance of his associates, I would have killed them all. Because I was not with you, all these misfortunes had happened to you. Only on my return to Dwaraka, the events of Hastinapura reached my ears. I rushed to see you on account of my worries for your sake."

Dharmaputra asked Krishna, 'Why were you not in Dwaraka? Where were you? What were you doing?'

Krishna explained, "Salwa was angered at me because I had killed Sisupala. He besieged Dwaraka believing that I was there, when I had not returned to Dwaraka after the completion of Raja Suya Yaga. There was a terrible war between Yadavas and Salwa. Pradyumnan, son of Rukmini, defeated Salwa. Salwa retreated and took refuge in an island in the ocean. On reaching Dwaraka, I came to know of all that had happened. I was keen to get rid of Salwa. I fought against him bitterly. He was great in deception by employing magical methods. I killed him by sending my Chakra. "

There is a big story in Mahabharatham about Krishna-Salwa war. Slaying of Salwa was as important as the slaying of Sisupala. That was another incident in which Krishna had to use Chakra to vanquish his foe.

5.3. Krishna Foils Sage Durvasa's Malicious Plan Instigated by Duryodana

Although Pandavas were spending their days in the forest experiencing many difficulties, Duryodana was bent on creating more and more problems for them and to tease them. As though to please him in that regard, a wonderful opportunity arose for him.

Sage Durvasa reached Hastinapura on a visit. He was accompanied by his one thousand disciples. Sage Durvasa was notorious for his outbursts of sudden anger. His anger would end up in unleashing a curse.

Duryodana and his brothers were extending to Sage Durvasa and his disciples a great hospitality, paying excellent attention to keep them fully satisfied. Duryodana was personally attending on the Sage, like the latter's servant. The Sage stayed there for many days. Duryodana was very alert and provided all possible comforts to the Sage, by taking due care, day and night. Durvasa, true to his nature, would subject Duryodana to tests of true fidelity. He would tell, 'I am extremely hungry. Bring me food immediately. I shall bathe and be back.' So saying, he would be away, return late wantonly, state 'I am not going to eat. My stomach is not well' and exit. Sometimes, he would meet Duryodana suddenly and ask him, 'I want to eat now' without any prior intimation. On a few occasions, he would wake up in the midnight and demand, 'I have to eat immediately.' After the food is prepared speedily and ungrudgingly, and with care, he would reject saying, 'No food for me.' Despite all these deliberate irritations, Duryodana was not perturbed. He did not retort with anger. He was not feeling embarrassed. He continued to conduct to the Sage, with due respect and submissiveness. Sage D'urvasa was very much touched by Duryodana's sincerity and said, 'I offer you a boon. I am very much pleased with you. Ask me what you desire.'

Duryodana had already anticipated this sort of outcome and had consulted with Karna and Duchhasana. He made this submission to the Sage,

"Oh! Revered Brahmin! You have honoured me by staying here as my esteemed guest. I request you to also spend a few days with Dharmaputra as his guest. He is known for his upright conduct. He is a big king. He is the most outstanding member of his family. He is the eldest. He treads on the path of Dharma (Righteousness). He is living in the forest, along with his brothers. Draupadi, who is laudable for her qualities, after serving food to the guests, and after her husbands eat, also takes her food, but lastly and then takes rest. You should reach them just at that time. You please go over there in the same way as you have graced me."

Sage Durvasa told Duryodana, "I shall go there for satisfying you" and left. It was obvious to him that the plan was a malicious one and he had no hesitation to collaborate. Duryodana was very happy and catching hold of Karna's hands he said that his expectation would be fulfilled. Karna told Duryodana, "You are very lucky. You have done a marvelous job. Your desire is going to fructify. Your enemies are going to plunge into the ocean of grief. They will have no scope to escape. Falling a victim to Durvasa's wrath, they will be burnt alive. Pandavas will be thrown into the deep hole in earth on account of their own misfortune."

One day, Sage Durvasa reached the place in the forest where Dharmaputra was residing, in accordance with Duryodana's special suggestion. His evil motive was to cause to Pandavas a tremendous misery, tease them, shake their mental equilibrium, confound them with no solution to face the situation and compel them to conduct themselves in such a manner that he would be infuriated. He made his visit taking with him ten thousand disciples in order to make the situation more arduous for Pandavas, whereas he was Duryodana's guest with only one thousand disciples. He chose that particular time to meet Dharmaputra, when the latter and his brothers were taking rest, after serving food to Brahmin guests and after they had consumed their daily food. Draupadi also had her meal and was taking rest. Dharmaputra, true to his in born nature, was elated to receive such a renowned guest who was a great sage and he extended a respectable welcome to Durvasa, with the utmost sincerity and uprightness, quite innocently and he was in the company of his brothers. He offered a proper seat to the Saga. He, with great humility, spoke to the Sage, telling him, "You please have your bath in the river; have your daily ablutions done; finish your prayers and then come back as soon as possible."

The Sage, with all his disciples, went to the river for bathing. He thought within himself, 'How are they going to feed me and my ten thousand disciples?'

Draupadi was horrified. She always had the utmost respect for her husband. She was wondering how the guests were to be treated respectfully and fed. She had no solution for the predicament. The only remedy left to her to seek was to pray to Krishna. She began to offer her prayers.

"Hey Krishna! The Eternal One! Son of Devaki! Vasudeva! Lord of the Universe! Supreme Almighty! Protector of Depressed! Creator of Universe! You are far more superior to those considered as superior! You are the origin of Universe. You are the origin of Wisdom, Intelligence and Uprightness. I bow to you with all humility. You are never tired of bestowing boons. You are the refuge to those who have none to help and nowhere to go. You are the most ancient. You are the life of all living beings. You are beyond comprehension. I surrender to you. Please protect me. You are the one with an attractive bluish complexion. You have eyes resembling the lotus flower. You are adorned with a white silk garment. You have Kaustuba Gem in your chest. You are the origin and you are the ultimate end. You are the origin of everything in Universe. Your holy face is the beacon light for all the directions. You had then saved me from Duchhasana. You release me now from the predicament in which I am caught."

The sincere prayers of Draupadi reached the ears of Krishna! Krishna's smart and elegant moves and their range and variations were always enigmatic. They were not comprehensible. When Draupadi's distraught prayers were appealing to Krishna, who desired to respond forthwith showing his mercy, he was in the company of his beloved consort Rukmini spending some time with her sweetly. He appeared before Draupadi suddenly. Krishna's advent was reminiscent of his mystical and divine attributes. Draupadi worshipped him with her heart choked in emotion and she explained how Sage Durvasa's sudden and untimely visit had caused her alarm.

Krishna told Draupadi, "I am now haunted by hunger. I must take food immediately. You give me food. After I eat, I shall take care of what is to be done for you."

Draupadi was ashamed. She pleaded, "The Akshya Patra (Vessel) which never gets exhausted and gifted to us by Sun God would be full until I consume my food daily. Oh! Loka Natha (Guardian of World)! I have already taken my food and cleaned the vessel. That vessel could not generate food again today."

(Akshya Patra was a divine container in which any food variety would appear as wished for, with no limit on quantity and for any number of persons to eat. Once all had eaten including Draupadi and the vessel was cleaned and kept aloof, it would not be available again to create food for the second time in the same day. Dharmaputra was blessed to have it, to enable him to pass through the twelve years of forest life, without hitch to extend due hospitality to Brahmin guests and for their own daily consumption of food).

Krishna asked her, "This is not the time for playing with each other. I am now in acute hunger. I am tired too. You bring the vessel here immediately. You show it to me."

Due to Krishna's insistence, Draupadi brought Akshya Vessel. Krishna had a close look at its interior. Only one cooked grain and a tiny portion of cooked green leaf were found sticking in a corner as though hiding, the vessel not having been cleaned properly. (Probably by divine grace). Krishna put those two (insignificant?) pieces into his mouth. He spoke these auspicious words to Draupadi.

"Let Bhagawan Hari, Primary Soul of Universe, get gratified happily on account of what I have taken from this vessel, derive the same happiness as He would out of the offerings in a Yaga and grace you."

Krishna called Sahadeva and asked him, "Bring here Sage Durvasa and all his disciples."

Sahadeva went to the river bank in order to meet Sage Durvasa and his disciples and to invite them, as instructed by Krishna. All the ten thousand disciples were then in the midst of the river water bathing themselves. Each one of them was seen running his hands gently over his belly. All of them felt that their stomachs were full. They all represented to Sage Durvasa,

"We have all come to the river for bathing, after asking Dharmaputra to arrange for food for us. Our stomachs are already full up to the neck. How are we to eat more? What will happen to the food got ready for us by Dharmaputra?"

Durvasa told them, "The food prepared for our sake by them would go waste. We have committed breach of trust to Dharmaputra, who is like a saint. If they happen to look at us, we shall be burnt and reduced to ashes. Dharmaputra has the same great power which sages have. I am aware of that. They have great intrinsic devotion to Bhagawan Hari.

Pandavas are noble persons. They are very sincere devotees. They are outstanding in wisdom. They are believers in vows. They earnestly adopt the principles of Dharma (righteousness). They have the powers conferred on them by penance. They owe allegiance to Vasudeva. If angered, they are capable of reducing evil doers to ashes. We shall be burnt like cotton balls. Oh! Disciples! Do not see them at all. You all run away." All the disciples ran away and hid themselves. When Sahadeva reached the river bank, none was to be seen. On enquiring with other sages, he was told that Sage Durvasa and all his disciples had run away to escape.

Pandavas were still waiting for them as they had no knowledge of what had happened. They were worried over the possibility of Durvasa and his disciples appearing suddenly in the night for food.

Krishna told them, "I came to know of the predicament caused to you. I came over here hurriedly. You will not expect any trouble from Durvasa again. After realizing your power of penance, they have all run away. No difficulty will ever confront one who is righteous. I shall get back. All good will happen to you."

Dharmaputra and Draupadi expressed to Krishna respectfully, "Like one reaching the shore with the help of a boat, at a time when he was drowning, we have been saved by you from a mammoth danger."

Krishna's grace is unparalleled.

6.1. End of Pandava's Forest Life - Consultation with Krishna

Pandavas had spent twelve years in the forest and one additional year, incognito, with no one identifying any of them, thus in all for thirteen years. The onerous burden, which Kauravas had placed on their head, had been removed. Pandavas were expecting that the kingdom would be restored to them. All of them were holding consultations among themselves in Virata Desa, where they were staying. Krishna and Balarama had also come to meet them. When Krishna's views were sought, he told them,

"You are aware how Dharmaputra had been defeated in the game of gambling due to the treachery of Sakuni. You are also aware how, as a result, Dharmaputra lost the kingdom and had to undertake the long forest life. Pandavas could have wrested under their control the whole world, because they had that much power and strength. Their chariots are capable of entering majestically Deva Loka (Heaven Above) and hold a parade there, with no restrictions as they could have on this earth. They are bound by Satyam (Truth). They have honoured their vow by remaining aloof for thirteen years. The troubles they have faced, the cruelties they have suffered, the tortures they have experienced and the threats they have got over, were intolerable. They had to carry out inferior menial jobs too. They now expect the kingdom usurped from them to be restored to them and to live comfortably. Let us now examine as to what will be just for Pandavas, what they are entitled to, what is appropriate for them and what should reach them legitimately with the same honour which was their's previously. Dharmaputra, who is righteous, would not aspire to attain even Deva Loka (Heaven Above) by resorting to unethical methods. He would accept even a village, only if it means that he is entitled to it justly. He had lost the vast kingdom, which he had inherited from his forefathers run by them for several ages, on account of the treachery caused to him by the sons of Dhritharashtra, who had committed the despicable act of cheating. He was not defeated by the exercise of valour by the enemies. Dharmaputra wishes prosperity for Kauravas. Pandavas expect earnestly to get back the kingdom, which was their's lawfully and by the show of their strength. Enemies had tried many times to eliminate them by resorting to cruelties and in fraudulent manners, since their boyhood days. Let us keep in mind the enemies' huge undue aspirations and Dharmaputra's respectable uprightness. Pandavas are united because of their mutual affection. They pursue Satyam (Truth). They abide by their promises. If they are hereafter going to be treated unjustly, let them kill Dritharashtra's sons. Dhritharashtra should counsel his sons and ask his well-wishers to pass on good words of advice to them. If Duryodana and others are having faith only in wars, they will all die. If Pandavas believe that they need a big army to support them, let us increase their army strength. We do not know what Duryodana's thinking is and in which direction he will move. Let us, therefore, send an emissary to them. That person whom we choose for this purpose must understand what righteousness is, must be upright, must have a good origin by birth in a respectable family and must be free from dubiousness. He must pave the way for Dhritharashtra to part with half of the kingdom."

Krishna thus expressed his views, which were full of mature ideas, in a dispassionate and righteous manner.

Balarama offered his views. He said, "Dharmaputra ought not to have played the game of gambling. He must resort to peaceful methods only for getting back what he has lost. Only that will last long. If conquered in war, there would be a lasting benefit, but, that will create bitterness and miseries."

Satyaki was very emotional when he said that war was the only option. Drupada said, "War may become inevitable. Let us make preparations for a war. However, we shall choose a highly noble Brahmin as our emissary. I suggest that my preceptor is sent."

Krishna accepted Drupada's suggestion. He spoke, "If Kauravas commend equal rights for us, we shall agree. If, instead of seeking peace, they prefer war path due to their contentious nature and arrogance, let us fight against them."

Krishna returned to Dwaraka.

6.2. Arjuna - Duryodana - Prayer To Krishna

The preceptor of Drupada was sent to Hastinapura as Pandavas' emissary. Pandavas were very brisk in identifying all their supporting kings of States and seeking them as allies in the event of war arising against Kauravas.

As each one was sent to meet the friendly kings, Arjuna went to Dwaraka to meet Krishna.

Duryodana had gathered information from his spies about the preparations being made by Pandavas in case a war became inevitable. Duryodana also reached Dwaraka to meet Krishna and seek the latter's support.

Both Arjuna and Duryodana reached Dwaraka on the same day. However, it was Duryodana, who was ahead of Arjuna in entering into Krishna's mansion. Arjuna entered later. But, Krishna was asleep, when Duryodana as also Arjuna entered into Krishna's palace. Both had a look at Krishna, who was still sleeping. Duryodana, who came first, saw a beautiful well decorated chair kept at the head side of Krishna's bed and sat on it. Arjuna was standing close to Krishna's feet with both his arms folded in reverence.

When Krishna woke up, he saw Arjuna first, who was standing close to his feet, in a manner that the latter was showing respect to Krishna with humility. Krishna saw Duryodana secondly, who was sitting in that decorated chair.

Krishna made his customary enquiries of both of them, first to Arjuna and then to Duryodana.

Duryodana was the first to talk to Krishna. He said, "It will be proper if you support us in a war. Your friendship with me as well as with Arjuna is on even terms. In the same manner he is related to you, I am also related to you. I am the one to come here first to meet you. Ever since the days of our ancestors, it is customary to show preference to that person, who has come over first. Krishna! You are the one with the most outstanding stature in the world! You should follow that precedent and offer to help me first."

Krishna replied, "There is no doubt that you were the first to arrive here. But, my eyes saw Arjuna first. I shall, therefore, offer to help you both. Scriptures say that it is the younger one who is to be chosen first for any preference. I shall, therefore, offer the first chance to Arjuna."

"There are ten crores of Gopas in my army. They are also known as Narayanars. Each one among them possesses as much valour as is needed even to defeat me. I shall place on one side that huge army and I shall personally align myself with the other side. However, I shall not fight in the war. I shall not touch a weapon. Arjuna! What do you choose between the two? I give you the first right to ask, in line with the tradition."

Arjuna requested immediately Krishna to offer to help him. Though Krishna was not to participate in the war directly, and fight, who was He truly? He was Sriman Narayana! He was the one who vanquished all those opposing Him. He was Lord Narayana's incarnation. He was the foremost among all Kshatriyas. He was God of Gods.

Duryodana chose Krishna's vast army. Ten crores of Narayanars were to be on his side.

Duryodana left after taking leave of Krishna. Krishna asked Arjuna, "Why do you prefer me even after knowing that I shall not take a direct part in the war?"

Arjuna replied, "There is no doubt that you have the capacity to kill all. I am also capable of doing so. You are the most outstanding person of all people in the world. I also possess as a single person the capability to destroy all. I shall, therefore, certainly win any war. Even if you are not going to fight in the war, you must help me as my charioteer. That is my desire. That is the aspiration which I have been nurturing in my heart since long days. I request you to please drive the chariot for me."

Krishna spoke with great magnanimity, "Arjuna! If you are equating yourself with me, you, in fact, deserve to do so. I shall drive the chariot for you. Let your desire get fulfilled."

Arjuna returned to Dharmaputra.

This is an important episode in Mahabharatham. Krishna was to be the driver for Arjuna's chariot. Krishna became PARTHASARATHI. He was not holding any weapon in the war. Yet, he led Pandavas on the path of success.

Duryodana had requested Balarama to help him in the war. Balarama refused to align himself in the side opposed to Krishna. He also assured that he would neither assist Pandavas.

6.3. Discussion About Krishna as Emissary

Drupada's preceptor, who was sent as emissary reached Hastinapura. Dhritharashtra, Bhishma and Vidura received him. He talked about the events leading to Pandavas losing their kingdom, about how, in accordance with their vow, they had completed the forest life as also the additional one year of living incognito and that they were desirous of securing back half of the kingdom. He also explained that, although they had experienced several difficulties all these years, they still sought to remain in peace with Kauravas and further that it was not their expectation to fight a war against Kauravas. He also disclosed that Pandavas had already collected an army with strength of seven akshouhinis, as a precaution in case fighting in a war became inevitable. He further stressed clearly that Krishna was on the side of Pandavas, that Krishna's wisdom to plan intelligent approaches and cleverness to comprehend correctly were guiding Pandavas and that Pandavas had the benefit of Krishna's superior strategic power assisting them.

Bhishma expressed the view that establishment of peace was essential. Karna took a tough stand that Pandavas might get back the kingdom, if they spent another thirteen years in the forest. Duryodana and others were opposed to the idea of showing any concession to Pandavas. Dhritharashtra decided to send Sanjaya as their emissary to talk to Pandavas.

Sanjaya met Dharmaputra, Krishna and others and spoke to them in great detail. Dharmaputra told Sanjaya very firmly that if a war broke out, Kauravas would not succeed. He then added, "Sanjaya! We are prepared to tolerate ourselves further for all the acts of injustice perpetrated against us by Kauravas. They should entrust to us back at least that portion of the kingdom which has Indraprastha as its capital."

Sanjaya again expressed as Dritharashtra's messages that war had to be avoided and that to remain content without a war would be the best course. With a view to clarify to Dharmaputra what justice meant, he conveyed, "You have no inclination to be unrighteous. You will not commit sinful acts on account of anger. You will not desire to acquire sins. Patience is the best for you to show. You should not attain prosperity by killing Bhishma, Drona, Karna, Duryodana and others. You may succeed in getting the kingdom. But, old age and death are unavoidable. You may win affection. But, the state of disaffection will also be there. You may find happiness and comfort. But, you cannot avoid difficulty also happening. Let there be no war. If you desire that you ought to go to war for the sake of pleasing others, let you dissociate from them and do not close the path which will lead you to Holy Heaven."

Dharmaputra reacted to say, "The path of righteousness is definitely laudable. You better talk after understanding whether I observe righteousness or seek unrighteousness. I am not the one to be blamed. Righteousness may appear to be unrighteous; unrighteousness may appear to be righteousness. But, it is essential that righteousness must appear to be righteousness and unrighteousness should appear to be unrighteousness. It is true that wise persons, with their proper sense of judgement, perceive everything in its proper perspective. Krishna is the Lord of Dharma (Righteousness). He is the best expert by possessing the correct knowledge of all royal codes and their implications in various dimensions. If I am accused that I do not seek peace, if there is an opinion prevailing that I am not observing the ethical codes established for persons like me, let Krishna who cherishes the welfare for both the sides offer his words of counsel and I shall not transgress them. Let him now talk."

Krishna started to talk elaborately, "Sanjaya! I am keen to seek the welfare for Pandavas, for their prosperity and for their overall good. In the same way, I desire for the everlasting prosperity of Dhritharashtra and his sons. I have been telling Pandavas always to secure peace and nothing else. I believe that Dhritharashtra also aims at it. Pandavas have shown what peace is by their demonstration in a rare and wonderful manner all along. Dritharashtra's sons have shown how over-ambitious they are. Why should a war break out in a big way between the two sides? Sanjaya! You are aware better than Dharmaputra and me as to what is right and what is wrong. For what reason do you find fault with Dharmaputra? Dharmaputra is a great pragmatic and enthusiastic person. He realizes fully what his duties are. He adheres to the traditional methods of maintaining good understanding with his relatives. Why do you say that his appreciable traits have been diminishing? You were talking about Karma (Duty). There are different opinions prevailing about it.

"There is a section of people who say that Moksha (Ultimate Union with Lord Almighty) will be attained by carrying out one's duties. There is another section of persons who oppose that opinion and say that Duty (Karma) aspect may be ignored and further that the path of Gnana (Transcendental Knowledge) would ensure Moksha. However, by taking into account the salient aspects of the high principles of the worthy elements, they do not agree to be satisfied by giving up Karma of 'intake of food'. Gnana alone generates good results, that they lead us to tread on the path of virtues and not others-these are their views. We see the result of Karma as fully evident in this world. One who is thirsty drinks water and is satisfied. The Creator of man has seen to it that through Karma, Karma again shows up. Therefore, fools and the weak accept that all those other than Karma are good enough."

"Gods in Heaven above distinguish themselves on account of their Karmas. Wind circulates because of Karma. Sun, who knows no sleep, who is never idle, produces the day and the night alternatively, non-stop. Moon, also, due to his inherent greatness, ensures the occurrences of Shukla Patcha (Growing Phase) and Krishna Patcha (Waning Phase) and months, unfailingly, sequentially, without sleep and without idleness. Agni (Fire) owing to his tireless attributes offers fire to the living beings on this earth and thus benefits them. Earth bears the heavy weight of its huge structure. Rivers allow waters to flow with speed for peoples' benefit. Indra gives us rains. Indra has attained his highly noble position because of Karma. Brahaspathi too is always engaged in virtuous acts, owing to Karma. In the same way, all planets, Rudra, Adityas, Vasus, Yama (God of Death)and others are in the performance of their respective tasks, incessantly, because of Karma. In spite of being aware of these amazing truths, why do you argue favouring Kauravas?"

"Dharmaputra learns Vedas at all times in order to enhance his knowledge. He has performed successfully Aswameda Yaga and Raja Suya Yaga. He has trained himself ably in driving chariots, riding on horses and in using bows, weapons and shields, in an efficient manner. If, without getting killed, Kauravas can secure beneficial results for themselves by resorting to other means, adherence to their own righteousness may be possible. But, if, on account of destiny, they, who are also susceptible to Karma, happen to lose their lives, their death is also praise-worthy. If you are keen to opt for peace, you answer to my single question. Does the duty of a Kshatriya lie on participation in a war or in abhorrence of war?"

"A Kshatriya has to protect his kingdom. He has to protect his people. He must be profusely generous to those who are pure and upright. He must perform Yagas. He must learn Vedas. Once married, he, in the company of his wife, must lead a worthy life, and get involved actively in righteous activities."

"A King, instead of engaging himself in subservient services to others, must function impartially in matters relating to his subjects and should never get caught in non-virtuous activities. If there is another person, who is superior to himself, and if he realizes that the other person possesses more virtuous qualities, he, by way of recognizing superiority of the latter, should facilitate flow of fruitful results from that person. An evil-minded king will not go along that path. The King who usurps the wealth of others and snatches away their prosperity loses his human nature and gets engaged in wars. Weapons and bows are made only for use in wars. Weapons are to be used to eliminate those indulging in nefarious activities. Righteousness, as a concept, has not taken root in Kauravas' affairs. They are not bound by justice, laws, rules and moral codes. Sanjaya! This is not at all correct. The sons of Dhritharashtra have plundered the inheritance of Pandavas. They have thrown into the wind the codes of ethics set for kings. A thief, irrespective of whether he loots hiding himself or before the very eyes of others, is to be condemned. Do you see anything different, so far as the son of Dhritharashtra is concerned? He claims as righteous what all he tries to acquire by his anger and what he aggrandizes unjustifiably by ambition. Pandavas have their share. Why should Kauravas misappropriate what is legitimately ours? If lives are lost in war, it is commendable. An inherited kingdom is more laudable than a usurped one. You please clarify these fundamental principles to Kauravas. They should know that they are approaching the gate of death."

"Draupadi was crying in front of those who were tyrannical and irrational. Bheema was shunted into such a position that he could do nothing. There were many youngsters on the side of Kauravas. There were elders too. Dhritharashtra did not do what he ought to have done then. If he had acted justly, his sons would have earned good. Duchhasana had dragged Draupadi forcibly to the assembly hall. She was put into shame in front of those who were like her fathers-in-law. Vidura was the lone person who spoke in support of Draupadi. You were also present in the assembly at that time, but you did not come forward to utter a single word. But, yet, you are now offering words of good counsel to Pandavas. Only Draupadi was able to stand good ultimately, opposing the evil. She was able to save Pandavas. What was Karna's satirical tirade against Draupadi? He abused her charging her, 'Oh! Draupadi! You now have no other go. You serve in Dritharashtra's house as a maid. Your husbands, defeated in the game of gambling, will no more be your husbands. Oh! Expert Lady in Love Making! You choose other husbands.' These words of Karna are horrifying. They are dangerously sharp like a knife's edge. They are piercing the heart deeply. They have hurt Arjuna like a burning fire, engulfing his heart in darkness. If I can maintain peace, without acting detrimentally to Pandavas, I shall be deemed to have acted righteously to them. Only good things will happen. I will have the satisfaction of saving Kauravas from destruction. I shall come to talk to Dhritharashtra. I shall stress by telling good words to them. I believe that Kauravas will show me due courtesy. If events are found to happen to the contrary, Dritharashtra's sons, who wander on evil paths, would get burnt on their own accord and would be eliminated totally from every amenity, as Arjuna fights remaining in his chariot and Bheema shows his brilliancy in encounters."

"Duryodana is a vast tree, but full of animosity. Karna is its trunk. Sakuni is its branch. Duchhasana is its flowers and fruits. Dhritharashtra is its root."

"Yudhishtra also is a big tree, but full of righteousness. Arjuna is its trunk. Bheema is its branch. Nakula and

Sahadeva are its flowers and fruits. I, Lord Almighty and Brahmins are its roots."

"Pandavas are worthy of admiration. They follow the path of righteousness. They are ready for war. They are in a state of readiness to fight. But, they seek peace and reconciliation. You apprise Kauravas of everything properly."

(What a speech! Wonderful! Astonishing! Only Krishna as Lord Almighty could have spoken thus.)

Dharmaputra, after talking to Sanjaya again in great detail, spoke about his determined view,

"Tell them. We ask for our share which is legitimately ours. If so done, there will be peace. We, seeking reconciliation, must obtain at least one province of the kingdom. If not, let us get five villages at least. Let there be no war. I am ready for peace. I am ready for war too."

Sanjaya, after taking leave, returned to Hastinapura. He was emphatic, talking to Dhritharashtra, Bhishma, Karna and Duryodana explaining to them everything that seeking Pandavas' friendship would be the most desirable step, and in the event of a war breaking out, Kauravas were sure to get destroyed.

6.4. Sanjaya's Conversation with Dritharashtra - Krishna Glorified

Sanjaya told Dhritharashtra in detail about his talks with Pandavas for seeking an amicable settlement. He expressed that the war could not be averted and Dhritharashtra on hearing that was extremely worried. Dhritharashtra asked Sanjaya, "You are aware of the factual conditions of Pandavas. In what way are they found to be superior to us? In what way are they inferior to us?"

Sanjaya replied, "I am not keeping anything as secret confining to myself. You please listen to me attentively. Arjuna and Vasudeva (Krishna) are both great experts in archery. Chakra (Holy Wheel) in Krishna's hand is a supremely mystic weapon. Its diameter may measure as small as the size of five fingers kept closed in one hand. But, the greatly brilliant Krishna, who uses it, is capable of putting that weapon into action in all incredible ways, with any sort of variations. His Chakra will carry out any silent commands of Krishna."

"That Chakra alone would annihilate Kauravas. On account of its enormous splendor, it presents an appearance of brilliant radiance. It comprehends the enemy's strength instantly and attacks. You may remember that Narakasura, Kamsa, Sisupala and others were killed by Krishna. Krishna is the first and foremost among all men. He is an upright Soul. He is highly noble. He is incomparable. He has the power to exercise full control on the entire earth, by his determination alone. In the same way, he can take control of Heaven above also."

"Krishna would distinguish himself as more powerful, if the entire world on one side is pitted against him on the opposite side, in a war. Krishna has the power to burn all the worlds together into ashes. Krishna is where there is Satyam (Truth); where there is Dharma (Righteousness); where there is modesty; where there is prevalence of uncorrupted human nature; where there is humility. Victory is found only there. It is Krishna, who directs this Earth, Sky and Heaven above. He is the inner soul of all living beings. All these are being done by him playfully. He is going to destroy all your foolish sons, using Pandavas as his device. Your sons are immersed in all evil activities. They show no value for this world. It is Krishna, who keeps the cycle of time (Kala Chakra) rotating. The world keeps rotating because of him. Yugas are his creations. Births and deaths happen as pre-determined by him. He is instrumental for all moving and non-moving objects to function in the manner they do. He is the lord of the world. His Karma is for this world to sustain. He, thus, with his mystic powers, makes the whole world to function. Those who look at him without prejudice are able to know of the true form manifest in him."

"Krishna is the cause of everything. He is integrated with all the atoms of any substance. He is immanent in the entire world. He is omnipresent. It is he who creates all. But, no one has created him. To him, Lord Almighty, who creates all, they reach and merge with him ultimately. For getting near to him, sense organs in us have to be under control. Krishna cannot be known and comprehended as to his true manifest form. He is called VISHNU because he is present everywhere (Omnipresent). It should be understood that 'KRISH' means that he has a form, for our eyes to see and 'NA' means that he possesses the permanent state of cool composure."

"He is known as PUNDARIKAKSHA. By PUNDARI, he is recognized as one permanently pervading everywhere and by AKSHA it is meant that he possesses no quality which needs to be abandoned."

"He frightens those who are cruel. He never quits out of purest of the pure entities (Satva). Satva entities never get detached from him. We see him through the eyes called Vedas. He also sees through the eyes of Vedas. His birth was not out of ordinary, which we know. He is unconquerable. He is unique among all Deities. He possesses everlasting fullness. He carries the whole burden of earth, on his hands. We call him NARAYANA. That is because, the entire humanity is dependent on him. He, who creates and protects, is also called PURUSHOTHAMA. There is nothing which he does not know. He resides permanently in Satyam (Truth). Satyam is rooted in him permanently. He is Satyam of Satyam. Familiarly known to us by the name VISHNU, he is also called JISHNU because he is the conqueror of all Deities. He had no end and so he is called as ANANTHA. He, known by the name GOVINDA keeps all his sense organs under full control. He transforms mystic objects to real ones. No one can comprehend the significances of his various activities which look casual (Leelas). He is the embodiment of all these qualities. He is always pure and clean. He is always virtuous. If he takes part in a war, no life, which deserves no existence, shall survive."

Bhishma advised that Pandavas were to be roped in as friends. Karna spoke excitedly that there should be no compromise with Pandavas. Duryodana also rejected any idea of conciliation. When Sanjaya told them, 'Pandavas expect to be offered at least five villages', Duryodana refuted emphatically, "It is clear that they are afraid of our strength. They cannot get even that much of land of the size of the tip of needle." And he paved the way for the war to take place.

6.5. Krishna Decides to be the Emissary

Dharmaputra, after expressing his points of view, spoke to Krishna, 'Krishna! I ask you to tell me what will be advisable for us to do, as I have always sought your guidance on such critical situations. I should not slip away from the path of righteousness. Good should also happen to the world. Excepting you, there is none else to consult with us and help us when we are in the midst of a crisis. Who else is more intimate to us as a friend? Who is there to take genuine interest for our good? Who else has the capability to weigh the pros and cons, after judging correctly what is likely to happen in the days to come? Who else, other than you, can predict correctly what is likely to be the result of my actions?"

Krishna told Dharmaputra, "I shall go to Kauravas in order to explore for good results to happen for both the sides. If a way can be found to reach a peaceful settlement, without detriment to our interests, I shall consider that as a victory. That will be the noblest act, consistent with Dharma (Righteousness). I shall see the end to the play of destiny, which is threatening Pandavas and Kauravas. Death should not be the net to get caught into."

Dharmaputra said, "Krishna! I do not wish that you go to Kauravas. However much you may talk in a friendly manner for doing good, Duryodana will not listen to you, lending his ears. It is not good for you to get caught in their midst. What will happen to you, if you are harmed by them? You should not imperil yourself in the process of trying to make us happy."

Krishna replied, "I am the one knowing fully the evil tendencies of each one of them. The world will blame us, if I do not go there to talk to them. If I was to be provoked and I get angered, even if all the kings on this earth are to unite for attacking me, they cannot stand before me in a war. They will not be a match for me in valour, like all animals before a lion. If they are to insult me at a time when I am trying to do good for them, I shall burn away Kauravas. That is my thinking. There will be no absence of an end. There will be at least some little advantage. Others will not blame us."

Dharmaputra told Krishna, "You shall do as you wish. You are indeed my brother! You are indeed my friend! For having got your intimate acquaintance, there is no sense of helplessness or instability and no worry bothering us. You please tell, whether it is pleasing to us or whether it is harsh to us so long as it is conforming to Dharma, endorsing Dharma and extolling Dharma."

Krishna said again, "We have heard Sanjaya. It is now clear what their way of thinking is. I am aware that you aim at peace. However, I see many bad omens. Our armies must get ready for the war. Duryodana will not come forward to offer the kingdom to you."

Bheema, after listening to their conversations, expressed his views.

"Krishna! You talk to them in such a way that peace may be attained. Do not threaten them, by talking in terms of war.

If peace is sure to be secured, we shall accept Duryodana's leadership. Both sides, with the same origin, should not be extinguished."

On hearing Bheema's words, Krishna said, "You have been all along declaring that we want war and that the cruel sons of Dhritharashtra should be destroyed. You were awake all the time with that view, not even sleeping slightly. You were always accustomed to pouring out frightening words in acute anger aiming at war. You have vowed saying, 'Sun rises in the East and is going round majestically with immense radiance; he sets in the West; and with the same assertion of the natural phenomenon which is eternally true, I shall smash Duryodana with my mace. This is my vow. I shall never give it up.' Is it the same Bheema now preferring peace? Bheema! Get up! No slumber!"

Bheema replied, "I am in fine spirits. I shall not hesitate even if the whole world is against me in a war. If I had spoken in favour of peace, that was due to the aspect of mercy. I am prepared to face any difficulty and any hardship."

Krishna responded, "Bheema! I know of your real caliber. You will take due responsibility if a war becomes inevitable, by participating in it and by guiding others. Arjuna will fight occupying his chariot. I shall be driving his chariot."

Arjuna spoke next. "Krishna! Your words are indicating that a conciliatory solution will not be feasible. I think that your point of view is based on the assessment of Dritharashtra's sons as over - ambitious and on our own weaknesses impairing chances of peace. Our ideal must be fulfilled, if we adopt an upright path. Krishna! You please endeavor choosing that path which will ensure peace. You work hard in order to get a solution which will do good to both the sides. Krishna! We shall accept what you desire to do after a thorough, mature and serious analysis. You decide whether it has to be war or peace. If it becomes absolutely necessary to get rid of them completely, you work towards achieving that as our goal."

Krishna spoke with determination, "I shall try to achieve that result which will ensure welfare for Pandavas as well as for Kauravas. Peace or war is both within my ability to bring about. Land gets rains by Karma called Rain. Without rains, crops do not grow. If there are no rains, water sources in the ground are to be tapped. If water irrigation is also ruled out, there will be drought. That cannot be prevented. Drought prevails due to God's will. That is why learned persons are of the view that the peoples' affairs secure good results due to God's grace as well as the vigorous endeavours of people. We have to undertake to do what is within the powers of men. I shall not try to change what has already been determined by God. Those wicked fellows have no inclination to tread on the righteous path. That evil minded Duryodana will not give you what you ask him. Karna and Duchhasana will not yield to concede even the slightest part of the kingdom. No solution will be possible unless Duryodana is killed. Your kingdom was usurped by them by conspiracy. They will not agree for peace, which means restoring the kingdom to Dharmaputra. You are aware that they had, in fact, even tried to separate me from you. They are terribly afraid of me. I shall endeavor for peace, by my acts and by my words. But, do not expect the enemy to be conciliatory."

Nakula and Sahadeva spoke next. They also entrusted Krishna with full responsibility.

Draupadi addressed Krishna with terrible grief. She could not accept Bheema's initial observations that a path must be explored for ensuring peace as the solution and only that should be their endeavor and not war, which meant huge deaths on both sides. She recalled to her mind all the unpleasant happenings experienced by her in the past and began to speak with enormous firmness.

"Krishna! You are aware that Pandavas have been deprived of happiness and worthy ways of living. You have understood what the trend of thinking of Kauravas is, after listening to Sanjaya. Dharmaputra has agreed for the solution of getting back at least five village. If that is not acceptable to them, we should not be surprised. Duryodana requires that conciliation which does not mean parting with the kingdom to us. Krishna! Pandavas shall secure certain victory, if war takes place. We cannot fulfill our ideal either by surrendering to them or by seeking peace compulsorily. You should not show mercy to them. They must be punished by you, by enlisting the cooperation of Pandavas. Only that will be commendable to Pandavas. Your honour will also grow. The race of Kshatriyas will find that giving them happiness. An over- ambitious Kshatriya must be killed by another well-meaning Kshatriya. It is sinful if a person is punished with death penalty, when he had committed no crime; it is equally sinful if a person is left free without punished with the penalty of death, when he had committed a crime warranting death penalty. That category of sin should not afflict Pandavas and should not extend to you too."

"Krishna! I wish to tell you one thing on account of my extraordinary faith on you. Is there another woman comparable to me in this world? I am Drupada's daughter. And I have risen from the sacred Yaga fire. I am your fond friend. I am the daughter-in-law of Maharaja Pandu. I am the eldest queen of Pandavas. Through my husbands I have given birth to five valourous sons. Despite all these credentials, I had been dragged into the assembly hall. I was insulted before the eyes of Pandavas. I was treated like a slave. Dhritharashtra who took pity on me, who was distressed, granted me a boon. I asked, 'They should be released along with their chariots and armies'. They were released but sent on exile to the forest. It is a shame on Arjuna's bow which is supposed to be invincible and on Bheema, who is supposed to be of incomparable valour."

"Krishna! Duryodana should not be allowed to remain alive even for a second. If it is true that I am being supported by you and that you have mercy on me, let your entire anger be directed against Dritharashtra's sons. Krishna! If Pandavas seek conciliation and peace, I shall ask my father to fight against Kauravas. My five sons will also fight. That arm of Duchhasana must be severed and thrown out. Thirteen years have elapsed. I am waiting. My heart's inner senses are demanding revenge. They are burning like fire."

Draupadi, after talking like that with great emotion stated weeping and her tears were warm. Her tears started flowing down to her abdomen.

Krishna consoled Draupadi and said, "Draupadi! You will very soon witness the wives of Kauravas weeping in great distress. As Kauravas, their relations and friends perish, those ladies will be seen crying profusely. I, along with five Pandava brothers, shall act to make that possible.

Dogs and foxes will eat their fleshes sumptuously. Himalaya Mountain may move; earth may crack; sky and stars may fall down, my words will not fail. I swear. You stop weeping. You will see your husbands attaining prosperity and their enemies suffering destruction."

(While Pandavas had left to Krishna to decide whether war or peace, Draupadi was firm on resorting to war. Krishna also felt that war would be inevitable).

Krishna told Pandavas, "I shall meet Dhritharashtra. I wish to show uprightness. I shall try to secure what is best for us and I shall aim to do what is advantageous to us."

7.1. Pandavas' Emissary

Krishna left for Hastinapura in the month of Karthigai, with Revathi star as the star of the day. Brahmins chanted auspicious hymns. Krishna wore exquisite dresses and ornaments. He worshipped Sun as also Agni. With auspicious omens found around and as Satyaki as the driver, Krishna got into the chariot.

On coming to know through the spies that Krishna was on his way to Hastinapura, Dhritharashtra spoke to Bhishma, Drona and Vidura.

"I hear strange news. It is very significant too. Ladies, children and elders in every family are talking about it with great interest. The most powerful Krishna is coming here on behalf of Pandavas. He is entitled to receive due honour and respect from us. The world's fate is in his hands. He is the chief guardian of all the living beings. Patience, forbearance, valour, wisdom, intelligence and skills are all centered in him. He is the leader for the mankind. He is to be revered by us for our own good. Only he is the eternal Dharma. We shall derive our happiness, if we worship him. Grief and sadness will happen to us, if we fail to show respect and honour to him. Our desires will get fulfilled if he is extended a hearty welcome to his satisfaction. Let arrangements be undertaken right now for showing proper veneration to him. There should be wonderful celebrations in the entire city. Banners and festoons and excellent decorative materials must be displayed everywhere."

All arrangements were accordingly undertaken and completed. The entire city presented an admirable appearance. Duryodana had himself taken the active lead in arranging for the splendid decorations.

Krishna reached Hastinapura. Without giving any importance to view all the decorations made in connection with his visit, he first entered into the house earmarked for his stay.

Dhritharashtra was talking to Vidura, "I shall hand over as gift to Krishna, sixteen chariots, eight elephants, one hundred servants and many precious gems. (He was going on listing out all his intended gifts). All my sons and grandsons, excepting Duryodana should be there to receive Krishna. Krishna should be requested to stay in Duchchasana's palace. That mansion is a huge one. Its beauty must be enhanced further making special efforts"

Vidura spoke to Dhritharashtra, "You should show special care to receive Krishna properly, with all your relatives displaying pleasant dispositions. They should be mature enough to be humble. On account of their impish and bad behavior, your sons and grandsons should not pave the way for their own destruction."

"You would have had a heap of gifts meant to be given to Krishna. In addition, you may offer to him many things including the whole earth. But, you have not got them ready with noble intentions of satisfying Krishna with intrinsic love and respect. I am telling the truth. You expect that those gifts and decorations would yield to you good results. These are evidences of your deceptiveness and evil motives. They are, therefore, not worthy. I know what your secret intentions are. Five Pandavas desire to get at least five villages. If you do not agree, there will be total annihilation and no peace. You are endeavouring to win him over to your side, by tempting him with precious riches. You are planning that by doing more in that way you will succeed in diverting him away from Pandavas. I am aware of Krishna's greatness. You cannot separate him from Arjuna. That is because, it is like taking away his life. You should receive him by keeping ready a pot of pure water, wash his feet with reverence and make sweet enquires with a pure mind. He will not see with his eyes all your offerings to him. Krishna wishes to bring about peace between Pandavas and your sons. You are the father. They are your sons. You should exert yourself as the father and they should respond as the sons."

Duryodana told Dhritharashtra,

"This entire world is to worship Krishna. But, taking into account the present circumstances, we should refrain from offering any gift to him. If it is war, there is no chance of peace at all."

"I shall not share my privileges of ruling and enjoying enormous comforts with anyone else. I have taken a firm decision in my mind. I shall capture Krishna and imprison him. Once he is kept inside our prison, Pandavas and the entire world will be under my control. Krishna will be coming to meet us tomorrow. We shall carry out our plan, with no one expecting that to happen. You all please tell me as to how this plan is to be put into action, with no danger to us."

Dhritharashtra was pained to hear those words and said, "Krishna is arriving here as an emissary. He is also very closely related to us. He has not committed any harmful act against us. How could he be imprisoned?"

Krishna went, at first, to meet Dhritharashtra and Bhishma. He was treated with great respect and honour. Krishna then went into Vidura's mansion. He, thereafter, visited his aunt Kunthi's house. He made this assurance to Kunthi, "You will, very soon, witness the laudable expectations of Pandavas getting fulfilled. Their enemies will be destroyed. Enormous beneficial results will be theirs."

Krishna then reached Duryodana's palace. Duryodana showed due respect to him. Duryodana invited Krishna to have food with him. Krishna, however, rejected the offer and refused to have food with Duryodana, in the latter's house. Duryodana spoke to Krishna, in a low tone, but with evil intentions filling up his heart.

"Why do you not agree to have food with me? You are seeking to do good for both the sides. You should, therefore, be impartial and show your kindness to both the sides. Further, you are related to us closely. You are aware what Dharma is. Oh! The Person holding Wheel and Conch! Tell me the reason."

Krishna raised both his arms and replied with a voice resembling the thunder in the midst of clouds. He spoke very clearly and very steadily and without any reservation.

"Emissaries will come forward to accept the offer of food only after the purpose of their visit succeeds. They will also accept the honour extended to them only then. You, therefore, fulfill my expectation. I shall then accept your courtesies."

Duryodana replied, "You should not resort to unjustifiable methods. It is my wish to please you by my offering to you a fitting reception, irrespective of whether I fulfill your expectations or not. Your response to me is not based on proper reasoning. I have no enmity against you."

Krishna spoke, "I shall not deviate from Dharma, by yielding to petty desires. Whether it is anger or hatred or undue inducement to receive only a gain or an urge to enter into arguments or to derive petty happiness, they shall not succeed in deviating me from the righteous path. If I have to eat the food offered to me by you, you should have mutual goodwill with me. Or else, I should be in such a desperate situation when I shall be compelled to eat your food. Duryodana! You do not have goodwill to me in your heart. I am not in a desperate condition either."

"You have been showing hatred against Pandavas, ever since their birth. What is the reason? They are keen to be affectionate to you. They follow the righteous path, by possessing virtuous qualities. Your animosity against them is not proper. Any animosity against them is the same as animosity against me. Any approach to them on the basis of uprightness is the same as showing it to me as well. I am united with Pandavas. Anyone inimical to them is an evil person. They are righteous and upright and they are your brothers, whereas you are avaricious and senseless, pouring in feelings of hatred against them, thereby proving that you are a slave to your own ego and prey to an angry nature. For such a person standing against Pandavas, no prosperity shall remain long. On the other hand, for the one who aligns himself with those who are righteous and upright, greatness and fame reach him."

"The food which you are offering to me has been prepared by those who are tainted by evil qualities and so it has lost purity. I shall eat only that food which Vidura offers to me."

Krishna left Duryodana's palace. He reached Vidura's mansion. He ate the food offered by Vidura with sincere devotion.

7.2. Krishna's Conversation with Vidura

Krishna stayed with Vidura. Vidura spoke to Krishna with great humility.

'I do not consider that your visit to this place has been planned properly with full fore thought. That fool (Duryodana) is found always to breach all norms of good behavior. Sense of anger governs him strongly. He never carries good opinion on others. He seldom treats others respectfully. But, he desires that all others should always give him respect. He never listens to the good words expressed by those elder to him. He violates the prescriptions of the scriptures. He never values words of good advice of others. He is a fool. He will not accept good words of advice. He does not trust Bhishma, Drona, Kripa and others. You are trying to bring about peace and reconciliation by placing good faith on those, who are like your brothers. They have already decided not to be conciliatory in their approach to Pandavas. Your words of advice will be futile. Duryodana is so avaricious that he wants to wrest control on the entire earth, with no one opposing him. You cannot expect peaceful solution from him. I have greater affinity towards you than I have on Pandavas. I am saying this out of my affection, respect and fondness to you."

Krishna replied, "You have uttered what a man of great wisdom would do. Your words are testimony to the real situation. I shall explain to you the purpose of my visit."

"I shall endeavor to bring about peace with all good intentions. Kauravas will be extinguished totally, if the war becomes inevitable. A great calamity is going to sink them completely. Karna and Duryodana are the cause for that. Others only follow them. If a person fails to stop them who face utter destruction and does not protect them, he will himself be deemed to be cruel. That person who fails to protect another person even forcibly, who is very intimate to him and who is sure to get caught in great danger, is fit to be condemned. Therefore, no blame is to be found in the person trying to be the savior. Dritharashtra's sons should respect my words and abide by them. I shall endeavor to the best of my ability for the good sense to prevail upon them. Duryodana may not have faith on me. He may even suspect me. However, so far as I am concerned, I shall have to carry out my duty, in order to prove that my heart is pure. I shall cease to claim the privilege of my being closely related to these brothers and my friendliness to them, if I do not try to bring about reconciliation between them."

"Those Kauravas are unrighteous idiots and are prone to show their evil nature. They should not blame me that I did not endeavor to establish peace, as they may view me as fully capable and possessing enough power to do so, at a time when they are otherwise bent upon engaging themselves seriously in a mighty war. The purpose of my visit is to establish a good harmony between them. I shall endeavor for peace. I shall not give scope for them to blame me. What is destined for them can never be prevented to happen, if they fail to accept to tread on the path suggested by me. I shall have to accomplish what Pandavas are entitled to. This is very important. Kauravas must accept this as the basis for peace to prevail. My effort will be commendable, if Kauravas accept my approach. Kauravas will escape from the grip of death. Kauravas will not escape from death if they refuse to accept my words and plunge into war taking for their support others and however much they may fight united with full vigour. That would happen before my eyes. What could other animals do before an enraged lion?"

7.3. Emissary of Pandavas (Continued)

The next day, Krishna arrived at Dritharashtra's assembly. The assembly was very largely attended. As Krishna entered, Bhishma, Drona and all others stood up in the same way as Dhritharashtra did, to extend a great reception. Krishna also reciprocated by greeting them duly. A great decorative seat was kept for Krishna and he occupied it.

(Duryodana had issued a strict instruction that no one should rise from his seat and stand by way of showing respect to Krishna, when the latter entered into the hall. However, propelled by the enormous, majestic and divine lustre of Krishna, everyone, without being conscious in any way of themselves and due to the excitement, stood up spontaneously to show respect to Krishna. Duryodana also, without being conscious of himself, spontaneously stood up like others, due to the awe of Krishna's divine personality. There is a story on these lines. But, the original text does not refer to this incident.)

After all in the assembly resumed sitting, Krishna started addressing with great dignity.

"Oh! Dhritharashtra! Let there be peace between Kauravas and Pandavas. Let no one lose his life on either side. I am here in order to bring about such a desirable outcome. I have nothing else to tell. You all should be aware of what is talked about greatly in this world. Your race is an eminent one, in the midst of several royal races. They possess a good knowledge of the scriptures. They have adopted measures which are meant to do good to one's life. It is fully righteous. Kindness, sympathy towards others who are oppressed by distress, elimination of evil tendencies, intrinsic mental attribute of integrity, pardoning others' mistakes, adherence to Truth are the qualities which are commendable to any race. One belonging to such a highly noble race should not allow himself to commit any act which is improper and which is undesirable. He should not be the cause of such an action. Kauravas should not be treacherous to others. Your sons led by Duryodana have deserted all canons of justice, uprightness and righteousness. These cruel persons, having lost their own self-respect, with their hearts vitiated by evil paths of avariciousness, have committed a fraud on their own close kith and kin. A great tragedy has been showing its ugly head signifying their peril. If that is still left unchecked, the entire earth will face extinction. If you wish, you may avert it. It is not impossible to secure peace. Oh! Great Man! Conciliation is within your hands. It is so for me too. Let you bring your sons to the straight forward path. I shall do accordingly so far as Pandavas are concerned. Your orders should be obeyed by your sons. Only that will do good for them. Let Pandavas acquire your friendship. Surrounded by them and with them in your midst, please allow righteousness and justice to prevail. There is none like them who will get united with you. If Kauravas and Pandavas are united, the whole world will be in your hands. The stage of invincibility against enemies will forever be established."

"In the event of war erupting, losses of many lives on both the sides are bound to be there. Pandavas have been trained in an admirable manner, in the utilization of weapons. All of them wish to have the war. But, it is necessary to escape from great annihilation. The message sent by Pandavas to you-

'Our respects to you. This is our most respectful and humble appeal to you. Due to your severe order to us, we had met with many acute agonies. We undertook forest life for twelve years. On the thirteenth year, we disguised ourselves and lived incognito and completed that ordeal too. We believe strongly that you will not breach the promise made by you to us. In the same way as we conducted ourselves to abide by your order based on your promise to us, you please give back to us half of the kingdom to which we are entitled. Keeping in mind the principles of Dharma and the moral codes of this world, you please act in such a way that we are benefitted. You are elder to us. We showed our patience for all these years for your sake. You please guide us as our father and as our mother. You please make us to tread on a clear path. Let righteousness be allowed to remain firm.'

"Oh! Dhritharashtra! You should exercise control on your sons."

Krishna ended his talk.

Dhritharashtra told Krishna, "Your words are all based on righteousness. They are meant to do good to the world. They will lead all to Holy Heaven. However, I am not my own master. You please try to change the wrong course being adopted by my cruel son Duryodana and put him on the right moral path. He does not abide by the directions contained in the scriptures. He does not keep me in happiness. He does not accept words of good advice."

Krishna spoke to Duryodana and counseled him. Bhishma also did so and warned, "Do not cause destruction to your entire race." Drona also gave him a good advice. Duryodana was not in a mood to yield to anyone. He addressed Krishna,

"Krishna! You are doing us harm because of your fondness towards Pandavas. All of you are finding faults with me. But, I have not committed any wrong. Pandavas lost their kingdom on their own as they were defeated in the game of dice, for which they had offered everything as their stake. How can I be held responsible for that? They undertook the forest life in order to save their own honour. What mistake have I done, if they are dragging me to the war? I shall not be frightened by their threats. My elders had bestowed half of the kingdom to Pandavas by way of cheating us, when we were young, although they had no such right. Somehow, I too agreed for that arrangement. They had lost the kingdom in the gamble. I refuse to return the kingdom to them, There is absolutely no fault in me. Pandavas will not get land even of the size of the tip of a needle."

Krishna spoke to Duryodana in a stern tone,

"You wish to sleep eternally! That will happen. You and your ministers will all be massacred. Fool! You claim that you are under no obligation in the matter concerning Pandavas. Having been envious of the supreme glory enjoyed by Pandavas, you dragged them to do an unrighteous thing on Sakuni's fraudulent instructions. They are honourable and they stick to righteous methods but they were compelled to participate in an unrighteous gamble in a treacherous manner. Gambling tarnishes the image of noble persons. Excepting you, who else would have forcibly pulled the wife of your step-brother to the assembly hall and exposed her to utter shame in the presence of several persons? How nasty were the words poured out by Duchhasana and Karna insulting Draupadi? You had plotted to burn alive Pandavas along with their mother. You had committed several audacious crimes against them. They will acquire what is rightfully theirs, only if you are all crushed and your rich possessions are snatched away. Having committed several atrocities against them, you still pretend that you have done no harm to them. You do not listen to the good words of advice given to you by Dhritharashtra, Bhishma, Drona and Vidura."

Duchhasana told Duryodana mischievously, "Duryodana! If you do not listen to their words, they will arrest you by binding you with a rope and entrust you with Dharmaputra." Duryodana was very much agitated. He walked out accompanied by his brothers.

Bhishma told Krishna, "You have done matters in accordance with your desires."

Krishna again counselled all and addressed Dhritharashtra,

"You please arrest Duryodana and bind him with ropes. Only then, disaster can be averted. Karna, Sakuni and Duchhasana should all be kept under arrest. One man is to be sacrificed to save one race; one race is to be sacrificed to save one village; one village is to be sacrificed if need be at least once to save one nation. Land is also to be sacrificed for the sake of one's own soul. Keep Duryodana tightly bound, arrest him, keep him in prison and establish peace with Pandavas. Kshatriyas will be saved from destruction."

Dhritharashtra called Vidura and told him, "Gandhari is farsighted. She has a vision for the future. Duryodana may listen to her words."

Gandhari was accordingly brought to the hall. Despite her forthright words of counsel, Duryodana was not changing his adamant nature.

Duryodana again staged a walk out. He was conversing with Sakuni, Karna and Duchhasana. He told them,

"Krishna, who is an expert in expeditious completion of even difficult tasks, is inducing Dhritharashtra and Bhishma for arresting me and binding me tightly. We shall, ahead of them, arrest Krishna and bind him. Pandavas, once they hear that Krishna has been captured by us, will be heart broken and will lose all their confidence and strength. It is said that Krishna offers protection to those who surrender to him! He, who grants boons, will be under our custody. Let us capture Krishna quickly."

This news reached Krishna. He told Dhritharashtra,

"They are thinking in terms of capturing me, in their angry mood. Let them try. I shall liberate them from their enraged conditions. I shall never do anything which is condemnable or cruel. They, trying to deny Pandavas of safe living, are themselves going to be deprived of safe living. Because of their preponderant outlook for mischief, chances of Dharmaputra's success have grown further. I can, in a moment, arrest and bind all Kauravas and their associates."

Dhritharashtra asked Vidura to bring Duryodana and all his associates inside the assembly hall. Duryodana, Karna, Duchhasana, Sakuni and others came inside. Dhritharashtra warned Duryodana,

"You cannot carry out what you are planning to. Your act will be condemned by the world and will defame you. Only an idiot will indulge in such a thing. The lotus-eyed Krishna cannot be subjugated. No one can stand before him. Do you wish to arrest and bind him, with the assistance of your wicked associates? Even gods in Heaven under Indra's leadership will not succeed in capturing him forcibly. You plan like a child wishing to catch Moon. Even gods cannot defeat Krishna in a war. Neither Gandarvas nor Asuras nor Nagas can go near him. In the same way circulation of air cannot be hindered by the living beings or Moon cannot be kept within the palm of a man or Earth cannot be borne over a man's head, Krishna cannot also be kept under control."

Krishna told Duryodana, "Duryodana! You are desirous of capturing me because I am here alone. Oh! Silly Man! Now see my true identity!"

Krishna then manifested himself in an unbelievably huge form (VISWA ROOPAM) (Cosmic Form).

Krishna smiled broadly. Then His body structure shined like a lightning. All gods were seen at the tips of His fingers, only of the size of a thumb, but shining brilliantly like the lustre of Agni. Brahma was seen in His eye brow. Rudra showed his appearance from His face. Adityas, Saandyas, Vasus and Aswini devas were also seen. Indra with Maruths, Viswe Devas, Yakshas, Gandarvas and Rakshasas were also seen emerging. Balarama and Arjuna appeared in His both eyes. Arjuna with his bow was on His right side and Balarama with his plough was on His left side. Bheema, Dharmaputra, Nakula and Sahadeva were seen behind Him. Andhakas and Yadavas, under Pradyumana's leadership were there. Important Army Generals holding several weapons were on His front side. Holy Wheel, Holy Conch, Mace, Sword, Saargam (Bow), Plough, Nandaka were all with Him and there were many holding powerful weapons, which were shining brilliantly. Rudra emerged from His eyes and ears, blowing out fire along with thick smoke. Lustre was seen spreading from the bases of His hairs. He possessed one thousand arms, one thousand eyes and one thousand legs. Naga Loka was at the bottom of His foot. Moon and Sun were His eyes. Planets, Stars and all the worlds were within Him. Rivers and oceans were his sweats. Mountains were His bones. Trees were His hairs. Day and Night were His eye blinks. Saraswathi was in His tongue."

All the kings in the assembly hall were trembling. They closed their eyes. Bhishma, Drona and Vidura alone were in a trance as though, as they saw Krishna's VISWA ROOPAM. Krishna had bestowed them with divine eyes for them to look at him. Musical instruments were played in the Heaven above. Gods showered flowers.

Dhritharashtra bowed to Krishna and prayed, "Krishna! Please bless me. I must have a look at you. I do not wish to see anything else thereafter."

Krishna acceded and said, "Oh! Dhritharashtra! Let your eyes too see me."

What a wonder! Dritharashtra's both eyes had the vision. He worshipped Krishna's VISWA ROOPAM. Then all bowed to Krishna respectfully. Earth trembled. Oceans rose. The kings were all in trauma.

Krishna resumed his usual form of a man. Dhritharashtra again prayed to Krishna, 'I had worshipped your VISWA ROOPAM. I do not want the vision to be restored to my eyes. I wish to revert back as a blind man.' Dhritharashtra was his old self again. He told Krishna, 'You have seen the actual type of respect shown to me by my sons. I also sought peace. But, I have lost respect. Do not suspect me. I do not bear ill-will against Pandavas.'

Krishna told Dhritharashtra, Bhishma, Drona and Vidura, "You were eye witnesses to all which have happened. We see Duryodana as devoid of wisdom and of human qualities. Dhritharashtra says that he has no hold on him. I shall apprise Dharmaputra of everything."

Krishna got into his chariot. He went straight to meet Kunthi.

Kunthi was extremely sad when she was told about Krishna's mission and the inevitability of war. She also realised that a war was essential. However, she was apprehensive that with Bhishma, Drona and Karna the three allied in favour of Kauravas, Pandavas were bound to face destruction. Kunthi also believed that Drona, having been Pandavas' tutor and trained them, might not kill them. She also further believed firmly that as Bhishma was Pandavas' grandfather, he might refrain from killing Pandavas. However, her fear was centered on Karna. Karna had been claiming loudly that his aim was to kill Arjuna somehow. She was nervous that Karna alone might succeed in killing all the five Pandavas.

Krishna met Karna alone and spoke to him. He said, "Karna! You were born to Kunthi. Pandu is your father. Pandu is to you, as he is to the other five Pandavas. Pandavas are your close kin paternally. Kunthi is also close to you maternally as she is a Yadava. You are, therefore, more intimately related to Pandavas on both the alignments. Let Pandavas come to know that you were born to Kunthi. Let them know that you are Dharmaputra's elder brother. They will prostrate to you and cling to your feet. They will accept you as their king. They will crown you with sincere celebrations on a grand scale. I shall also be aligned with you."

Karna replied, "Krishna! What all you have said is out of goodwill, fondness and friendliness and I have no doubt about it. I accept that I am the son of Pandu. But, I have been abandoned by Kunthi. I cannot get separated from those who have brought me up. I shall never sever my link to them even if the entire earth is offered to me or enormous riches become mine or out of fear. I have been a ruler for thirteen years due to the generosity shown to me by Duryodana. I shall not betray Duryodana, neither because of possibility of getting killed nor because of being held captive nor over the chances of acquiring enormous riches yielding to improper temptations. No one should know about this conversation between us. Particularly Dharmaputra must not become aware of this secret because he will at once abandon all desire for getting back the kingdom and totally sacrifice all such desires. Even if I succeed in the war, I shall offer everything to Duryodana. Krishna! Let this conversation between us be kept a secret."

Krishna told Karna emphatically, 'The war will commence on the full moon day, seven days from today.'

Krishna left for meeting Pandavas.

Kunthi thought over deeply and had decided to meet Karna, disclose to him that he was her son and to persuade him from dissociating with Duryodana in order to get united with Pandavas.

Karna was no doubt gratified to acknowledge that he was Kunthi's son. But, he declined to get into the fold of Pandavas. He was emphatic that he would never betray Duryodana by severing his bond with the latter. He also promised to Kunthi that excepting for Arjuna, he would not kill the other four Pandavas. He expressed strongly that he would fight against Arjuna certainly, but at the end, either he or Arjuna would escape alive and, in all, Kunthi would still be left with five sons either way.

7.4. Arrangements for War

Krishna met Pandavas and reported to them about the actual developments in Hastinapura. He said,

"I explained to them what was upright and what would do good. But, it was futile. There is no alternative to war, now. Duryodana did not lend his ears to all the good words of advice expressed by many in the assembly hall. Let us get ready for war, without delay. Kurukshetra is waiting for the process of destruction to commence."

Dharmaputra also endorsed that war was inevitable, in the absence of any other alternative. He had already begun to form an army consisting of seven Divisions (Akshouhini). He had nominated seven, one to head each division. Consultations began to nominate a Commander for the entire army. Dharmaputra called upon others to come out with their views.

Sahadeva suggested King of Virata.

Nakula mentioned Drupada's name.

Arjuna was in favour of Drishtadyumna.

Bheema chose Sikandi.

Dharmaputra requested Krishna to offer his suggestion. Krishna said, "All those, whose names have been suggested so far, are fit to be the Commander. Each one of them would fill the hearts of Kauravas with fear. But, in the ultimate analysis, the choice of Arjuna namely, Drishtadyumna may be accepted to be the Commander."

Balarama told that he would remain neutral and so would not take part in the war.

Bhishma was chosen as the Commander of Kaurava army. Bhishma did not wish to assign any crucial role of senior most position for Karna. Karna, who was bitter and heart-broken, made a vow that he would not fight in the war as long as Bhishma functioned as the Commander.

Armies of both the sides were ready in the war field.

Dharmaputra, after surveying the army position of Kauravas on the opposite side, told Arjuna, 'The army of the enemy is vast. Our army is smaller. We should concentrate on strategic aspects where we should intensify our attack instead of spreading out our army aimlessly. Let us therefore march our army in such a way that they resemble a needle.'

Arjuna went into the interior of the army to have a look at all. Krishna was the driver of his chariot. He had a look at those wearing war ward robes. He became heavily agitated in his mind when he saw Bhishma, Drona and other respectful personalities ready to fight. He began to introspect, 'Am I here to kill these persons who are close to me?' Out of utter dejection and filled with remorse and pity, he threw away his great bow GANDIVA. He did not want the war to take place. Krishna chose that occasion to impart to Arjuna with the delicate aspects of prudence, wisdom and realization of self and soul and stressed why Arjuna must fight. Those lessons of Lord Sri Krishna form SRIMAD BHAGAWAD GITA. This is a gospel. Srimad Bhagawad

Gita contains the noblest teachings of Lord Krishna. It lays emphasis on the following principles, inter alia.

- How one has to perform his duty. Arjuna being a Kshatriya has to fight and cannot run away from the war field.
- How one has to perform his duty, without expecting the result, with no desire, with no aim to gain or with no fear of loss.
- How the life of a man has to be led.

There are several other sermons meant to uplift the mankind.

Bhagawad Gita is a part of this book but is found as the last Chapter, for the sake of convenience of reading.

Arjuna regained his poise and his mind became clear.

The war started.

8.1. The War

Everything was set for the war to begin. At that time, armies on both the sides were astonished to witness an incident, which was absolutely unexpected. Dharmaputra had removed all his weapons, got down from his chariot and started walking towards the other side where the Kaurava army was in readiness to fight. Everyone was perplexed, not able to guess what the motive of Dharmaputra was and there was total silence in the war field. Dharmaputra kept on moving towards Kaurava army, with no words coming out of his mouth.

Arjuna, who was confused, jumped down from his chariot and ran towards Dharmaputra. The other brothers as also Krishna went along with Arjuna. They were all aware of Dharmaputra's basic and in born nature and so they suspected that true to his nature, he must be planning to opt for a compromise, ready to concede anything to the enemies and prepare for abandoning the war and Dharmaputra must be approaching the enemies only to disclose his late intentions. They were struck with fear of the consequences of Dharmaputra's sudden mysterious conduct.

Arjuna asked Dharmaputra, "Oh! King! Why are you moving towards the enemy army's side, which is inexplicable, at the time when the war is about to start? You have not told us anything. The enemies are fully geared up for the war. They are all seen covering themselves with shields and armed with weapons and are going to attack us. But, you, without shield, with no weapons and with none of us accompanying you, are walking towards them. What is your motive?"

Yudhishtra did not reply but he kept on moving.

Krishna knew what was likely to be preponderant on Yudhishtra's mind, at that stage. He expressed, "Dharmaputra's intention is to bow to the elders and secure their blessing, before the commencement of the war. He should have realised rightly that it would not be proper to take part in such an important adventurous challenge, without first seeking the blessings of the elders. He is perhaps proceeding to bow to Bhishma and Drona for the purpose. That is why he is not wearing the shield and not carrying weapons. He is doing what is appropriate. He is fully conscious of good conduct and believes in uprightness. His approach at this juncture is laudable."

Duryodana and his associates were joking, saying, "This Dharmaputra, wishing to have peace and seeking reconciliation, and as he is scared of war, is coming to us to surrender. This man is a disgrace to our entire Kshatriya community. Why was this coward born in our eminent race?"

As correctly guessed by Krishna, Dharmaputra's objective was to bow to Bhishma, Drona, Kripacharya and Salya and seek their blessings, before the commencement of the war.

Dharmaputra paid his respects to Bhishma and sought the latter's blessings. Bhishma was immensely pleased with Dharmaputra's conduct and indicated that success in the war would be Dharmaputra's despite his fighting in the war on the side of Kauravas. Dharmaputra requested with no hesitation and no feeling of ill-will but in a straightforward manner, "Oh! Grand Father! I ask you as I bow to you. You are blessing me with success in the war. But, you are on the opposite side. How will death be caused to you by your enemy?"

Bhishma replied at once, "There is no one who can defeat me in a war. The appointed time of my death has not yet arrived. It may occur in the days to come."

After listening to Bhishma, Dharmaputra met Drona and offered his sincere and heartfelt respects. Drona told Dharmaputra, "You have decided to have the war. I would have cursed you that you should meet with defeat in the war, if you had not come to me for offering your respects to me, before the commencement of the war. Oh! Sinless Soul! I feel happy. I have been honoured by you. I give you permission. Fight! Be victorious!"

"Drona continued, "You are sure to be victorious. Krishna, of course, is there to guide you properly with his masterly wisdom. Where there is righteousness, there Krishna is! Where there is Krishna, there victory is."

Dharmaputra also asked Drona with great humility and with no bad motive but frankly, "You cannot be beaten at all in a war. How do we defeat you in the war?"

Drona, with no hesitation, gave the reply. "You will never win, if I am fighting against you. You should, therefore, take away my life, by you surrounding me with all your brothers."

Yudhishtra asked him "What is the way for taking your life? I cling to your feet and request you to tell me. I bow to you."

Drona replied, "I am not aware of an enemy who can defeat me once I step into the war field. If, in anger, I start discharging arrows incessantly, I can never be defeated. But, if, I, on my own, prefer to abandon the weapons, after preparing myself to die, and cease to be cognizant of what all are happening around me, and I lie down senseless, I may be at that time killed. I am saying this to you. If I happen to hear from a supremely reliable source news which will not be bearable to me to hear, I shall then abandon all my weapons and expose myself to death with no attempt to protect myself."

Dharmaputra thereafter met Kripacharya and Salya also and offered his respects. This conduct of Dharmaputra in meeting his respectful elders for seeking their blessings was very noteworthy. Drona had given indication as to how death could be caused to him. Bhishma did not share such information immediately. But, he did take Dharmaputra into confidence in that important matter, when the appropriate occasion arose.

8.2. First Ten Days of War - Bhishma Falls

Pandavas' army suffered a setback on the first day of the war. Dharmaputra was upset. Pandavas approached Krishna for their mental relief. Krishna consoled them saying, "Oh! Yudhishtra! Do not fear! Lord Almighty has blessed you with brothers of remarkable valour. Why this futile apprehension and suspicion? Satyaki, Virata, Drupada, Drishtadyumna and other highly skilled valorous persons are on your side. I am with you. Therefore, there is no need for mental depression! Sikandi is with us only for taking away Bhishma's life."

While the result of the first day's war was dampening Pandavas' spirits, Duryodana was ecstatic immensely. He appealed to Bhishma for intensifying further the attack against Pandavas and the war on the second day began ferociously. Bhishma was massacring the soldiers of Pandava army mercilessly.

Arjuna spoke to Krishna, "We have been demoralized. Our army, in its entirety, will be annihilated, if Bhishma is not checked. We must have to kill Bhishma."

Krishna told Arjuna, "Dhananjaya! Get ready! You see Bhishma's chariot there." Krishna drove Arjuna's chariot towards Bhishma's chariot.

The war between Arjuna and Bhishma was furious. Bhishma tried to dominate by his intensive showers of arrows. Arjuna was undaunted and by shrewdly deploying his arrows, he caused Bhishma to lose balance. Krishna's handling of the chariot was superb. Duryodana was worried about Bhishma's safety. He declared to Bhishma, "In spite of you and Drona remaining with me, the combination of Krishna and Arjuna would succeed in crushing our army, eliminating us. You should forthwith knock down Arjuna."

On the third day, the war between Bhishma and Arjuna was very furious. Even gods in Holy Heaven had assembled to witness the bitter fight between them.

Krishna halted the chariot for a while, on finding that Pandavas' army was getting decimated by Bhishma and he spoke to Arjuna, "The moment which you have been waiting for, is just ahead of you now. You attack Bhishma with immense intensity. If you do not do so, you will be a senseless loser. You have given me an assurance that you will kill Dritharashtra's sons and by taking a leading part in the war, you will kill Bhishma and Drona, who are opposing you in the war. Let your words prove to be true. I find that your army is facing destruction in all the directions."

Arjuna asked Krishna to take his chariot to the area in which Bhishma was fighting.

Bhishma, on seeing Arjuna and Krishna, roared like a lion and began to cover Arjuna's chariot by the shower of his powerful arrows. Krishna was also wounded. However, he managed to use his extraordinary skills judiciously. The fight between Arjuna and Bhishma reached the crescendo. Bhishma pierced the bodies of Arjuna and Krishna with his sharp arrows. Even Krishna felt depressed. Krishna was astonished to witness the mighty valour of Bhishma at its best display. Krishna felt that Arjuna too, without putting forth his best ability, was showing leniency towards his grandfather. The most excellent Krishna, who was capable of subduing his enemies, who was the true symbol of greatness, saw the happenings around him. He realized that the possibility of Pandava army getting fully crushed might become unpreventable. He decided within himself, "I shall wear the shield. I shall kill Bhishma today, for the sake of Pandavas. I shall reduce the heavy burden oppressing Pandavas. Arjuna is not found to operate adequately, to his full potential, in the manner he ought to, in these challenging circumstances."

Krishna spoke loudly, unable to bear the predicament of Pandava army, who could not witness the blistering attack of Bhishma. "I shall hold on my hand Holy Wheel (CHAKRA) which will vanquish all my enemies, in order to kill Bhishma. Bhishma and Drona must be killed. I shall also kill all the sons of Dhritharashtra. I shall hand over the kingdom to Dharmaputra."

Saying so, Krishna threw away the reins of the horses. He jumped down from the chariot. Holy Wheel was rotating brightly in his arm. That was a rare sight. Its edges were very sharp. Its splendor was like Sun's. It had the combined power of one thousand Vajra Ayutha (Indra's Thunder Bolt). Krishna dashed towards Bhishma. Earth shook. The border of Krishna's yellowish silk garment was shining like a lightning. CHAKRA resembled a lotus flower and with its stem longish in Krishna's arm, it looked as though a lotus flower was just blossoming. Krishna was himself appearing like a vast lake. It looked as though that Krishna was himself turning into the devastating fire at the time of deluge, in order to reduce the world into ashes.

Bhishma saw Krishna of such dimensions. Bhishma, holding his bow and arrows, with absolutely no fear, told Krishna, "Please come over! Please come over! Oh! The First among Gods! You have the Universe as your abode! You are always seen with Holy Conch, Holy Wheel, Holy Mace, Holy Sword, which are mighty. I bow to you! Oh! Lord of Universe! You please push me down forcibly from my chariot. You are the ultimate refuge for all the living beings. Krishna! If I am killed by you in this war, the enormous divine grace which I shall acquire will be astonishing, not only in this world but in Holy Heaven too. You have bestowed on me an unparalleled honour in the three worlds. My prestige will be fit to be celebrated in a grand manner."

Krishna went near Bhishma and said, "You are responsible for this world's destruction. You will see Duryodana's life becoming extinct today. You are like a minister full of wisdom. You should have condemned the king who was indulging in gambling and other evil activities. You ought to have abandoned the king who had deviated from the principles of Dharma and rightful duty."

Bhishma replied, 'Fate alone is most powerful.'

Arjuna got down from his chariot and ran towards Krishna. He used both his hands to circle round Krishna and to hold him. Krishna ignored Arjuna. Nay, pulling Arjuna also with him, he went near Bhishma like a huge tree uprooted by storm. Arjuna caught hold of Krishna's feet.

Arjuna succeeded in stopping Krishna, only after Krishna had taken ten steps forward. Arjuna appealed to Krishna, "please! No anger! You are the refuge for Pandavas. I swear in the name of my sons and brothers, I shall never retreat from the promises I have made. I shall destroy Kauravas."

Krishna condescended. He got into the chariot again.

Arjuna caused very heavy casualties on Kauravas' side in the terrible war which then ensued.

The war was taking place continuously. Dharmaputra, along with his brothers was holding consultations with Krishna. He told Krishna, "The most powerful Bhishma is causing a great disaster to our army. I have doubts about our victory in the war. I shall undertake the forest life again. I shall withdraw from the war, because Bhishma is crushing our army."

Krishna told Dharmaputra, "Do not feel sad! You are bound by Truth! There are many valourous persons with you. You give me permission, by virtue of our mutual friendship. You utilize me for killing Bhishma. I shall fight against him. I shall knock him down, as the army of Dhritharashtra sees it happening. Once Bhishma is gone, victory is yours. What is antagonistic to Pandavas is antagonistic to me also; what is the privilege of amity to Pandavas, that is the same to me also. Arjuna is my friend, relative and disciple too. I shall sacrifice my life for his sake. He will also sacrifice his life for my sake. I shall fight on your behalf."

On the ninth day, Duryodana's nagging of Bhishma was on a peak scale. He expressed his deep disappointment. Bhishma also spoke to him in great distress.

"I have been fighting by sacrificing my life, like the pouring of ghee in the sacred fire of Homa. Why are you harassing me, in spite of my giving away the utmost for your sake? You have still not understood what is right and what is wrong. The seed of hatred and enmity that you have sown has now sprouted and grown to this extent. We shall fight to the best of our ability. I shall never deviate from my duty. But, I shall never fight against Sikandi. I see him as a female. Further, I shall not kill Pandavas, with my own arms. These two factors do bind me. I shall vanquish all others. Let us continue to fight in the war. We shall take into account the norms applicable to Kshatriyas. The ultimate result, whatever it is, will bring us fame."

Bhishma fought very furiously that day. Pandava army was smashed. They began to run away to save their lives. The situation became unmanageable for them. Krishna told Arjuna, "Arjuna! Today is the day you were waiting for all these thirteen years. Do not forget that you are a Kshatriya, as long as you do not hesitate to kill Bhishma."

Arjuna was wavering still. But, Bhishma was unrelenting. His torture was on a mammoth scale. Krishna was unable to control his temper. He told Arjuna again, "Arjuna! You are not fighting at all. You are not using your full skill." Krishna, saying so, jumped down from the chariot. He had the Holy Wheel in his arm and ran towards Bhishma.

Bhishma started praying Krishna, "Oh! Lotus eyed! Let my soul be separated from my body by you. Please come on. Please come on."

Dharmaputra who was in the scene spoke to Krishna, "We can achieve anything, with your support. But, you should not participate in the war directly on our behalf. That is your vow. Bhishma had given me a notable indication, before the commencement of the war. He told me, 'I shall give you proper counseling. But, I cannot become a part of your army. I shall fight on behalf of Duryodana only.' I shall, therefore, meet Bhishma and ask him to reveal to me the exact means by which his life can be taken away."

Dharmaputra, along with Krishna and his brothers met Bhishma. Dharmaputra requested Bhishma to let him know, "We shall have to win. We shall have to get back the kingdom. Our army should not be devastated. How do we contrive so that you may face death?"

Bhishma replied, "You cannot score victory so long as I am alive. Once I die, victory shall be Pandavas. Neither gods nor Asuras can kill me. Even Indra cannot defeat me in a war. If I hold weapons in my arms, there can be no harm to me and I shall be invincible. However, if I cease to hold any weapons, any warrior will be able to kill me. If I am confronted by one who has lost his own weapons or by one who stands defeated by me or one who has run away from the war field or by one who due to excessive fear tends to be ineffective to fight or by one who has surrendered to me as a slave or by one who is a female or by one who has the manners of a female or by one who has physical handicap on his body or by one who has only one as his son or who is mean minded, I shall refuse to fight. Sikandi, Drupada's son, is no doubt valourous. But, by birth he was a girl and he has transformed himself into a boy now. You must be aware how this strange phenomenon had occurred. Let Arjuna, with Sikandi in his forefront, attack me with sharp arrows.

I shall not counter even though weapons may be with me. Let Arjuna use this opportunity and succeed in piercing my body with his arrows. With the exception of Krishna and Arjuna, there is none who can kill me in a war."

Dharmaputra returned to his army camp along with the others. However, Arjuna told him, 'I shall not kill my grandfather' and was emphatic in his refusal. Krishna counselled him saying, "You have promised that you will kill Bhishma. You cannot fail in your duty as a Kshatriya. Without killing Bhishma, you cannot win the war. Bhishma's end is imminent. That has been ordained so by Fate. What has already been determined by Fate is bound to happen certainly. Excepting you, no one else will be able to knock him down. There is a law that if one is elderly or merely elder in age or he has been found adhering to Dharma, he can still be killed if he has turned out to be an opponent in a war. A Kshatriya cannot dissociate himself from the war."

Arjuna accepted to launch the attack against Bhishma, by keeping Sikandi in the forefront.

Tenth day war started. Kaurava army under the leadership of Bhishma began fighting with enormous vigour. Countless persons were getting killed, making a vast heap of dead bodies. Bhishma was disgusted in his life and he did not want to remain alive any longer. When Dharmaputra had gone to Bhishma's vicinity, the latter had told him, "Yudhistra! You are well learned in scriptures. You please listen to my words. They are within the realms of justice. They are the means to lead one to Holy Heaven. I have become disgusted with my own life. I have massacred countless persons in the war. If you are inclined to do any good to me, you may do so in a glorious way and that is to kill me, by asking Arjuna to attack me, keeping Sikandi in the forefront."

Dharmaputra sent Arjuna along with Sikandi accordingly.

Bhishma was seen relentless in attacking Arjuna. But, the moment he saw Sikandi in the chariot in front of Arjuna, he was getting wretched and by sternly looking at Sikandi, it appeared that by his very eyes he would burn Sikandi. As Sikandi was a female by birth, Bhishma did not relish attacking him. Arjuna asked Sikandi, "Attack Bhishma forthwith. There is no one in our army excepting you, who can kill Bhishma."

Arjuna and Sikandi, sitting in the chariot, began to attack Bhishma. Bhishma did not counter attack Sikandi. But, Sikandi sent several arrows with great speed in order to unsettle Bhishma. Bhishma's body got pierced by Arjuna's arrows. Sikandi's arrows also did likewise. But, Bhishma was able to recognize Arjuna's arrows as also Sikandi's arrows distinctly. Bhishma was even at that collapsing stage commented about Arjuna's superiority as an archer, saying, 'That arrow piercing through my body and attacking my life bearing nerves making me to lose my balance, is certainly Arjuna's and not Sikandi's'. At last he fell from the chariot. It was just before Sunset and his head was in the eastern direction. As his body was fully covered by arrows, it was not in contact with the ground.

Bhishma had a boon according to which he can choose the exact moment of his death. He cannot be killed in a war. As he fell down, there were rain showers. Earth shook. That particular day was in Dhakshinayanam period as Sun was still in the southern part in relation to Earth's rotation. That was not considered as auspicious. Bhishma had, therefore, still retained his life, the soul remaining in his body. He was waiting for Uththrayanam period to commence, for breathing his last and shedding his life.

Arjuna made a bed of arrows for Bhishma to lie down. Bhishma lauded Arjuna's act.

Krishna told Dharmaputra, "You were fortunate to win. Bhishma, who cannot be killed by any man, has been knocked down. Fate, with you as the means, has fallen him. There is no weapon which he cannot counter. But, your angry countenance has burnt him down."

Dharmaputra responded to Krishna respectfully, "Victory became ours due to your mercy to us. When you are in anger, the adversary gets killed. You alone are our refuge. One, who is fortunate to secure your grace, wins. With you as our guardian, anything happening to us does no surprise to us."

Who knows Krishna's methods!

9. Krishna Saves Arjuna

Dronacharya became the new Commander of Kaurava army. The war was being fought bitterly under his leadership. An idea struck Duryodana for winning the war quickly. He thought that if Dharmaputra was captured alive, that would mean end of the war and victory for him. He, therefore, asked Dronacharya to intensify the war and concentrate on capturing Dharmaputra alive. Dronacharya was also not in favour of killing Dharmaputra in the war. He, therefore, found Duryodana's strategy as a good one for him to accept. That would, of course, mean that the war had been won by them. Dronacharya was pleased that Dharmaputra and the other four Pandavas would be saved from death, as he never wanted to take the lives of Pandavas.

Dronacharya undertook very strenuous steps to isolate Dharmaputra and expose him for easy capture. On learning about that new strategy, Pandava army became extremely alert and was strictly vigilant to protect Dharmaputra. Duryodana got involved in several conflicts simultaneously with a view to divert the attention of Arjuna and prevent him from guarding Dharmaputra solely. Bhagadatta, a great warrior, was chosen for the purpose of engaging Arjuna in an intensive fight. He had in his command a very powerful elephant called Supritika, which was of the size of a huge giant. Elephants are themselves huge in size and Supritika was a giant of giants. Supritika started causing havoc and trampled to death a vast number of soldiers in Pandava army. Bheema who tried to prevent its onslaught was himself caught by that elephant and had to manage to escape with great difficulty.

Bhagadatta engaged Arjuna in a ferocious combat. Arjuna smashed all the weapons of Bhagadatta. Finding no other alternative to attack Arjuna, he took on his hand the goad of the elephant Supritika, invoked Vishnu Mantra (Attributed to Lord Vishnu) and hurled it against Arjuna. If that strange weapon had attacked Arjuna, he would have died instantly. Krishna, very shrewdly, intercepted that weapon and made himself its victim. That weapon turned into a flower garland and adorned Krishna's chest, shining brilliantly. Arjuna asked Krishna,

"Why did you volunteer to take upon that weapon, making yourself its victim? You are my driver only. I am there to fight." Krishna replied, "My dear Arjuna! You do not seem to understand. If it had hit you, as intended, you would have been dead. That weapon, with Vaishnava Mantra invoked into it, is after all mine. It, therefore, reached to whom it belonged rightly."

Arjuna was saved from a mighty danger by Krishna. Arjuna thereafter killed Bhagadatta as also Supritika.

10.1. Abhimanyu's Daring Fights

Duryodana, as usual, was expressing his deep disappointments over his setbacks to Drona and accused the latter of leniency towards Pandavas, thereby revealing his despondency. Drona told him that as Arjuna was bent on protecting Dharmaputra, no harm could be caused to the latter. If Arjuna was compelled to divert his concentration elsewhere, and Dharmaputra, denied of superior protection, would be susceptible for easy capture."

In accordance with that plan, a great battalion of Samsaptakas was getting ready to attack Pandava army, expecting Arjuna to step in in support of his army. It was not only a large battalion, but it consisted of many supremely powerful warriors. When they challenged Arjuna, the latter had, in accordance with the war codes, to respond and he accepted their challenge. Arjuna, therefore, was away from Dharmaputra. He left to others the task of protecting Dharmaputra.

Drona formed Padma Vyuha of his army to launch the attack against Pandava army. Dharmaputra was at the center of Kaurava army's offensive. Bheema, Satyaki, Drishtadyumna, Drupada, Gatothgaja and others surrounded Dharmaputra for guarding him. Nevertheless, Drona intensified his attack and his opponents were struggling to withstand the onslaught. Dharmaputra called Abhimanyu, son of Arjuna and told him, “Drona seems to be irrepressible. Arjuna also has gone elsewhere due to compelling circumstances. We should not get defeated, although Arjuna is not here with us now. There is no one else who can face Drona and resist him. Only you are capable of successfully opposing him.”

Abhimanyu was very young. But, he was a very great archer. He said, “I shall oppose Drona. I have learnt from my father the strategy to be adopted to break Drona’s Padma Vyuha. But, I have not been taught about the strategy for emerging out successfully, after I fight inside and there is need for me to exit.”

Dharmaputra told Abhimanyu, “You march inside after breaking Padma Vyuha. We all with our huge army shall follow you from behind. Once we are with you, you will not be exposed all alone inside.”

Bheema also endorsed Dharmaputra’s words.

Abhimanyu was Arjuna’s son. His mother was Subhadra, Krishna’s sister. He said, “I shall fight, for the sake of my father and uncle Krishna and I shall make them proud.”

He got ready to fight. The driver of his chariot cautioned him, saying, “Drona is a very great expert. There is no one comparable to him. You are also, no doubt, an expert, but he is far older than you. Well trained, he has also rich experiences.”

Abhimanyu told him, “I am Krishna’s nephew and I am Arjuna’s son. Who else possesses as much credit? I am absolutely fearless. The enemies cannot claim to be capable of even one sixteenth of my valour. Do not hesitate. Drive fast.” Abhimanyu showed enormous courage.

With Abhimanyu marching in the front, Pandava army followed him. Kauravas were scared and they feared that Abhimanyu was more skilled than Arjuna.

Abhimanyu launched a virulent attack to smash Padma Vyuha, like a lion in the midst of elephants. Unable to withstand his ferocity, there was a crack in Padma Vyuha. After the crack, it broke. Abhimanyu succeeded in crashing Padma Vyuha, before the very eyes of Drona. Abhimanyu surged inside. Pandava army should have also marched inside, following Abhimanyu closely. However, Jayadratha, an important army leader of Kauravas, who was Sindu's king and son-in-law of Dhritharashtra, succeeded in closing the breach caused by Abhimanyu very fast with the quick assistance of his vast army. Pandava army could not get inside, to follow Abhimanyu. Abhimanyu had to continue with his fight inside Padma Vyuha, alone and unassisted.

Kaurava army attacked the lonely Abhimanyu. But, like the flies surrounding a lamp and getting burnt, Kaurava army was massacred by the rapid flow of Abhimanyu's arrows. They were unable to withstand Abhimanyu's onslaught, though he was left alone. Drona, Aswaththama, Kripa, Karna and others resisted Abhimanyu. They also had to struggle to retreat.

Pandava Army, which was prevented outside, tried to fight strongly in order to reach Abhimanyu and assist him. Jayadratha was also a formidable warrior. Further, he had a very big army to back him. He blocked the entry of Bheema and Pandava army.

Abhimanyu was killing many Kaurava soldiers as also some very prominent persons of that side continuously.

He succeeded in unsettling the leaders like Karna, Drona, Aswaththama, and Kripa who were unable to face him and were in a quandary. Unable to bear with the terrible destructions caused by Abhimanyu, Drona called Karna and told him in a cowardly manner, "Kill the horses of Abhimanyu attacking them from standing behind Abhimanyu."

Karna did accordingly and killed Abhimanyu's horses but from behind Abhimanyu. He did not show that he was an honourable opponent, as he did not fight against Abhimanyu positioning himself in the front. Karna did likewise to break Abhimanyu's bow, without fighting from the front side. Abhimanyu lost his horses, chariot and bow and was forced to fight standing on the ground. He took his sword and was on spree in killing mercilessly many Kaurava army people including some leaders and sons of leaders, by swirling his sword unimaginably fast. Drona found Abhimanyu even more aggressive than his father and he realised that Abhimanyu posed a real threat to them all. Drona sent an arrow to hit Abhimanyu's sword which fell down. Karna smashed Abhimanyu's shield all in a non-chivalrous manner.

Abhimanyu was still not deterred. He removed the wheel of his chariot and using it as a weapon by revolving it fast in his hand, he still massacred many Kaurava army prominent personnel. It looked as though he was gifted with the Holy Wheel of Lord Vishnu. Many in Kaurava army put into joint action for immobilizing Abhimanyu. Abhimanyu fell down. When he was struggling to rise up and resume his attack, the son of Duchhasana hit Abhimanyu with his powerful mace. Abhimanyu fell down dead.

Abhimanyu's daring fights ultimately ended in his death. He was a lonely fighter. Those who attacked him were Drona, Karna, Kripa and other prominent leaders of Kaurava army. The entire Kaurava army had fought against him, violating all codes of war and unjustifiably.

Arjuna and Krishna were returning to the army camp, after Arjuna had killed most of Samsaptakas.

Arjuna was somehow feeling restless as he was still in the chariot driven by Krishna. And he told Krishna, "I do not know why! My mind is passing through some unexplainable vibrations. My heart is beating fast. Some great tragedy should have occurred. Is it possible that Yudhishtra is in danger?"

Arjuna was not aware that his son Abhimanyu had taken part in the war on that day in his absence.

Krishna told him, "Do not worry about Yudhishtra. He and your other brothers are well."

Krishna was Lord Almighty. Would he not have seen in his inner eyes what had happened to Abhimanyu? But, his actual reply to Arjuna was cryptic. How could he hint to Arjuna about the fate of Abhimanyu?"

Arjuna and Krishna arrived at the place where Pandavas had assembled. Arjuna, coming to know of Abhimanyu's cruel death became extremely sad. He cried, "Has my son reached Yama's abode? How did Yudhishtra, Bheema, Drishtadyumna, Satyaki and others fail to prevent Subhadra's son Abhimanyu getting killed by the enemies? How will it be possible for me to console Subhadra, Draupadi and Utthara?"

Krishna told Arjuna, who was immersed in the sea of grief, "Do not get overpowered by grief! Those, who are born as Kshatriyas have to live and to die surrounded by weapons. Valourous persons must have to prepare themselves to face death, sometime or the other. Abhimanyu was still very young. But his destination is that Holy Heaven, where many elders reach after getting killed heroically in wars. If you still plunge yourself in grief, your brothers would also be doing so and you will be left crippled. You console yourself. You console others too and pick up courage."

Arjuna lost his consciousness for a while due to excessive grief afflicting him. After regaining consciousness, he declared his vow, "It was Jayadratha who had executed the plan to murder my son Abhimanyu. He is responsible for my son's death. I shall kill Jayadratha before sunset tomorrow. If Drona, Kripa and my other Acharyas stand in the way of the fulfillment of my vow, I shall kill them too."

After declaring so, he pulled the string of his bow which produced a thunderous sound. Krishna blew the conch. Bheema said, "The sound of the string of Arjuna's bow and the tremendous blare of Krishna's conch would result in the death of Dritharashtra's sons."

Kauravas came to know of Arjuna's vow. Though it caused worry to them, they felt strongly that if Jayadratha was very well protected and saved before the next day's sunset Arjuna, getting disappointed that his vow could not be fulfilled, would enter fire and give up his life. With this feeling they were, in fact, ecstatic, anticipating that Arjuna would no longer be in the picture. Their plan for the next day was not to allow Jayadratha to appear before Arjuna's eyes and to protect him with extraordinary vigilance.

Vriddhaksha was the king of Sindu. Jayadratha was his son. When Jayadratha was born, the hidden divine voice from Heaven announced, "This son of yours will attain great fame. But, getting killed in war, he will reach Holy Heaven. That person, who is the most powerful of all valourous ones, will sever your son's neck and your son is destined to die thus."

Vriddhaksha was worried. He cursed, "That person, who severs my son's neck resulting in my son's death, will find that his own head cracks into pieces, if the severed head falls down on earth."

Therefore, even if Jayadratha's head fell down resulting in his death, that person responsible for his death with his head falling on Earth would also die with the perpetrator's own head cracking into pieces.

Jayadratha took a decision to return to Sindu at once, as soon as he heard about Arjuna's vow, without participating further in the war. Arjuna was the foremost among all warriors. If he got involved further in the war, he feared that he might get caught, with the divine voice's caution proving true and might die in the hands of Arjuna. But Duryodana pacified him saying, "Karna, Salya, Duchhasana, Drona and many other powerful leaders of Kaurava army will save you from any threat and the entire Kaurava army will for one day function only for protecting you. You should not return to Sindu."

Jayadratha agreed to stay on.

The protection for Jayadratha was strengthened manifold before the war started on the next day. Jayadratha was twelve miles behind Kaurava army, besides a large army surrounding him keeping vigil. Karna, Aswaththama, Drona and others were in readiness for preventing Arjuna to penetrate into Kaurava army.

Durmarshanan and Duchhasana, who were prominent leaders in Kaurava army, were the first to fight against Arjuna, but they had to retreat as they were defeated by Arjuna.

Drona engaged Arjuna in a fiery fight. Drona was not able to defeat Arjuna. Arjuna also could not go beyond Drona and make progress in his march towards Jayadratha. Krishna told Arjuna, "Time is getting wasted. There is no need for a fight against this Brahmin." Saying so, Krishna diverted Arjuna's chariot to the left of Drona and drove forward.

Drona tried to prevent their movement crying, "Stop! Do not go ahead without first defeating me."

"You are my Acharya. You are not my enemy. I am like your son. There is no one in the world to defeat you." Arjuna saying those words was moving ahead fast in the chariot.

Sruthayutha, a great warrior, opposed Arjuna. He was in possession of a mace, which had divine blessing. That was obtained by him, owing to a severe penance undertaken by his mother. She did a special penance seeking a boon from Varuna and her payer was, 'My son Sruthayutha should not get killed by any enemy at all.' Varuna granted the boon, but with a condition, "I shall hand over to your son a mace with divine power. He will become victorious in all wars, if he uses that mace. No one can either defeat him or take away his life. But, if he aims that mace against one, who does not fight, that will rebound and kill your son."

When Arjuna was opposing Sruthayutha, the latter, in utter desperation directed his mace towards Krishna. Krishna was only the driver of the chariot. He was not fighting at all. That mace, instead of attacking Krishna, rebounded automatically and hit Sruthayutha killing him at once. With the 'curse' proving to be true, Arjuna was saved by Krishna.

Arjuna, thereafter, defeating many army generals of Kaurava army, one after another, was marching towards Jayadratha.

10.2. Bhurisravas

Many heroes in Kaurava army had tried to prevent Arjuna from advancing towards Jayadratha. As Arjuna was kept engaged by others thus, on one side, another very significant event was taking place in a different area.

Bhurisravas was the king of Pahilka. He was Somadatta's son. Somadatta had a long time rivalry against Yadavas. Fascinated by Devaki's beauty, who was then a young girl, Somadatta had invaded Devaki's father's capital in order to capture Devaki and marry her forcibly. Vasudeva was desirous of marrying Devaki. Sini, a friend of Vasudeva, fought against Somadatta and defeated him. Vasudeva married Devaki. That being the case, enmity between two families of Somadatta and Sini was growing enormously.

Satyaki was Sini's grandson. He was a very great warrior and a very good friend of Krishna. Both were very intimate with each other. Satyaki was also driving the chariot for Krishna when the latter undertook the role of ambassador for Pandavas.

In Kurukshetra war, Satyaki was a close ally of Pandavas. Bhurisravas was with Duryodana. Bhurisravas was a very formidable warrior.

It was the fourteenth day of the war. Arjuna was found fighting elsewhere. Satyaki had fought many battles vanquishing many Kaurava men, big and otherwise strong, and was already very much exhausted. He was really not in a condition to face another combat. Bhurisravas, because of his long time enmity against Satyaki drew him for a fight which was going on furiously. Satyaki, who was already tired, was about to be defeated by Bhurisravas. Bhurisravas was ruthless and he was found dragging Satyaki brutally like a lion dragging a weak animal. Satyaki was thus caught inextricably, which Krishna saw to his bewilderment and utter shock. As Satyaki was very intimately friendly with Krishna, Krishna drew the attention of Arjuna for witnessing that pathetic scene. Arjuna was still busy in attacking the resistance against him by Kaurava army and he also did not like the idea of going to the rescue of Satyaki who was fighting against another person. Bhurisravas was now lifting his hand possessing a sword and was about to slay Satyaki mercilessly. Krishna grew panicky and he asked Arjuna to intervene without any delay. Arjuna precisely at that very moment sent an arrow and severed Bhurisravas hand holding the sword. Bhirisravas did not expect at all that such an incident would happen. Satyaki was saved miraculously. Bhurisravas began to abuse Arjuna bitterly and Krishna particularly as he believed that Krishna was responsible for what had suddenly happened much to his total surprise. Bhurisravas felt that he was attacked by Arjuna in an unjustifiable manner, as his fight was against someone else and not Arjuna. When Arjuna retorted how Bhurisravas was not justified in forcing Satyaki for a fight when the latter was totally exhausted and not fit to fight and started dragging Satyaki like an animal mercilessly, Bhirisravas was feeling bitter about his own beastly conduct. Bhurisravas took the blame on himself and threw away his weapons. He began to sit in Yoga posture. Satyaki regained his consciousness and before Arjuna could stop him, he killed Bhurisravas with his sword.

(Duryodana would be condemning Krishna later on that only Krishna was the cause of Bhrisravas's death in an unjust manner.)

No doubt Arjuna was engaged in another war. But, he was forced by Krishna to get diverted, at the most appropriate time to go to the rescue of Satyaki, when the actual fighting was between Satyaki and Bhurisravas and Arjuna should not be expected to interfere. Satyaki was Krishna's intimate friend. It was Krishna's timely act which saved Satyaki. Bhurisravas was bitter against Satyaki due to old family rivalry and had tried to take revenge in an unjustifiable manner and Krishna found nothing wrong in rescuing such a victim of bitterness.

10.3. Jayadratha Killed

Duryodana was extremely worried as he found Arjuna advancing rapidly. As usual, he started blaming Drona for being lenient towards Pandavas. Drona handed over his own shield to Duryodana and told him, "You cover your chest with this special shield and fight against Arjuna. Arjuna would be stalled as a result and he would not move forward. I am now not in a position to confront Arjuna. In some other area, Pandavas aggrandizement is found to be fierce. They have to be crushed."

Arjuna was making very good progress in his aggressiveness to reach Jayadratha. Duryodana chose to fight against him, with his full vigour. He was wearing Drona's shield. Duryodana had not been fighting with that much furiousness, until then. Krishna was surprised and spoke to Arjuna, "Arjuna! I keep wondering! Why are your arrows not troubling Duryodana at all? This is the first time I find that Arjuna's arrows, despite hitting the targets, are not causing serious harm to his opponent. Why? Have your weapons lost their potential? Has your Gandiva bow lost its striking power? Why? Your arrows, though surging towards Duryodana, are not effective, but fall down with no avail! This is mysterious!"

Arjuna smiled and replied, "This Duryodana is wearing Drona's shield. But, he has not spread it on himself in a proper manner. He has just thrown the shield on his chest, just like what a bull will do. Please now see the amusement."

Arjuna, at first, attacked Duryodana's horses of his chariot. The driver was then knocked down. Duryodana was forced to strand on the ground. Arjuna then broke Duryodana's bow. Duryodana was left with no weapon. Arjuna sent several needle like arrows to attack Duryodana. As Duryodana had not covered his chest properly with Drona's shield, there were several holes exposing Duryodana's chest. Arjuna's needle like arrows and the sword dispatched by him, pierced through the holes exposing Duryodana's chest and Duryodana was thrown out of balance. He ran away retreating from the fight.

Arjuna succeeded in crushing Kaurava army and went very close to Jayadratha. The war, therefore, became intense. Jayadratha army was endeavouring its best to block Arjuna's further advancement. Sun was moving down in the western horizon and Sunset was not quite far away. Arjuna could not still manage to see Jayadratha even from a distance. Arjuna at last reached the exact place where Jayadratha had been kept, securely protected. Arjuna killed the driver of Jayadratha's chariot. The chariot was also smashed. Jayadratha fell down from his chariot. At that time, Sun, on the western horizon was moving down fast and Sunset was not far away at all.

Krishna warned Arjuna saying, "There are six different warriors of enormous strength surrounding Jayadratha and protecting him carefully. You have to go near Jayadratha, after crossing those guards and overpowering them. You will not be able to go near Jayadratha and kill him, after knocking down those six guards and before Sunset. All your sources of tremendous strength will not be of adequate use to you, at this crucial short moment. I shall hide Sun at once through my own power. Jayadratha will believe and see that Sun has already set. In his ecstasy believing that his life has been saved, and to rejoice himself to see you destroying yourself for the reason that your vow has not been fulfilled, he will come out from his hiding. You should exploit this rare opportunity for your own benefit with your judicious alertness. Do not allow this moment to slip away from you, thus interpreting that Sun has already set."

Arjuna said, "Let things happen as contrived by you."

Krishna, with his divine power, spread darkness at once. Kaurava army was delirious. They were delighted that Arjuna was finished. Kaurava army and Jayadratha lifted their heads to look at the western direction, to see that Sun was missing. Jayadratha, particularly, lifted his head to look anxiously at the western horizon. Krishna told Arjunan, "Arjuna! See there! Jayadratha, with his fear of you vanishing, is there, with his head lifting up, as he wishes to see the Sunset. This is the most important moment, for which you have been waiting for. Sever Jayadratha's head forthwith. Fulfill your vow."

Krishna removed the darkness. Sun was thus seen in the horizon but not precisely set. Arjuna aimed the most appropriate arrow to sever Jayadratha's head.

Krishna, at the top of his voice, cautioned Arjuna, "You should send arrows in quick succession, so that the head of Jayadratha which has been severed from his trunk, does not fall on earth and is carried by relay to fall on Vriddhakshara's lap."

Arjuna's arrows carried Jayadratha's head, as though floatingintheatmosphereanddroppedfastonVriddhakshara's lap and then fell on earth. That was an unforgettable scene. As soon as that happened, Vriddhakshara's head got cracked into several small pieces, as technically the head of his son was fallen by him.

Arjuna's vow was fulfilled due to Krishna's unbelievable strategy.

11.1. Gatothgaja's Death

Pandavas were devastating Kaurava army. Duryodana placated Karna and Karna devised novel measures for repressing Pandava army. Arjuna told Krishna, "I shall oppose Karna. Either he should die or I should die today." Krishna spoke, "Karna has reached the height of fury with his immense powers pouring out all his potential. His splendor today matches with Indra's. You no doubt have the full capability to oppose him and to control him. Gatothgaja also possesses that much power. But, that destined time for you to fight against Karna has not yet come. Karna is in possession of Sakthi weapon given to him by Indra. Karna has earmarked that Sakthi weapon with care, just for killing you. With Karna possessing his Sakthi weapon with a view to take away your life, and in today's circumstances when he is fully charged to show off his fury, he may aim that Sakthi weapon against you. Gatothgaja is always devoted to uphold your safety. He is keen to do his best for your benefit. Let Gatothgaja oppose Karna. Gatothgaja, born to Bheema, is capable of whirling round like wind, without any chance of getting killed. He is fully conversant with all varieties of weapons generally in the possession of Gods, asuras, Rakshsasas and others. He will score victory over Karna certainly."

Gatothgaja appeared before Krishna and Arjuna. He bowed to Krishna and Arjuna respectfully and was overwhelmed by the confidence reposed on him by them both. Krishna told him, "You have my blessings. You please listen to me with rapt attention. Time has come for you now to put into display your splendid valour. No one else will get such an opportunity. For Pandavas, who are sinking, you are the boat. You possess several weapons. You are a master in resorting to Rakshasas' illusory techniques. Karna is destroying Pandava army. Pandava army is unable to withstand his attack. There is no one, excepting you to oppose Karna and to put an end to his atrocities. You, therefore, succeed in blocking Karna's onslaught, true to your great valour. Fathers give birth to sons only with the expectations and belief that they will be duly protected. You, therefore, protect your father and his brothers. You have the mental temperament for showing righteousness. Your valour and power in war are formidable and unparalleled. None can defeat you in a war. For Rakshasas, power gets enhanced manifold, once darkness spreads. You also possess power to create illusions. You should kill Karna."

Gatothgaja was immensely pleased.

The war fought by him was note-worthy. He crushed Kaurava army people of several cadres mercilessly. He chopped many with his sword. He made a heap of corpses of Kaurava army people, by murdering them with his weapons. As the darkness spread, his powers grew enormously. With his magical powers, he created Rakshasas and caused several devastations of unimaginable magnitude. When Karna confronted him, Gatothgaja unsettled him and tortured him in different ways. Karna's chariot was broken. His horses were killed. Kaurava army people appealed to Karna,

"You must kill Gatothgaja." Karna put into use several of his weapons to attack Gatothgaja. Gatothgaja used his illusory powers to vanish in one place and reappear elsewhere and harassed Karna.

Karna was utterly confused as to what to do to contain Gatothgaja. Finding no other alternative, he decided to aim Sakthi weapon given to him by Indra. Karna had all along preserved that special weapon, earmarking it to kill Arjuna, with that determination in his mind. Karna was permitted to use it only once and it would be ineffective if used for the second time. That was the condition attached to that weapon when Indra offered it to Karna. Sakthi weapon was like fire emitting flames. It would kill any opponent irrespective of who it was.

Karna aimed his special Sakthi weapon at Gatothgaja. Gatothgaja had no means to escape. He fell down dead. As he fell down, because of his enormous weight, one Akshouhini (Battalion) of Kaurava army was crushed. Many enemies were killed by him even as he was dead.

Kauravas hailed Karna.

Pandavas were in immense grief. They cried. But, Krishna alone felt greatly relieved and he was happy. He even danced as a result. He embraced Arjuna very tightly. He was not only a divine figure, with no mental inhibitions, but he had deep far-sightedness. Arjuna finding that Krishna was in mirth asked him, "At a time when we are all plunged in grief, you are found very happy. We are broken to find Gatothgaja dead. Pandava army is choked in sadness. Our grief is beyond measure. Tell me truly. What is it that is making you glad? Your act is inexplicable."

Krishna replied, "What I am going to tell you will not only dispel your grief, but also cause happiness. With Karna having already used his special Sakthi weapon against Gatothgaja, Karna is as good as dead now. If Karna had kept in his possession that Sakthi weapon, he would have remained invincible. No one could conquer him. It is your good luck that the special Sakthi weapon has been dislodged from him. Neither Indra nor Kubera nor Varuna has the power to defeat Karna, as long as he is in possession of that weapon. With that weapon no longer with him, he is like a snake under the charm of Mantra, with its venom fully extracted out. He is like fire sparks doused by water. He was all along full of pride that your life was in his hands. You have now escaped. Hereafter, his life is in your hands."

11.2. Drona's End

Drona, at the height of his fury, used Brahma Astra at Pandava army, causing them unbearable devastation. Pandavas were troubled beyond measure. They were perplexed, unable to find a counter. This was due to the enormous pressure put on Drona by Duryodana who was suffering one serious setback after another.

Krishna told Arjuna, "Drona cannot be defeated in a war. He can be killed only if refuses to hold any weapons with him. Oh! Pandavas! Dharma has to be given up, and some other means has to be chosen to win the war. Before Drona succeeds in killing us all, if Aswaththama is killed by us, he will dissociate himself from the war. Therefore, there should be someone, among us, who should convey to Drona that Aswaththama has been killed."

Arjuna was not accepting that idea. But, others endorsed it. Yudhishtra also agreed to it, though after initial reluctance. Bheema took on his hand his mace and he went to kill a very huge elephant, called Aswaththama, which could have destroyed many enemies, with its own enormous strength. As that elephant Aswaththama had been killed, he announced to Drona, 'Aswaththama is killed,' in a loud voice.

Drona heard those words which wounded his heart. His limbs started losing vigour. He was fully aware of his son

Aswaththama's tremendous valour. He thought the news conveyed to him was false. He regained his full strength and in the war which ensued, he killed thousands in Pandava army. At that time, the Great Seven Sages, who could not bear seeing Drona annihilating a large number of army people in utter fury, met Drona and told him,

"You are wrong in fighting like this in war. The destined time of your death is around the corner. You throw away your weapons. Look at us. Such cruel acts on your part hereafter are unwarranted. You are well learned in Vedas. You have to adhere to Truth and Dharma. You are a Brahmin. Murdering others is not your profession. Give up weapons. You cease to tread on the sinful path. You seek the eternally virtuous path. Your days to linger in this world have shrunk. You have, with the aid of Brahma Astra, taken away thousands of lives who have not at all heard about it. Your act is not all laudable. You should not do any more such sinful act."

Drona got disgusted about himself, when he heard those words of eminent sages. He met Dharmaputra. He believed firmly that Dharmaputra, whatever be the compelling circumstances, even if the rulership of the three worlds was offered to him, would not utter a lie. Krishna was horrified. He felt that if Dharmaputra spoke the truth, there will be no salvation for Pandavas. He told Dharmaputra,

"Drona, if infuriated further, will trounce you all beyond recognition in a half day war even. You save us from Drona. In the circumstances in which we are now placed, a lie is more valuable than truth. It will not be sinful if a lie is uttered, for the sake of saving several lives."

Bheema came to them and said, "I have killed a very huge elephant with the name Aswaththama. I announced to

Drona of the death of Aswaththama. He does not trust me. Brother! You accept Krishna's advice."

Dharmaputra yielded to the belief that Fate was unalterable. He said, "Aswaththama was killed, the elephant." His voice when he said, 'Aswaththama was killed' was audible, but his subsequent words, 'the elephant' were in a lower tone and were therefore meant to be inaudible.

Until that moment when Dharmaputra uttered those words, his chariot used to move four inches above the ground, without touching the ground in recognition of his principles of Dharma (Righteousness). But, when he degraded himself to say those words, his chariot dropped down to touch the earth, like any other's chariot. It was clear that Dharmaputra did not utter any words of falsehood, but his intention was not pure!

On hearing Dharmaputra saying those words, Drona believed that his most beloved son Aswaththama had been killed and he was plunged in great grief. His heart pricked as he admitted that he had committed grave injustice to Pandavas. The news about his son's death choked his mind with pity. He was unable to fight again.

Drishtadyumna was born on this earth just for killing Drona. Drona was aware fully of that fact. Drishtadyumna was very busy that day for attacking Drona with his arrows. Drona, who was initially showing his disinterestedness, began to hit back very ferociously. Pandava army was unable to face his attacks. Bheema tried his best to contain Drona. He failed to withstand Drona's offensive. Bheema got frustrated and he uttered these words which Drona heard clearly.

"Brahmins, after shirking their duties prescribed for them in scriptures, are found to cling to weapons like Kshatriyas. To protect lives is Dharma (Righteousness). Brahmins are like the roots for Dharma. You are an eminent person among Brahmins. But, you, like a lowly born chandala (butcher) are found to be committing the atrocious deed of murdering many lives. Are you not ashamed to be indulging in such contemptuous deed, contrary to the codes of your highly eminent Brahmin race and degrading it just for your family's sake and for the sake of your son? That person (your son) for whose sake you possess all these weapons and for whose sake you live on Earth, is elsewhere lying on Earth, behind your back. It is not proper on your part to suspect the words of Dharmaputra."

Drona threw away all his weapons at once. He cried, "Karna! Kripa! Duryodana! You show your valour in the war. I have abandoned my weapons."

After throwing away all his weapons, he was crying aloud, 'Aswaththama' and reached the top portion of his chariot. He sat on yoga posture, closing his eyes. Drishtadyumna, carrying in his hands the bow, arrows and the sword, went near Drona immediately. Drona was still in deep meditation (Yoga). He was chanting the sacred hymns. He concentrated his mind on Paramathma, Lord Vishnu. He moved his face upwards, sat erect with his stiff chest, eyes closed and got himself merged with OHM, the Pranava manifestation of Lord Almighty, and was resplendent with great halo around him. He reached Holy Heaven in the trance created by his deep meditation. When he, in the upper region, was thus transporting his soul, a feat which no one could ever perform, it looked as though there were two Suns. That great brightness vanished after a while.

Drishtadyumna saw Drona's body, with life extinct. He dragged Drona's body and severed the head from the body.

Drona had already reached Holy Heaven. What Drishtadyumna had claimed to have done, was that he severed the head of a body from which the soul had already got separated.

The manner of Drona's end was astonishing.

11.3. Aswaththama - Narayana Astra

Aswaththama could not bear with the death of his father Drona and the manner it took place and he spoke in great consternation,

"I heard that my father was killed when he, after abandoning all the weapons, was in meditation with his eyes closed. Those who boast themselves of as the followers of Dharma have committed this sinful act. Dharmaputra, the symbol of Dharma, has himself done this loathsome act mercilessly. War may end in victory; it may end in defeat. It is no doubt highly admirable to lose life in a war. That sort of death will not cause sadness, if it had taken place in a just manner. My father had fought straight-forwardly. But, he was eliminated unrighteouly. He had met with this end, even when I am still alive. Dharmaputra is responsible for this detestable act. This earth will taste today his blood. Drishtadyumna has perpetrated this dastardly crime. I shall not fail to take away his life today. I shall kill him with whatever means are available to me, whether by deliberate open violence or by a concealed strategy. They will see today my true valour in action, in the very presence of Krishna. Neither Gods nor Gandarvas nor Asuras nor Rakshasas will be able to conquer over me. I shall use my unique divine weapon in the same way as Sun burns with his scorching rays. No one whether Arjuna or Krishna or Bhima or Dharmaputra will be aware that I am in possession of that divine weapon."

"Long time ago, Lord Narayana graced us by visiting my father. Supreme God was pleased with the high respects shown to Him by my father, and he offered a boon. Narayana Astra was thus gifted as the boon to my father. He also commended saying, 'No one can fight in a war comparable to you. But, this Astra is to be put into use only for a well intentioned purpose, after a very great deal of deliberation and proper thinking. That person against whom it is aimed will die certainly. I am not aware whether there is anyone who can escape from it. That will kill a man even if he claims immunity against death. Therefore, it ought not to be used hastily. This Astra is not to be aimed against one who abandons his chariot and remains helpless or one who has given up his own weapons or who prays for mercy or one who seeks surrender or one who has no one to protect him. This Astra will rebound and attack its user, if he aims at such exceptional targets.' My father has handed over to me that Astra. I shall kill all Pandavas and Panchalas with this Astra."

Aswaththama undertook the needed steps such as cleansing himself thoroughly and to recite the sacred hymns for invoking Narayana Astra. When Narayana Astra attained the critical stage of getting into action, strong wind blew from the opposite side. Thunders were heard from the sky. Earth shook. Oceans rose up. Peaks of mountains were scattering. Darkness spread.

There were speculations galore among Pandavas. They apprehended that all those bad natural phenomena were precursor for a vast disaster to occur, as the evil consequences of Drona's death in an unjust manner.

Krishna met Pandavas and hurried them up, cautioning, "You all throw away all your weapons with nothing remaining in your hands, immediately. You get down from your chariots or other means of carriage forthwith. All must stand on the ground. Aswaththama is about to release Narayana Astra. This will be the only way to escape from its onslaught. Narayana Astra will not kill anyone, who, without holding any weapons or without using any chariot or other means of carriage just stands on the ground helpless unassisted in any manner. Even if one plans in his mind to counter it, will find attacked lethally and killed by it."

Immediately on hearing Krishna's counsel, all in Pandava army threw away all their weapons on the ground and stood on the ground with bare hands. No one entertained any thought in his mind that he was a participant in the war. But, only one among them had the temerity not to do so. Bheema did not abide by Krishna's advice, but he said on the contrary, "Everyone may retake his weapons and hold them in his hands. I shall, single-handedly, counter that weapon and crush it into pieces", and he was getting ready for the counter attack foolishly. Aswaththama was in great joy, when he found that Bheema had been caught. Narayana Astra started the process of encircling Bheema. It was about to penetrate into his head. Arjuna was in a quandary and he was contemplating to counter Narayana Astra with his Varuna Astra and to neutralize the former. Narayana Astra reached its most dangerous stage of swallowing Bheema. Krishna and Arjuna hurried to reach Bheema's vicinity closely. As they both were Nara and Narayana respectively, they inherited within themselves their inherent divine power. They pushed down Bheema forcibly from the chariot. They threw down on the ground all his weapons. Krishna condemned Bheema saying, "What has happened to you? If there is a way to counter Narayana Astra, would we all have thrown away all our weapons and seek refuge standing in the ground for protecting ourselves?"

As Bheema was also pushed to stand in the ground, with no weapons to protect him, Narayana Astra became silent and was inactive. It got its original status restored to it. When there was a demand to use it again, Aswaththama admitted, 'Once discharged, it will not return to the user. If I recall it, it will destroy me instead. You would have seen how Krishna has neutralized Narayana Astra.'

12. Arjuna Abused Dharmaputra

Dharmaputra fought against Karna. But, he was unable to withstand Karna's attack. Arjuna intervened in order to save Dharmaputra and engaged Karna in a bitter fight. Arjuna fought ferociously and dislodged Karna so badly that Karna was frightened for his safety. News spread even that Karna had lost his life. However, it became necessary for Arjuna to move elsewhere for attacking others. Karna had not, in fact, lost his life. Dharmaputra was expecting that Karna would have been killed, but hearing that Karna was still alive, he spoke to Arjuna very harshly. He said,

"My brother! Your battalion has been pushed to a shameful plight today. You have not handled the war properly. How is it that you were born to Kunthi? If you had admitted that you were incapable of killing Karna, we would have arranged for an alternative strategy. You had vowed that you would kill Karna but now you are looking for breaching that. We were expecting quite a lot from you. Our beliefs and expectations have all been shattered. At the time of your birth, there was a divine voice from Heaven which announced, 'There will be no superior and no greater archer than this child. There will be no one to defeat him in any war.' But, you have been rendered ineffective by Karna. You have earned for yourself a chariot, which is divinely blessed.

You have Krishna to drive your chariot. If you had handed over your bow to Krishna praying him to fight and driven the chariot yourself, Krishna would have killed Karna. If you find it impossible to fight against Karna, you may pass on your Gandiva bow to the one who is superior to you. Oh! I pity your Gandiva bow! I pity your flag which carries the image of Hanuman! I pity the divine chariot gifted to you by God of Fire!"

(Dharmaputra was never seen exhibiting his anger to that extent. He was furious against Arjuna, because his most eager expectation of Karna getting killed had not been fulfilled.)

After hearing Dharmaputra abusing him, rather abusing his Gandiva, Arjuna drew his sword and took it on his hand. He had decided to kill Dharmaputra. Krishna, pretending as though that he was ignorant, asked Arjuna, "I do not find any enemy confronting you for you to use your sword now. Dritharashtra's sons have been killed by Bheema. You have seen Dharmaputra alive, on your return for the day from the war field. We should all be immersed in happiness at this hour. There is none to be seen around you for you to kill using your sword. Who is there for you to fight against? Have you lost control on your brain?"

Arjuna, with his eyes staring at Dharmaputra angrily like a snake hissing, told Krishna,

"I must sever the head of one who insults me asking me to hand over my Gandiva to someone else. This is my secret vow. Now, this most valourous gentleman has rebuked me with that tenor, in your presence. I shall not pardon him. I shall kill him and fulfill my vow. I am bound by Truth.

Krishna! What is left to me to do in these circumstances? Oh! Lord! You know fully about this Universe's past, present and future. You please give me your answer."

Krishna spoke very beautifully.

"You are angry in a funny manner but at a welcome time. There is some scriptural background relating to your stance. It has some very delicate aspects. Someone who has acquired knowledge of that, will not be able to behave in the manner you have done, now, today. That man who carries out that great sin, unbecoming of him, is to be condemned. You are perhaps not aware of the words of men of wisdom. It is not easy to know what ought to be done and what ought not to be done. Scriptures illustrate all. But, you are an alien to them."

"When I find that you are as though aware of the scriptures dealing with moral codes and that you endeavor to adhere to them, it is very clear that you are ignorant of them. You seem to believe that you are acting righteously. But, it is not really so. How is it that you are wishing to kill your own elder brother, like any ordinary man? You are telling me that you have made a vow. It is childishness. You, out of utterly wrong application of mind, are trying to do another disgraceful act, in an unrighteous way. Righteousness is a very delicate subject. One who adheres to Truth is a believer in God. There is nothing superior to Truth. But, one must first understand what really is meant by Truth. Truth does not come out of one's tongue easily. A tongue utters lie easily. Truth may appear to be a lie and a lie may appear to be Truth. Lie may be uttered, if there is threat to a life or if a marriage is to fructify or if wealth is to be saved from plunder."

Arjuna asked Krishna, "I have heard your words of high wisdom. You are my father and mother. You are my refuge. There is nothing in the three words, which you are not aware of. Dharmaputra is foremost in practicing Dharma. He is not to be killed at all. I shall tell you what occurs in my heart. I have made a vow that I should certainly kill one who ridicules me saying, 'You hand over your Gandiva to someone superior to you.' My vow shall remain honoured. Dharmaputra must not lose his life at the same time. Is there a solution?"

Krishna said, "Dharmaputra is very much tired. He is also feeling disgusted. He is irritated because of sharp arrows aimed at him by Karna. Karna has also attacked him by hurling at him very many cruel abusive words. Under these circumstances, he has used against you those improper words in his anger. Dharmaputra has also expected that if you are rebuked harshly, you may be incited to react adversely against Karna with greater determination and driven to fight with the utmost vigour for killing Karna. Dharmaputra should not lose his life. Your vow should also not be belied. Dharmaputra's life should not be taken away. But, a parallel non-lethal non-violent situation must be created in which Dharmaputra must be deemed to have been killed symbolically but not dying actually. An honourable man in this world must be moving about with due respect always shown to him. It would amount to death if he is exposed to an extreme sorrowful degradation of having to receive abusive verbal attack, though he may be left physically alive. Arjuna! You show lot of respect to Dharmaputra. Let you now hurl at him contemptuous words of censure and put him to shame. Although he is elder to you in age, you address him using second person singular 'you'. Sage Adharva and Sage Angirasa have suggested such a compromise in SMRITHI. When you censure him, he will experience as much humiliation as death itself. Let you thereafter fall on his feet and console him with kind apologetic words."

Arjuna started to abuse Dharmaputra accepting Krishna's suggestion.

"You should not abuse me and find fault with me. You were placing yourself at a distance of two miles in the battle field. You should not blame me without proper reason. I have been fighting honestly and diligently, without respite, using my full strength and power. I have killed thousands of elephants, horses and valourous soldiers making a heap of their dead bodies. You should not cast aspersions on me revealing your ignoble attitude, by remaining in the company of Draupadi over your bed always. I have been performing with great vitality in the war for your sake. You should have lost the seriousness in the war only because you have found me fighting with immense energy and concentration. That is why you have now resorted to mischief. I have never enjoyed happiness from you. You should not get back the right to the kingdom. You have great temptations for gambling. Having committed the sins and having indulged in activities in which only the inferior persons delight themselves, you are now expecting us to help you to retrieve you from your enemies. In spite of being fully aware of the enormous evil consequences of gambling, you had taken part in them and threw yourself to suffer acute misery. As you were immersed in gambling, we did not gain anything.

You being the cause of all the mischievous activities are now throwing abusive words against me. This Great War is for your sake. Thousands of people have died for your sake. Only you played in the gamble. Only you are responsible for the loss of the kingdom. If we have been driven to misery, it is because of you." (Throughout, Arjuna used second person singular 'you' disrespectfully for abusing Dharmaputra.)

After rebuking and abusing Dharmaputra, Arjuna was sad and filled with remorse. Drawing a heavy breath, he again took the sword in his hand. Krishna asked him, "What has happened? Why this sword?"

Arjuna, with his heart broken cried, "I have committed a sin. I shall destroy myself."

Krishna told Arjuna, "Dharma and laws of justice are very delicate. Why this suicide? That will be more heinous than killing one's own brother. You now begin to extoll your own virtuous qualities, your own admirable qualities and your own great valourous deeds and let you be seen as indulging in self-praise. That will tantamount to committing suicide."

Arjuna responded immediately saying, "My dear elder brother! Excepting for Lord Siva, there is no one equal to me in archery. I am capable of perishing all and everything in this Universe, by the power of my valour. It was I who had conquered all the kings in this world and brought them under your subjugation. If Raja Suya Yaga was performed successfully, it was because of me. I am incapable of getting defeated in any war, thanks to the auspicious marks in my arms and legs. I have killed all the enemies spread in the four directions of east, south, west and north. In this war, I am only responsible for killing more than half of the enemy army.

I do not eliminate ordinary persons. I kill only those who are well trained and well experienced in the use of weapons. Krishna! Let us hurry up! Karna has to be destroyed. Karna's life should be extinct certainly today. I shall not remove my army dress until Karna's life departs."

Arjuna then prostrated before Dharmaputra.

13. Karna is Killed

Let us recall the episode of Gatothgaja's death at the hands of Karna. Gatothgaja was Bheema'son. He was very mightily strong as he was a Rakshasa too. Krishna made him take a very prominent part in the war and he had a special reason to do so.

As he was a Rakshasa, Gatothgaja's power would increase manifold after darkness. He took part in the war, intensifying his attack against Karna and Kaurava army in the night time. Thousands were perished. Duryodana could not bear the plight of his men getting destroyed by that single Gatothgaja. He pleaded with Karna, 'You kill Gatothgaja at once.'

Karna stepped into the war field and fought against Gatothgaja. Gatothgaja had inflicted several injuries in Karna's body. Karna was perplexed as to how to stop Gatothgaja's further onslaughts. Indra had blessed Karna offering a special spear which would take the life of the opponent immediately whom it struck. But, Karna could not put that use more than once. Karna had preserved that special weapon earmarking it exclusively to take away Arjuna's life. But, that night, Gatothgaja's fury in the war against Kaurava army was mammoth and uncontrollable. As a result, Karna and Kaurava army were thrown into severe battering. Besides, darkness had spread enhancing Gatothgaja's striking power.

All these factors propelled Karna to retaliate quickly and he, in a fit of extreme annoyance, and without further thought, took that special weapon given to him by Indra and aimed it at Gatothgaja. That killed Gatothgaja immediately. But, Arjuna had been saved. That was because if Karna had not lost his patience against Gatothgaja and had spared it for using it against Arjuna, the latter would not have escaped death.

Krishna, in a way, planned intelligently, for ensuring that Arjuna was not attacked by Karna, with the latter using that weapon.

In that day's war, Kaurava army sustained several crushing defeats and Duryodana and others started losing confidence. Salya, the driver of Karna's chariot, instigated Karna to fight against Arjuna. Arjuna and Karna were engaged in a very ferocious fight. Karna had with him Naga Astra with the sole aim of killing Arjuna by attacking him with that weapon. Karna took that weapon in his hand and aimed it against Arjuna. That weapon emitting fire was surging towards Arjuna. Krishna sensing that as a serious danger to Arjuna and acting with his divine power to save Arjuna, pressed the whole chariot down to dig into the ground five inches deep. On account of Krishna's swiftness, Naga Astra, failing to hit Arjuna's face attacked his crown instead, which was knocked down. Arjuna was thus saved. However, he felt ashamed that his crown was thrown down by his enemy. In great indignation, he stepped up his virulent attack against Karna revealing his full skill in archery. Karna was struggling very hard to retain his balance. As a precursor of his imminent death, the wheel in his chariot got stuck in the ground. He got down with the object of lifting the wheel up. At that time, he addressed Arjuna,

"Wait for a while! My chariot is sunk in the ground. You are a great warrior. You are aware of the principles of war fare. By taking undue advantage of the mishap which has happened to me, you do not attack me in an unfair manner. You fight against me after I lift my chariot up."

Arjuna showed hesitation. Karna had suffered another curse, as the result of which the hymns which he ought to chant for his Astras to be activated were forgotten by him at that crucial moment. Karna was not able to put into use any of his other vital Astras. Krishna spoke to Karna, "Karna! It is strange that the great principles of justice, righteousness and uprightness are occurring even in your mind now. Those principles are perhaps appearing in your memory at a time when you are in peril. What happened to those principles of justice, righteousness and uprightness when you, Duryodana, Duchhasana and Sakuni were responsible for dragging Draupadi to the assembly hall exposing her to utter shame? You had all deceived Dharmaputra only because he was not aware of your conspiracy and fraud in gambling. Is it justice that you have rejected the kingdom to Pandavas after they had completed successfully twelve years of forest life and one additional year of living incognito? What happened to your share in the execution of the plot to poison Bheema and kill him? What happened to your share in the conspiracy to burn Pandavas alive in the palace full of lac and other inflammable materials? When those cruel arms fell on Draupadi for perpetrating that contemptuous act, were you not an accomplice and to rejoice and celebrate? Did you not shout at Draupadi saying, 'Your husbands have failed to protect you? Go! Marry another husband!' and you jeered at her. Your tongue, which had unleashed those shameful words, is now inducing you to utter the sacred words of justice, uprightness and propriety. What happened to your role in murdering unjustly the young boy Abhimanyu, who was isolated and thrown helpless? You should not utter the words justice, uprightness and propriety, because you have never given them any importance."

Karna turned his face down in great shame after hearing those words of Krishna. He was not able to respond and did not speak a word. He again tried to lift his chariot up. He failed. He was not able to retaliate against Arjuna as the curse afflicting him had its effect.

Krishna told Arjuna, "There should be no further delay. Send your arrow and kill your cruel enemy."

Arjuna showed hesitation. However, honouring Krishna's words, Arjuna sent his arrow to sever Karna's neck even as Karna was still struggling to lift his chariot up.

14. Gandhari Tries to Offer Full Protection to Duryodana

In the Great War between Pandavas and Kauravas which was going on, Gandhari's ninety nine sons had been killed. Duryodana alone was still alive. Gandhari, as his mother, had a very strong fondness towards him. Finding that only he had survived, and because of her worry for his continued safety, she had taken a decision to offer full protection to him against death by any weapon attack. She was reputed for her pure chastity. Out of sympathy for her blind husband, she also did not wish to have vision in her both eyes and she had covered voluntarily her eyes with a piece of black cloth. She found a way to save Duryodana from death in the war, by the power of her chastity. She called Duryodana and asked him to bathe and appear before her fully naked. She did not explain why. Duryodana also did not query. Her belief was that if Duryodana appeared before her fully naked, and she cast her open eyes on him after removing the black cloth blocking her vision, her grace as the chaste woman towards him would render him immune against attacks with any weapon by an adversary and no limb of his would be harmed.

Duryodana first abided by his mother's direction and bathed. He also was fully naked. He was about to walk across to stand before Gandhari. But, will Krishna allow

Duryodana to live perennially, giving an opportunity for Gandhari to carry out her aspiration? Having guessed correctly what Gandhari had planned to do, he appeared before Duryodana suddenly and told him, "If you are to meet your mother, why do you go naked" and laughed.

Duryodana felt ashamed. He covered his hip with a small piece of cloth. That piece of cloth had covered both his thighs. He went and stood before Gandhari. She, not knowing what had happened, in the meantime, had removed the black cloth blocking the vision in her eyes, with immense happiness, and looked at Duryodana with her gifted eyes. Duryodana's body, owing to the sanctification transmitted by his mother's unique grace, became partially immune to the ill effects of any weapon attacking him. However, that vital portion of his body, from the hip down up to the thighs, which was hidden by the piece of cloth worn by Duryodana, did not secure protection. Gandhari was shocked. Her desire did not fructify.

Bheema's pledge was to smash Duryodana's thighs and kill him. Due to Krishna's shrewdness and timely intervention, the measure taken to offer Duryodana full protection by his mother was frustrated.

(There is no such episode in the original text of Mahabharatham)

15. Duryodana's Death

Excepting Duryodana, all in Kaurava army had been killed. Duryodana was getting ready to fight, holding the mace in his arm. But, unexpectedly, he happened to enter into a water storage and was lying there in great dejection.

Dharmaputra was accompanied by his brothers and Krishna in his search for Duryodana. He saw Duryodana in the midst of water and asked, "Duryodana! After hastening all in our eminent race to tread on the path of death and getting killed, you are now trying to escape by hiding inside the water. What has happened to your self - pride? Are you not ashamed? Come out! Fight!"

Duryodana replied, "I have not come here to hide myself out of fear. My body is burning like fire. I have no desire to live. My ambition for the kingdom is no longer there. This world is now yours."

Dharmaputra spoke very sternly. "Has this liberal mood become yours only now? You had refused to give us even that small piece of land of the size of the tip of a needle. I begged for conciliation and peace. You threw away my offer then. We have not fought this war, for the sake of the kingdom. Shall I narrate all your sins? Our mental distress may somewhat subside, only after your life is taken."

On hearing this, Duryodana came out of the water. He was holding the mace in his hand. He challenged, "Come on! One by one! I am solitary. I presume that you, all five joining together will not attack me who am now without a weapon, but instead fight one by one."

Yudhishtra replied, "If you do not want that we, all five, together should not fight against you, how was Abhimanyu killed by you all? Did not all of you, joining together kill that young boy, who was left isolated and helpless? Is consciousness of the principle of righteousness showing itself in you only at the time of your distress? You wear a shield and fight. You may choose any one among us five."

He continued, "Duryodana! I offer you one concession. We, Pandavas, are five. If you desire to fight against any one of us and kill him, you will be the king. If you are killed, you will reach Heaven. What is your choice?"

Duryodana, with his self- pride still intact said, "I shall kill all the five of you, one by one."

Krishna was extremely angry with Dharmaputra and told him, "How irresponsible and foolish are your words, without proper fore-thought! You are agreeable for Duryodana to choose any one of you for the one to one fight. What will be the consequence if he chooses you or Arjuna or Nakula or Sahadeva? Duryodana has trained himself very seriously with the aim of killing Bheema. You have shown a desire for securing for him an unexpected fortuitous gain. You have allowed a very good opportunity to slip away from you. Bheema alone is the proper match for Duryodana. It is doubtful whether even Bheema can defeat Duryodana. Your offer has created a very good chance for your enemy to derive consolation and to find a way to protect himself. You have paved the way for the kingdom, which is in your hands, to slip away from you. With all the enemies already vanquished, only he is left alive. He is also caught in a desperate condition, with no means to escape. Why do you show this concession to him? Even if Bheema fights against him, it is a big question whether success will be Bheema's!"

Bheema told Krishna, "I shall conquer Duryodana in the fight. See us fighting. I am capable of conquering the three worlds as also gods in Heaven!"

Duryodana told him, "Why do you waste words? Bheema! You fight against me. I shall subdue you."

The fight between Bheema and Duryodana began. It was a virulent one. Both were great warriors. The fight was going on equal terms. As they both were at the height of their respective power and strength, Arjuna sought Krishna's opinion on the trend. Krishna told him, "Both are eminent warriors. Bheema possesses superior strength. Duryodana has trained himself very well. Duryodana has a greater skill. Both have worked hard. Bheema may not achieve success, if he fights in an upright manner. He will be able to kill Duryodana only if he resorts to devious techniques. If Devas (Gods) had defeated Asuras, that was due to their deceptive means. Indra defeated Virochana in a similar manner. There are several such precedents. Bheema also should seek such means, in addition to the display of his valour. Bheema had taken a pledge that he would break Duryodana's thighs, owing to the post-gambling circumstances. Let Bheema now fulfill his pledge. If Bheema is defeated, Duryodana will regain the kingdom."

Immediately, Arjuna attracting the attention of Bheema gave a strong blow to his own left thigh.

Krishna said, "Bheema will now fulfill his pledge successfully. Did he not swear in the assembly hall that he would smash Duryodana's thighs?"

Bheema heard those words of Krishna spoken to Arjuna. The pledge made by him struck his memory only then as he was fighting with all the force at his command. Like a lion, he leaped fast on Duryodana and broke Duryodana's thighs. Duryodana fell down. He was at the doors of death. Bheema stood over Duryodana's body, hit the latter's face with his leg, and he started to dance in wild fury.

Dharmaputra told Bheema, "You have redeemed your debt. Duryodana was a king. He was our brother too. You should not kick his face with your leg."

Krishna told him, "The life of this cruel man will depart very soon. You may all go away in your chariots."

On hearing these words, Duryodana, without in any way showing regret over what all had happened, started to utter invective words.

Krishna spoke to Duryodana, "Why are you throwing useless blame on others? Extreme avarice and self-pride had directed you to commit innumerable atrocities. What you have sown before, you have reaped now."

Duryodana was more indignant. He retorted saying proudly, "Oh! Wretched Man! I was distinguishing myself as an eminent Prince, so long as I was alive. I had innumerable friends. But, I am a formidable enemy. I had enjoyed all sorts of happiness with great rejoice. For a Kshatriya, shedding life is a reward. Let Bheema trample on my face. I will not be bothered."

As the war was thus nearing its end, Balarama arrived there. He saw with his own eyes the undignified act of Bheema breaking Duryodana's thighs. He shouted, "I am conveying to you all my mental agony. Will any Kshatriya fight in such a way that his opponent is hurt below his navel? Bheema has transgressed the rules of war."

He moved near Krishna and said, "You may be watching all these as a fun and tolerate them. I cannot bear with this type of imprudent act."

Saying so, he stood before Bheema, with his weapon (Plough) lifted up. He was preparing to strike at Bheema.

Krishna was aghast. He stopped Balarama immediately and uttered these words,

"Pandavas are our dear friends; they are our close relatives too. They are the victims of the very many nefarious activities of Duryodana. At the time when Draupadi was put into shame in the assembly hall, Bheema had sworn, 'Duryodana! One day, in a war, I shall smash both your thighs. I shall kill you.' All were hearing Bheema making that pledge then. A Kshatriya must carry out his pledge with certainty. Bheema did only that. Your anger should not drag you into a wrong path. Do not show unfairness towards Pandavas."

"You take into account the acts of injustice and atrocities perpetrated by Kauravas to Pandavas, before you step in to punish the latter. You should not accuse a man by pointing out only his ultimate act, without analyzing the circumstances in which he has committed it and without proper regard to the various concomitant incidents succeeding them. You should not judge on the basis of a single act, without examining how such an occasion arose. Kali Yuga era is on the advent. The principles of the previous eras will not suit Kali Yuga. Bheema cannot be deemed to have acted unfairly, when he had hit Duryodana below the navel of the latter. It is so because the enemy whom he has attacked in that manner had tried many times to take away his life creating unjustifiable circumstances. It was due to Duryodana's ill advice, Karna had broken Abhimanyu's bow by aiming an arrow from that boy's backside. Abhimanyu was, at that time, isolated and yet was managing to fight against several powerful warriors. When Abhimanyu's chariot got broken and he was rendered helpless in an isolated condition and still fighting, he was murdered in a cowardly manner. Bheema has committed no sin in killing Duryodana. Bheema had suppressed his pent up anger for thirteen years. Duryodana was always remembering Bheema's pledge about him. When Duryodana called upon Pandavas to fight against him, he chose Bheema only with the intention that Bheema should honour his pledge. Why do you consider that Bheema has erred?"

Though Balarama had not changed his view, his anger subsided. He was disgusted and did not want to remain there any longer.

Dharmaputra and Arjuna were also not happy over Bheema's action in trampling on fallen Duryodana's face and dancing. However, all in the gathering were talking contemptuously of Duryodana. Krishna told them, "The enemy, who has been defeated, is lying on the ground. His life is about to depart. There is no need to continue to condemn him. He was bad himself. He mixed with bad men. Let us go."

Those words of Krishna fell on the ears of Duryodana. He was furious. He commented,

"Oh! Wretched Fellow! Born to a Slave! Did not your father Vasudeva serve under Kamsa as a slave? You are never in the habit of moving with princes and mingling with them. You are talking like a shameless and deceitful man. Only you had induced Bheema asking him to break my thighs. Pretending as though you were talking to Arjuna in a disinterested manner, you, showing out your own thighs as a signal for Bheema to attack me that way, you made Bheema to ignore the rules of war. Bheema and I were up to then engaged in the war on equal terms. You do not have sympathy. You have no sense of shame. Only you conspired to bring about Bhishma's death. You made Sikandi to be in the forefront when Bhishma was to be opposed. You were aware that Bhishma would eschew fighting against females. He refused to fight and out of disgust he fell down after sustaining injuries with no effort to counter the enemy. You made Dharmaputra to utter a lie so that Drona would be nearing the gate of death. You are the father of that lie, which Dharmaputra had uttered. When Drishtadyumna cut down Drona, who had already abandoned all his weapons and sat on Yoga posture in deep meditation, you had not expressed your disapproval. On the other hand, you had rejoiced. If Karna had used his divine spear to kill Gatothgaja, it was due to your strategy to save Arjuna. Karna had spared that unique weapon until then only with the intention of killing Arjuna. But, you had maneuvered to divert Karna in order to save Arjuna. Only you had asked Satyaki to kill Bhurisravas, after making the latter feel disinterested to fight any longer and who was in meditation. When Karna was struggling to lift his chariot up, only you had directed Arjuna to kill Karna at once. You had indulged in illusory tactics for bringing about Jayadratha's death."

Krishna spoke to him, "Why are you causing increasing pains to your body on account of your anger? Your wrongful actions have only drawn you to your end. Do not throw the blame on us. Only you are responsible for the death of Karna and all others. I shall tell you all about your very huge crimes. Will any punishment suffice for your atrocious conduct towards Draupadi? Your cruelties and evil deeds are innumerable. You should not condemn others, with those deeds of yours as the basis. It became necessary for us to undertake those measures about which you are accusing us, only because they were the results of your own cruelties. You have redeemed your debts in the war only due to your own ambitions. You have a place in Holy Heaven meant for Kshatriyas, who have shed their lives in wars."

Duryodana said, "Krishna! I shall reach Holy Heaven along with my associates and relatives. You and your associates will continue to live in this world experiencing distress." The adamant nature of Duryodana had not deserted him even then.

Krishna conceded at last saying, "You could not have been killed in a fair manner. Oh! The Expert in War!"

16.1 Burning of Arjuna's Chariot

All had returned to their camps. Krishna was driving the chariot of Arjuna as usual. As soon as they reached the camp, Krishna asked Arjuna, "Please get down taking with you your Gandiva bow and the arrows. I shall get down after you do so. It will be to your good if you get down first."

Accordingly, Arjuna got down from the chariot, taking with him his Gandiva bow and the arrows. Krishna after releasing the reins of the horses got down. Immediately after Krishna got down, Hanuman as the symbol of the flag atop the chariot disappeared. That chariot was burnt in fire completely. Arjuna's remnant arrows, horses, reins, yokes and iron bars were all reduced to ashes. Arjuna was astonished. When he asked Krishna, the latter replied,

"Arjuna! This chariot should have been burnt already as there were many attacks of weapons. Because I was sitting on the chariot when the wars were going on, it did not crack and was not burnt. Now that I have got down, it has been reduced to ashes."

Krishna later on told Dharmaputra, "You have won because of your good luck. Your enemies were all destroyed. You five have escaped. You had prayed to me saying, 'Krishna! Arjuna is your brother; your friend. You should save him from all dangers.' I said, 'I assure you. I shall do so.'

Arjuna was always under my protection. You have scored the victory."

Dharmaputra told Krishna respectfully, "We were protected by you in spite of Drona, Karna and others putting into use the weapons of Lord Brahma. Samsaptakas were destroyed because of you. Due to your grace Arjuna did not face any defeat at all. My brothers and I have attained the happy end of the war."

"Sage Vyasa had pronounced, 'Where there is Krishna, dharma and success will be there.' That has proved to be true."

16.2. Dritharashtra's Embrace

The war had ended. The entire Hastinapura was weeping. Dhritharashtra in Kurukshetra was weeping. Dharmaputra came to meet him and bowed respectfully. Dhritharashtra drew him towards him and embraced him. But, there was no real fondness in it. Bheema was the next to be invited for a similar embrace. Krishna, who was there at that time, knew what was going to happen because of his fore sight. He had already arranged for the iron image of Bheema to be brought there. Duryodana used to practice giving terrible blows to it in his preparation for an eventual inevitable encounter with Bheema. Krishna pushed Bheema away. Bheema's iron image was before Dhritharashtra. Dhritharashtra was blind. Believing that he was embracing Bheema, he got that iron image in his firm grip. Dritharashtra's inner thoughts were full of ire against Bheema, as it was Bheema who had killed all his hundred sons and with that animosity reflecting in his strong arms, he embraced that iron image so tightly that it crashed into pieces. He cried, 'Ha! My anger has thrown me out of balance and I have killed Bheema.'

Krishna told Dhritharashtra, "I anticipated this event. I have prevented the occurrence of a great disaster. You have crushed the iron image, which I had arranged to be kept before you. Has your anger subsided? Bheema is alive."

Dhritharashtra became cool and blessed Bheema.

16.3. Krishna Met Dritharashtra and Ghandhari

Next day, Krishna left to meet Dhritharashtra and Gandhari. Pandavas were perplexed as they were not aware of the purpose behind Krishna's visit.

Krishna told Dharmaputra, "Gandhari is a highly holy woman. She has the power to reduce the three worlds to ashes, when in anger. She should first be consoled with agreeable words."

Krishna, at first spoke to Dhritharashtra after weeping a little. He said,

"There is nothing you are unaware. Pandavas endeavoured their utmost to avert all these destructions, on account of their respect for you. If Fate strikes, is there an escape? Pandavas are free from blame. You and Gandhari should not show hatred towards them. Dharmaputra shows very much affinity for you and is fond of you. He is not at all happy, as he grieves for your sake and for Ghandhari's sake. He is hesitating to meet you as he is ashamed."

He then spoke to Gandhari. "What an amount of wise counseling you had passed on to your son! You had reprimanded Duryodana! You also warned him that Dharma will be rewarded with success. Your words have proved to be true. Please do not grieve. Please do not wish for Pandavas destruction."

Gandhari replied to Krishna, 'Krishna! You have spoken the truth. My heart is now in peace on hearing your words.'

16.4. Aswaththama - Brahma Siras Weapon

As Krishna was talking to Dhritharashtra and Gandhari, he learnt that Aswaththama, son of Drona, was indulging in some seriously harmful activity. He told Dhritharashtra, 'I seek your permission to leave. You need not have to be sad. Aswaththama, son of Drona, has been planning for some evil act. I am leaving urgently only because of that.'

Finding that Duryodana had been fatally hit and in an unfair manner, Aswaththama, Kripa and Krithavarma were passing through a forest area in utter disgust. They sat under a huge tree. In the night, Kripa and Krithavarma fell asleep. Aswaththama alone, not able to sleep, was releasing heavy breath in anger and was restless. He was violently shocked about Duryodana's death and the unfair manner it had happened.

Aswaththama looked up at the tree branches. Many crows were sleeping in their nests peacefully. But, an owl came there flying silently. That owl killed many crows which were still in sleep. Aswaththama had a close look at that event. He spoke to himself, 'I learn a lesson from this owl. I will not be able to kill Pandavas in war. I shall end up losing my life instead in the war. I should kill Pandavas when they sleep in the night.' Thinking seriously on those lines, he woke up Kripa and Krithavarma. He disclosed to them his plan. They, at first, objected to the plan saying that it was sinful to kill someone in sleep. As Aswaththama insisted on executing the plan, they agreed.

They reached the resting place where Pandavas were expected to sleep. Aswaththama stationed Kripa and Krithavarma at the entry point of the rest place and he entered into it. He, at first, killed Drishtadyumna who was asleep. He then killed all the sons of Panchalas. Sons of Pandavas were his next victims. Aswaththama thus carried out his most nefarious activity of killing many who were asleep. Aswaththama mistook the sons of Pandavas as Pandavas sleeping there and so killed them. He was immensely pleased that his revengeful act had been accomplished successfully.

That night, Pandavas and Krishna had left that rest place earlier and gone elsewhere.

When the tragic information reached Dharmaputra, all Pandavas and Krishna reached the rest place. Dharmaputra, on seeing the tragedy, fell down like one struck by thunder, due to extreme sadness. Bheema was fretting and fuming in extreme anger. Draupadi was unable to bear with this mammoth tragedy. She made a pledge, 'There is a gem in Aswaththama's head, born with him. He must be killed at once and that gem in his head must be taken away and given to me.'

Bheema started immediately in search of Aswaththama in great excitement with the firm resolve to kill him. Krishna cautioned Dharmaputra, 'Aswaththama possesses a supremely powerful weapon called Brahma Sirsa. Drona had given that weapon to his son. If Aswaththama uses that deadly weapon, the whole world will be destroyed. You also go for saving Bheema.'

Krishna left in the chariot with the remaining four Pandavas. Bheema, who had left earlier, was in the vicinity of Aswaththama. Aswaththama finding Bheema very close to him apprehended that his own death was imminent at the hands of Bheema. For saving himself and to destroy Bheema, he took on his hand a Dharbha (Sacred Dry Grass), chanted the hymn appropriate for Brahma Sirsa weapon and released it.

Krishna alerted Arjuna saying, 'You should forthwith neutralize Aswaththama's missile which has acquired immense destructive power, by discharging your own Brahma Sirsa to counter that.'

Accordingly, Arjuna discharged his counter Brahma Sirsa missile.

In such a tragic surrounding, it looked as though that the whole world would be destroyed. Finding that the situation was becoming over charged and out of control, Holy Sages led by Sage Vyasa assembled together appearing in the scene suddenly and pressed both Arjuna and Aswaththama to use their own counter missiles (Upa Samharam) in order to nullify both Brahma Sirsas in action. Sage Vyasa further stressed that if the two Brahma Sirsas were not withdrawn by the proper application of recital of appropriate hymns, all in the world would get destroyed. Arjuna had learnt how Brahma Sirsa discharged by him could be withdrawn. Owing to his commitment for ensuring the welfare of the world, he immediately withdrew his missile. However, Aswaththama had learnt the methodology for discharging it only. He was not taught the methodology for withdrawing it. Sage Vyasa condemned him. Aswaththama told him, 'I shall divert my Brahma Sirsa missile in such a way that Pandavas are deprived of their heirs with no one to succeed them and my Brahma Sirsa will destroy the fetus in the wombs of their wives.' That compromise was agreed to in the absence of an alternative. Sage Vyasa asked Aswaththama, 'You take away that gem in your head and give it to Pandavas.'

Aswaththama removed the gem in his head and gave it to Pandavas. His weapon had the effect of destroying the heirs of Pandavas, even as they were growing as fetus in wombs.

Uthara, wife of Abhimanyu, was at that time pregnant. The fetus was growing in her womb. Aswaththama's weapon had attacked it and taken away its life. Krishna stepped in and pronounced with his divine voice, 'Let this child get back its life. This child will live long.' That lone heir to Pandavas was thus saved. Pandavas had one heir left alive thanks to Krishna's divine grace. Parikshit was that great child.

Krishna cursed Aswaththama.

"You are a coward. You are timid. You are abound in sins and are condemnable. Being used to commit sins, you have killed the children too. You should suffer due retribution for your inimical deeds. You should face consequential miseries. You will wander on the earth for three thousand years. No one will be friendly to you. No one will give you company. You will not be able to talk to anybody. You will roam in several far off places like a recluse. You will be cast away from the society and discarded by them. Pus and blood will bleed from your body spreading hateful bad odour. You will live inside a dense forest. All diseases will haunt you. Parikshit, Uthara's son, will shine as a powerful king. He will, before your very eyes, regain life although you had burnt the child with your weapon."

Aswaththama's gem reached the hands of Draupadi. She gave it to Dharmaputra asking him to wear it.

16.5. Ghandhari Cursed Krishna

Gandhari, along with Dhritharashtra, went to the battle field. Although her eyes were covered by a black cloth, Sage Vyasa had blessed her with vision for looking at the dead bodies lying in the war field.

Gandhari saw everything. Broken chariots and swords, crushed bows and arrows, dead horses and elephants were all in heaps. Thousands of corpses with crushed bones and in pool of blood were also seen. Some corpses without heads and some heads without trunks were also there. Eagles and vultures were circling round and wolves and foxes were very brisk as they had sumptuous food to eat.

Gandhari, on seeing that loathsome sight, was at the peak of agony. She wailed, within herself thinking, 'My son Duryodana's greed and foolishness have caused all these tragedies.'

Sage Vyasa asked Dhritharashtra to perform the obsequies for those dead and he left.

Pandavas and Krishna went with Dhritharashtra and Gandhari. Daughters-in-law of Gandhari were trying to identify the bodies of their respective slain husbands. There were many similar women in acute distress and tears.

This scene plunged Gandhari to deep misery and she spoke to Krishna.

"Krishna! Have a look at the sorrowful plight of my daughters-in-law. Those eyes which were full of hatred and animosity against my sons would now rejoice. Why did you allow for this punishment? What were their sins? The bodies of Bhishma, Drona, Karna, Salya, and Drupada are found to be shining. They might have been dead now, but they had enjoyed tremendous privileges and comforts. They were accustomed to wake up in the morning hearing the sweet music instruments singing for them. They are now hearing wolves and foxes howling."

"Krishna! How do you bear with this sight? Is it the consequence of your greatness? Weeps, cries, wailings and agony are everywhere!"

Gandhari said these words with her sorrowful throat choking.

Krishna did not utter a word. He kept on accompanying Gandhari. Gandhari saw Duryodana's body. Her wailings burst out loudly. She cried.

"My son Duryodana! What has happened to you? Dusts and sands are spread on you! I am your mother! Get up! Bow to me! Krishna! Krishna! Look at my son Duryodana! When he was preparing to march into the battle field, he came to me seeking my blessings. I told him, 'Dharma will conquer!' Krishna! Do you know why I chose those words to bless him? I certainly anticipated that as the stringent penalty for the injustices and atrocities perpetrated against Pandavas and Draupadi in the assembly hall, Dharma will conquer and Kauravas would be routed one day. I blessed Duryodana with those words, as the memory of the past deeds was always lingering in my mind."

"I have not been supporting and never justifying the deeds of Duryodana even though he happened to be my son. I have told him, 'It is laudable to die in the war, rather than retreating from the war field facing defeat. Now, with him lying dead, I am crying."

"Krishna! Duryodana is lying on the ground. All my sons have departed. They have deserted me and my husband and gone away. Vidura also had pleaded with my husband."

"Duryodana had conscripted a huge army of eleven Akshouhinis. All have perished. That is not due to the fate of my sons! They are the effects of the bad deeds of me and my husband."

Krishna did not utter a word.

Gandhari's wailings were uncontrollable. She had a look at the remains of every one and after crying, she told Krishna,

"Krishna! You gave wise counseling in the assembly. This great catastrophe would not have occurred, if your words were listened to and honoured. Events had happened in the way you had warned. You are the cause of this destruction and calamity. Without making proper efforts, you stopped with utterances of words of justice and propriety. You should have used your force and authority for preventing both the parties stepping into the battle field. Would it not have been possible to avert the crisis? Many noble persons were there. But, all of you have conspired, by grouping together. You have failed to establish peace. You all should bear responsibility for this great massacre."

"Krishna! You have in fact enacted the drama of trying for peace, with the aim of bringing about the end of

Duryodana. Only you have instigated the mutual enmity and hatred between Pandavas and Kauravas. Your mission ended in failure on account of that. All these are your creation."

"Krishna! Listen! If it is true that I, throughout my life time, have been truly loyal and devoted and upright to my husband, your entire Yadava race will get destroyed due to the mutual bickering of one against another. This is my curse. For the cruelty which you have caused to our race, you will also be killed cruelly thirty six years from now. Your body will lie on the ground with no one caring for it. This is my curse."

Krishna smiled and said,

"Oh! Mother Gandhari! Your curse to me is nothing new. There is already a curse to us. Yadavas had once offended a sage. He had cursed that the entire Yadava race would be destroyed. Due to Lord Almighty's grace, those very same words have been uttered by you also. There is, however, an underlying secret. No one will be capable of eliminating Yadava race completely. They should, therefore, be killed by themselves, one killing another, on and on. Your curse confirms another curse already pronounced. Oh! Mother Gandhari! Let the obsequies required, be allowed to be done."

Krishna and Gandhari joined with Dhritharashtra. As they were walking, Krishna told Gandhari, "Oh! Mother Gandhari! Are you not aware of the evil deeds committed by Duryodana and Duchhasana? Neither I nor Bhishma nor Drona even could prevent them. Their cruelty and their nefarious tendencies alone have resulted in the war. How will I be held responsible for that? Let you put an end to your sorrow. You are the mother of outstanding warriors. They fought and lost their lives in war. They have attained a noble place in Heaven, after their death."

16.6. Bhishma and Krishna

Mahabharatha war had ended, but Dharmaputra's agony was still persisting, despite his victory. Kauravas were all killed. Acharya Drona was dead. After coming to know that Karna was his own brother, Dharmaputra's grief was enormous.

Arjuna requested Krishna to console Dharmaputra. Krishna spoke to Dharmaputra and pacified him. Dharmaputra was also crowned as the king. He told Krishna, "This kingdom has become ours because of your blessings, your wisdom and your help."

He prolonged his submissions to Krishna, reciting hundred sacred names of Krishna, by way of STUTHI (Prayer).

Dharmaputra again met Krishna and bowed to him respectfully. Krishna was in deep meditation, as Dharmaputra was going on with his prayers to Krishna. Dharmaputra sought Krishna's clarifications as to why the latter was closing his eyes in meditation. Krishna replied to him,

"Bhishma, who is lying on the bed of arrows, is meditating with deep concentration on me. He is learned in the four Vedas. He knows how to put into use the divine weapons. He is the storehouse of knowledge of every kind, all those to be learnt. He has full control on the vital senses. My mind was centered on him and made me to meditate in response to his. Dharmaputra! You should approach him and learn from him all the scriptural lessons. Let us go to him."

Krishna accompanied by Dharmaputra met Bhishma. Bhishma worshipped Krishna and began to offer his prayers to Krishna. BHISHMA STHUTHI forms a prominent part in Mahabharatham. It is very elaborate. Let us absorb a few to ourselves.

"Krishna! You are absolutely pure. You are found in an absolutely pure surrounding. You have a highly exalted stature. You are superior to everything. You are PARA BRAHMAM (Supreme Soul). You have no beginning. You have no end. You are the lord of the world. You create the world. No one can comprehend your real form. All the worlds and all the living beings are merged in you. You are the resort for the whole world. You make the world function. You have thousand faces; thousand arms; thousand legs and thousand eyes. You are smaller than the atom; you are bigger than the biggest; you are mightier than the mightiest. You are the never perishing origin for everything. You cannot be comprehended. You are beyond imagination. You bestow Sun and Agni (Fire) their resplendence. You are represented by the single word OHM (Pranava).

You have taken the incarnations of MATSYA, KURMA, VARAHA, NARASIMHA, VAMANA, THRIVIKRAMA, PARASURAMA, RAMA, BALARAMA, and KRISHNA. You will be incarnating as KALKI. The five vital senses (Gnana Indriyas), the five vital organs (Karma Indriyas), Mind, the five elements (Pancha Bhoothas), are enclosing you, but your form is different.

You are the embodiment of Gnanam (Transcendental Knowledge). You grant Moksha (Liberation). You are bereft of Anger (Kopa), Hatred (Dwesha) and Moha (Passion) and other evil qualities. Everything is in you. Everything has emanated from you. You are the brightest part of everything. Everything is your manifestation. PRAKRUTHI, MAHAT, AHANKARAM, MANAS, BHUDDHI, INDRIYAS, PANCHA BHOOTHAS all have you as their basic form. You are there in all the three Kalas (Time) namely the past, the present and the future. I bow to you, the Protector of the World. I bow to you, who is beyond the Five Elements, and who is Nitya Muktha (True Emancipation). I bow to you who are prevalent in all the worlds. I bow to you who are prevalent in all directions. I bow to you, who create and protect the worlds. I bow to you who are non-conquerable. Krishna! I bow to you!"

Krishna requested Bhishma to impart the laws of the world to Yudhishtra. When Bhishma expressed that he possessed no physical strength to do so, Krishna granted him a boon. Bhishma was endowed with all the strength needed to teach Dharmaputra. These lessons constitute a prominent part of Mahabharatham

16.7. Uthangar

Uthangar was a great sage, possessing a very great resplendence. He had observed several penances, attaining supreme inner power. He used to spend most of his time in deserts. Krishna, who was returning to Dwaraka on the completion of the war, saw Uthangar. As Uthangar was bowing respectfully to Krishna, the latter reciprocated similarly.

Uthangar had not known about Mahabharatha war. He, after making the usual courteous enquiries of the welfare of all, asked Krishna,

"Have you succeeded in establishing friendly ties and restoring brotherly affections between Pandavas and Kauravas? Have you brought about unity between them?"

Krishna explained,

"I, at first, tried to conciliate Kauravas. I could not succeed. War became inevitable. Kauravas along with all their relations and associates had perished. Neither with brain power nor with physical power, could God's methods be transgressed. Bhishma, Vidura and I had endeavored to counsel them to follow the upright path. They fought and reached Yama Loka (Land of Death). Five Pandavas are alive."

Uthangar was very indignant. With his eyes turning red, he told Krishna,

"In spite of your potentialities, you had not protected Kauravas. You should have prevented them with all the force at your command. You are an expert with great capabilities. But, you had acted with deceit. I am going to curse you surely."

Krishna spoke to him,

"I shall explain in detail. You are a sage, rich in penances. After hearing my philosophical view points, you may release your curse. You cannot humiliate me with your mere saintly power. I do not wish that your saintly power should get extinguished. Your penances are mighty. It has brightness. I am aware of your higher spiritual power which you have cultivated from your boyhood. You should not destroy your spiritual power, earned by you with great difficulties." Krishna paused.

Uthangar said, "You narrate truly what all had happened. On hearing that, I shall either compliment you or curse you."

Krishna uttered these eminent words to Uthangar.

"Satvam, Rajas and Thamas are the three Gunas which have emanated from me. I am carrying the duties of Brahma, Vishnu and Siva of Creation, Preservation and Destruction respectively. I adopt Thamo Guna as Rudra, Rajo Guna as Brahma and Satva Guna as Vishnu. I am the form of Pranava. I am omnipresent, in all moving and non-moving substances. Rudras and Vasus have their origin in me. All living beings are in me. I am in all the living beings. Let you know from me that all Asura groups, Yakshas, Gandarvas, Rakshsas, Nagas and Apsaras have their generation in me. Sath (Truth) and Asath, Akshra (Indivisible) and Kshara (Divisible) are my manifestations. All the righteous rights and religious duties prescribed for all the four divisions of people are all my manifestations. I am God of gods. There is nothing superior to me. Let you know that I am Omkar (Pranava) originating from Vedas, Yupa in Yagas, Soma which reaches Devas (Gods), and Homas. I am Hotha, I am Havyam, I am Havis, and I am Udgatha for great Yagas. Those who perform emancipation rituals for freeing themselves from sins, those who chant Shanthi Sthuthis and Mangala Sthuthis are only offering their prayers to me. Dharma is my breath. My Dharma is to show mercy to all the living beings. I am with those who adopt Dharma and who desert Adharma in all their various births. For protecting the world, for establishing Dharma, I adopt appropriate forms and am omnipresent in all the three worlds. Vishnu, Brahma and Indra have their origin in me. I am the creator of all the various forms of life. I am the destroyer of all. With Yugas (Eras) keep on succeeding one after another, I am, in order to do good to the people, incarnating in their midst, build the bridge called Dharma for eliminating Adharmas. While I am born in the midst of Devas, I do all as God. While I am born in the midst of Gandarvas, I do all the duties of Gandarvas. While I am born in the midst of Nagas, I do the work of Nagas. I do likewise in regard to Yaksha race and Rakshasa race. Now, when I am here as a man, I beseeched Kauravas very humbly. They were idiots. They were intoxicated in power mongering. They did not accept my words. I even threatened them. I had shown them my true form. They, who were unrighteous, had been killed righteously in the war, at a time, when they had reached their life's end, and they have reached Heaven. Pandavas have secured fame in the world. I have told everything."

Uthangar told Krishna with the utmost respect, "Janardhana! I now know you as the one creating the worlds. My inner conscience has now become fully clear. My anger has vanished. If I enjoy your grace, I am eager to see you in your cosmic form (VISWA ROOPAM)."

Krishna was happy and he showed to Uthangar his cosmic form (VISWA ROOPAM) in the same way he had done for Arjuna before.

Krishna changed himself to VISWA ROOPAM. He had long arms. His splendor was equal to one thousand Suns. His form was immanent all over the sky. His face was seen spread everywhere.

Uthangar began praying Krishna,

"Oh! The Mightiest possessing multifarious forms! Paramathma! Padmanabha! Pundarikasksha! Madhava! I bow to you! I bow to you! You are in the form of Hiranya Garbha! You lift all people to rise above family bonds! You are the most ancient! You are the symbol of peace! Your colour is bluish! You are Sun dispelling the darkness called Agnanam (Ignorance). You are the best medicine for the disease called family bond. You are my refuge. You are to be comprehended through Vedas. You are Vedas incarnate. You love your devotees. You should eradicate my sadness and my wrong passions. Please protect me from all the sinful activities. You are, in fact, seen in the form of everyone's duties. You are Viswathma. You are the source from which all worlds have been created. This entire earth bears your holy feet. The sky above bears your holy face. The space between the sky and earth is borne by your stomach. The directions are borne by your arms. All worlds are you. Please compress your form, which is free from flaw and which is the most noble. Please repossess your original form of Krishna."

Krishna offered a boon to Uthangar. Uthangar told him, "I have worshipped your VISWA ROOPAM. I have no other desire left to ask."

As Krishna insisted, Uthangar sought this boon. "If you are granting me a boon, I should have access to water for drinking, wherever I am and whenever I want."

Uthangar was usually wandering in deserts. The boon he sought had this as the background.

Krishna granted that boon remarking, 'Only that! Let that happen.'

One day, as Uthangar was passing through a desert, he was thirsty and he invoked Krishna's boon. A hunter, who was ugly and wearing dirty clothes had appeared before him, carrying a leather pouch containing water. Uthangar, who was a pure Brahmin, hated to drink the water offered to him by that unclean hunter. He admonished Krishna remarking, 'Is your boon so regrettable?'

That hunter disappeared immediately. Krishna appeared before him. He said,

"Keeping in mind the boon you had sought from me, I asked Indra to bless you with Amritha (Holy Nectar) and to offer it to you in the form of water. He hesitated on the ground that a mortal man, with the limited life span, should not be rewarded with Amirtha, which would render him to live eternally and thus freed from death. It was I who had arranged to bless you with Amirtha in the form of water and for putting you in test. You possess full Gnana. You make no distinction between high and low. I accepted, therefore, his approach. It is unfortunate that you have conducted yourself in this manner, as the result of which I have been defeated by Indra."

Uthangar was perplexed in utter disappointment.

17. Krishna's Incarnation Concluded

The curse had acted. On conclusion of his incarnation, Krishna was reaching his abode in Heaven. He was worshipped by the congregation of sages and he rose upwards spreading brightness everywhere. Indra, Aswini Devas, Rudras, Adityas, Vasus, Viwedavas, Sages, Saints, Gandarvas, Apsaras all extended a hearty welcome to Krishna. Krishna, who is the cause of creation of worlds, who is imperishable, who is Yogacharya, who is Paramathma, becomes SRIMAN NARAYANA and with his great splendor, He gave brightness to the sky and earth and He occupies His abode in Vaikunta. Devas offered their prayers to Him. Flowers were strewn on Him. Sriman Narayana gave His vision, with His four arms.

Srimad Bhagavad Gita

18.1. Introduction to Srimad Bhagawad Gita

Sri Krishna's divine sermons to Arjuna, on the eve of the Great War of Mahabharatham constitute Srimad Bhagavad Gita. Arjuna was the recipient of these gospels, enunciated to him by Sri Krishna.

Srimad Bhagavad Gita (We may refer as Gita) occupies a very prominent part in Mahabharatham. Krishna is the heart of Mahabharatham. It is the heart which bears the life and keeps a man alive. It is the heart which circulates blood to every part of the human body making it possible for it to function. Brain is the most important organ among all the organs in the human body. It is the brain which issues commands to all the organs in the human body to carry out their respective functions. In the same way, Krishna plays such a crucial role in Mahabharatham. Every event in Mahabharatham has a link to the utterances of Krishna in Gita. Srimad Bhagavad Gita has no story of its own. A question may arise as to why Mahabharatham alone is not to be read and assimilated to the exclusion of Srimad Bhagavad Gita. A human body needs energy. Food generates energy. It is not enough if food merely is consumed. That food must be capable of generating energy. All the organs must function. Brain activates the body. Heart makes it possible for the brain to operate. It is, therefore, necessary to understand

Srimad Bhagavad Gita. By understanding Gita, we can understand Krishna.

The world has Sriman Narayana for its origin. Sriman Narayana creates, preserves and destroys the worlds. Sriman Narayana had incarnated as Krishna for the sake of the people's welfare. Great scholars consider that the entire Gita has its full essence in one sloka.

SARVA DHARMAAAN PARITHYAJYA MAAM EKAM SARANAM VRAJA

AHAM THWAAM SARVA PAPEBYO MOKSHISHYAMI MAA SUCHA.

If one learns this one sloka, with its underlying significant messages, that will pave the way for understanding the entire Gita.

Vedas preach that Sriman Narayana is PARAMATHMA, which message is contained in Upanishads too. Gita also expatiates on this truth.

Krishna tells in this sloka, " MAA SUCHA - no need to worry". Worry is about what? He tells again that 'I shall liberate you from all sins.' 'MAAM EKAM SARANAM VRAJA. - You surrender to me alone. 'This is his gospel'. 'Is it enough if you surrender to me alone?' Yes! 'SARVA DHARMAAN PRITHYAJYA' - That is to say, 'Relinquish all Dharma. Surrender to me alone.'

Sri Krishna preaches to the entire human community, 'Surrender to me alone.'

What is surrender? What are the means for surrendering? What is meant by the words, 'Relinquish all Dharma?'

There are several commentaries for Gita. Sri Ramanujacharya, Sri Sankaracharya and Sri Madvacharya have given us their extensive and wonderful Bhasyams (Commentaries). Their comments are very famous. Sri Alavandar in his GITHARTHA SANGRAHA has given us very short and sharp commentaries in one sloka each separately for the eighteen Chapters of Gita. Sriman Vedantha Desika has provided us with his THAATHPARYA CHADRIKA which illuminates us with his brilliant epitomized commentaries on Gita.

Gita has seven hundred and forty five slokas. There are eighteen chapters. Gita ends almost with the sloka starting SARVA DHARMAAN PARITHYAJA..., the sloka which we have seen above. Let us try to succeed to have a grasp of Gita, by going through the splendid messages it conveys in a short form as far as possible, in this book.

Sriman Narayana has preached Gita. Sri Krishna emphatically tells in Gita that it is Sriman Narayana who is to be surrendered to for securing Moksha (Liberation). For attaining Sriman Narayana, Bhakthi Margam (Path of Devotion) alone is ideal. Although the other two means namely Karma Yoga and Gnana Yoga have been expatiated in Gita for taking us to Sriman Narayana, Gita touches upon the doctrine that those two Yogas also lead us towards Bhakthi Yoga (Path of Devotion) and unites us with Sriman Narayana. Surrender is the means for Bhakthi (Devotion). Gita pinpoints on this salient aspect to take deep root in us.

The great significance of the term 'Surrender' (Charanagathi) is revealed at the very commencement of Gita. Arjuna was in deep anguish and dejection on looking at his agnates (same lineage brothers, cousins, grandfather and other relations), Acharyas (Teachers, Gurus, Preceptors) and other relations holding weapons, ready to fight and prepared for sacrificing their lives in the war set to commence. He was mentally agitated as to what was required to be achieved by killing them all. He said that even if others were preparing themselves to take away his life, he would not wish to kill them. He was determined that even if he were to secure the leadership of the three worlds by killing them all, he would not embark on the inimical act of murder. He threw away his famous Gandiva bow and arrows. He entrusted himself to Krishna pleading to the latter to accept him as the disciple. He surrendered to Krishna praying for a noble path to be chartered for him.

Krishna was in the war field for the purpose of driving Arjuna's chariot. Arjuna was, therefore, the master and Krishna his servant, on account of their respective roles. But, in reality, it happened that Krishna was the Acharya (Guru-Teacher) and Arjuna was the disciple.

Arjuna saw in the battlefield the eldest in his family of ancestors, his grandfather (Bhishma); he saw Drona who had taught him archery and every branch of warfare; close blood relation, cousin Duryodana; he saw several close relations. Should they be killed? Arjuna had made up his mind not to fight.

Krishna's divine sermons started flowing.

18.2. First Chapter and Second Chapter

Arjuna! You are sad that Bhishma, Drona and others are going to be killed. Death is inevitable. It is the body which dies. The Soul in the body does not die. Like boyhood, youth and old age, which occur naturally to a body, death also occurs. Body perishes, Soul does not perish. Body undergoes changes. Soul was not different at birth. Soul was residing in some other body. Soul keeps on leaving one body after another, and is occupying that body where it presently is. After that body perishes, it will occupy another body. Soul is beyond birth and death. Soul is never born. Soul is never dead. It is eternal. Like the process of one removing his old cloth and wearing a new one, Soul forsakes the old body and enters into the new body.

Weapons do not destroy the Soul. Water does not drown it. Air has no effect on it. It cannot be comprehended by the vital senses. No inner feeling can reach it. If this truth is understood, there will never be any realization on the part of a man that he either kills or is killed. So, do not grieve that a body is dead.

Fighting in war is Dharma for a Kshatriya. Kshatriyas must fight necessarily in war. Refusing to fight in war is contrary to Kshatriya Dharma. If he wins in the war, that means fame; death in war also means fame. To retreat from war or to refuse to fight in war is contrary to Kshatriya Dharma. That will result in losing fame. It means not only losing fame, infamy also will be attached to him. Death in war assures a place in Holy Heaven. Victory in war will fetch you the kingdom. For a Kshatriya fighting in war is righteous. Refusal to fight is unrighteous. It will tarnish the fame. You will be dubbed as a coward. Victory is kingdom. Death is Holy Heaven. Destroying enemies is not sinful.

A Kshatriya, once getting involved in war and setting his foot on the battle field, should attack his enemy who opposes him, irrespective of who that enemy is, whether that enemy is a relative or older in age or an Acharya, making no distinction whatever.

You carry out the prescribed duties for you irrespective of the result, treating as equal whether joy or sorrow, gain or loss, victory or defeat. No sin will occur. In that dispassionate outlook, nothing is deemed as deprived from you. There is no contrary consequence. If the duty is undertaken even to the slightest extent but righteously, fear is thrown out and protection is secured.

Those who are slaves of aspirations and attachments, treat a place in Holy Heaven after death or ample pleasures and comforts in this worldly life as supreme expedients to enjoy. Those who are attached to the likes and dislikes in their duties are like the fragrance in the flowers and attract others to their points of view. Fragrance in the flowers does not last long. Flowers fade. One should not fall a victim to their flowery words and get thrown down in temptation. He cannot attain the firm wisdom for seeking identity with Paramathma (Lord Almighty).

Krishna had his sermons telling that Body is different and Soul is different. He also stressed that a Kshatriya must fight in war and that will be righteous. He now will deal with the subject of Karma Yoga and the means to be adopted for Moksha (Liberation).

Krishna instructs Arjuna—

The three Gunas (Qualities) normally seen in men are Satvam, Rajas and Tamas. You should be free from the influences of these Gunas. You should dissociate yourself from the results of pairs of opposites namely, joy-sorrow, profit-loss and victory-defeat. You should be free from attachment towards Yoga and Kshema. (Yoga normally means fulfillment of future desires. Kshema normally means fulfillment of present desires.) You should concentrate on the pursuit for identifying yourself with Paramathma. When you have a large reservoir of water, there is no need for a small pond. In the same way, those who learn the broad principles enunciated in Vedas and the teachings contained in Upanishads, living in accordance with them and remaining detached are Gnanis and Mahapurushas (Enlightened and greatly eminent persons). They do not attach any value to pleasures and comforts, wealth and material power.

Your right is Karma (Duty). You have no right on the fruit of Karma. Do not exert yourself for securing the fruit of Karma and to enjoy it. You should not think in terms of abandoning Karma. Keep on doing Karma and carry them out treading on the path of righteousness. But, shed attachment. You accept equally, whether victory or defeat. Detachment is Yoga. Abandon desires. The Mind should be free from delusion. Do not hear anything to the contrary. You should generate hatred towards hearing that.

By forsaking attachment towards wealth and relations, keep on doing your Karma (Duties) observing Yoga (Equanimity). Whether success or failure, irrespective of the result, or remaining completely indifferent to the result, maintain equal poise. Such a state is called Yoga.

The outlook should be centered on Soul. Desires appearing in Mind are to be totally eradicated. Gnanam (Enlightenment) will be gained by such a person only. Sadness should not pull you down. Pleasures and comforts should not elate you. Fear and anger must be given up. Vital senses are to be kept under strict control. If left at the mercy of the vital senses, they corrupt Mind. One who keeps vital senses under control remains stable with Gnanam (Enlightenment.)

Attachment towards possessions leads to desires. Desire results in anger. Anger generates confusion (Lack of clarity). Confusion means misjudgment. Misjudgment clouds wisdom. A man thereby gets totally destroyed or is lost.

There should be clarity in approach. Clarity dispels sadness. Clarity in Mind stabilizes the brain. If the brain is not steady, there can be no meditation. There can be no contemplation. Without meditation, there can be no peace. Without peace, there is no contemplation and no happiness.

Storm in the ocean sinks a ship. In the same way, desires dislodge the vital senses and Mind finds itself confused and wisdom gets dented. Gnanam of one with controlled vital senses is stable.

Those ordinary men who have no control on vital senses, will not be involved in exercises seeking identity with Paramathma; they will have their brain corrupted and would be lost in the 'night' called passion. But, during their 'nights', Gnanis who have self-control remain awake. They are immersed in the contemplation of Paramathma. As ordinary men, though awake and are enjoying comforts and pleasures, and are earning wealth and are spending them, Gnanis during those periods would be deep in meditation peacefully seeking self-realization. For those ordinary men the 'night' in slumber struck by the corruption of Mind, is 'day' for Gnanis. The 'day' for ordinary men is the 'night' bestowing peace for Gnanis.

Ocean does not get stirred. Although waters from the rivers reach the ocean, the ocean is not agitated. In the same way, although the desires may find their way into a man, he must not get affected but he must seek peace. If passion has a hold on a man, he, in a state of disequilibrium, struggles. Therefore, one, who suppresses all passions, discards attachments, gives up ego and selfishness, alone attains peace and Mukthi (Liberation). Even if he reaches that stage during his last days of life, he attains Mukthi.

18.3. Chapter Three (Karma Yoga)

Gnana yoga and Karma Yoga are two. One, who ceases to get inv olved in action (Karma), will not be deemed as not entitled to action. By merely sacrificing everything, one does not get Siddi (Perfection).

It is not as though that one remains inactive even for a moment, avoiding to act altogether. All, due to their in born nature, are involved in some action (Karma) or the other, without their own awareness.

He, who, while restraining the organs of action, falls a slave to the effects of the vital senses, is called a hypocrite (A thief of conscience). He becomes a farcical entity. However, he, who controls within himself, within his mind, all the desires emanating from the five vital senses, is able to put into action his sense organs by entrusting them with actions (Karmas) and by undertaking them with due regard to integrity of purpose, and without attachment, is considered as noble, eminent, pure and perfect.

You should be doing those acts, prescribed duties, meant for you to do. By doing so, being obliged to do so, you will be superior to the state of total inaction. That will be commendable. Inaction will not help even for taking care of the body.

Among actions, excepting for those pertaining to Yagnas and for pleasing deities, others will have the effect of binding men in some way or the other. You continue to carrying out the duties of the former nature, without attachment and with proper devotion.

Brahma, in his process of creation of men, also created Yagnas alongside. He wanted Yagnas to be performed in increased scales. He said that by spreading Yagnas, the mankind would be more and more benefitted. He also expressed that Yagnas would fulfill all the wishes of the mankind. According to him, Yagnas would distinguish themselves by offering anything and everything wished for like Kamadenu. He wanted Devas (Gods) to grow more and more. Devas (Gods) are responsible for the growth of living beings. In this way, growth of one results in the growth of another, and so on, with mutual enhancements. Devas, who are benefitted by Yagnas, bestow the living beings with all those required for their good life. Those who do not offer to Gods through Yagnas, but appropriate for themselves all pleasures, are evil persons. They are thieves. Those who consume the remnants of the offerings to Gods in Yagnas are virtuous and are of a superior kind. They are saved from sins. Those, who cook food for their own consumption, are sinners. What they eat is sin!

Lives emanate from food. Food grows because of rains. Rains are possible due to Yagnas. Yagnas are performed as Karmas. Karmas are from Vedas. Vedas are the products of Lord Almighty, who is imperishable. Therefore, Vedas are consummate due to Yagnas.

One, who does not believe in this circle of events, lives for no purpose. He leads a guilty life. He is ruined due to the bad effects of passionate tendencies of the senses.

One, whose mind derives joy in itself, by self – glorification and by possessing such a mind is gratified with the Self, has no action to perform, by way of compulsion of duty.

There is nothing left for him to attain by his Karma. By not executing his right for Karma, he does not lose anything.

There is no need for him to be dependent on another, just for the sake of acquiring any benefit.

For such a man, there will be no impact, whether due to an act performed or an act not performed. There is no need for him for obtaining any benefit from any other man.

One should continue to be performing acts which are meant for him to do, but without attachment. One who does so attains Mukthi (Liberation).

Let you be doing acts, which are commendable, adhering to good principles, always and everywhere, but without attachment.

Janaka and other wise men, with no selfish motives, and for the welfare of the world, were always involved in Karmas, reaching Siddhi (Perfection). Let you also, for the sake of the uplift of the world, contemplate judiciously and undertake noble Karmas. What an exalted man, an illustrious man, does an act whichever way he chooses to do, whatever he does, and whenever he does, other people emulate him. The world accepts as noble, whatever that man carries out as one of an admirable nature.

Arjuna! There is nothing for me to do for my own sake, in the three worlds. There is nothing for me to attain for my own sake. There is nothing which I had not attained. However, I keep on carrying out Karma. Action, action...... is my character.

It is only because that I seldom take rest, because I have totally eliminated lethargy, because I have not deserted my Karma, every man adopts the path which I have set for myself. If I give up attending to my Karma, worlds will perish. There will be unholy mixture of communities. I will be accused of spoiling lives.

In the same way, those who are not very learned in scriptures take up Karma as though they have faith in Karma. The enlightened persons, without attachment, just for the sake of the uplift of the world, with their inner dynamism, must carry out their duties. Even if they are not enlightened, when they are keen to perform Karmas, they should not be led towards obsession in their mind. With great enthusiasm, apart from their own initiatives to do Karma, they should cheer up others too to get involved in Karmas.

The qualities innate by nature in a man are responsible for leading him to undertake Karma and to carry them out. However, because of ego, with his mind getting clouded, he claims, 'Yes! Done by me' and boasts himself. But, the one, who is governed intrinsically by action as well as by his innate quality, realizes that only the qualities within him tend him to identify them as actions and that his qualities alone are found to be reflected in actions and he discards attachment.

Leave all actions with me. By discarding desires, devoid of ego and selfishness, shedding grief, fight.

(You should set aside desires. You should give up ego. You should eliminate attachment. You should dispel the turbulence in your mind. Fight. This is Krishna's message to Arjuna.)

Those, who follow these principles of mine, without any envy and reservation but with faith, stand released from the bondage of Karmas.

But, those, who are envious, do not accept my dictums and hesitate to follow me. They are unwise. They are idiots. They are in bewilderment not distinguishing unwisely between good quality and bad quality. They are led to destruction. By their folly, they have wasted their birth. An enlightened man absorbing the innate qualities born with him conducts himself according to their guidance. All living beings follow, in fact, their natural tendencies intrinsic in them. There will be no use, if they are prevented from doing so.

Likes and dislikes are the products of the vital senses only. One should not be influenced by his vital senses, because they are the enemies of a man. There may be some principles being adopted by others. One may like them. However, compared to them, one's own principles are superior and remarkable. It will be advisable even to face death, by adhering to one's own principles. The principles of others are fraught with fear.

A man, despite his lack of interest, is tempted by another to get involved in violence and he commits sins and crimes as a result of the outsider's influence.

Desire and anger lead a man to be sinful and to commit crimes. Desire and anger are born out of the quality of Rajas.

The quality of Rajas attracts anything to its ambit. It is wicked. It is a man's enemy, foe.

Smoke covers fire. Dirt covers mirror. The embryo inside the womb is not visible to the eye. In the same way, desire blocks wisdom.

Even Gnanam of Gnani (Enlightenment of Enlightened) is itself covered by the enemy called desire.

Vital senses, Mind and Brain are the seats of desire. They only hide the intellect, kindles desire and throws him into a daze.

Arjuna! Let you first control your vital senses. Acquire the wisdom and experiences found in the scriptures and give up desire totally, which destroys the intellect.

There are some men who admire senses as superior to body. Mind is superior to senses. Brain is superior to Mind. Soul is superior to Brain. Soul is superior to wisdom. You should thus absorb within you that which is superior to Brain, conquer Mind by mind and kill the enemy called desire.

18.4. Chapter Four

Krishna said,

"When in the world, righteousness is on the decline, and unrighteousness is on the upswing, I take incarnation."

"In order to protect the noble men and to annihilate the evil men and for establishing righteousness, I take incarnation in Yuga (Era) after Yuga (Era)."

He continued,

One, who learns truthfully about my absolutely pure and divinely shaped births and my deeds and assimilates them, is never reborn. He derives the great gift of reaching me.

Those, who by giving up desire, fear and anger towards objects and wholly absorbed in me and by surrendering to me, get purified by the penance called Gnanam (Enlightenment) and they become one with me.

Whoever it is and in whatever way he is devoted to attain me, I accept him as such and offer my blessings to him. Men are accustomed to their own methods of worship and they do so always and everywhere.

There are those who worship gods, seeking the fruition of the purpose of their prayers. That is because, by doing so, they enjoy the results of their actions quickly.

I have created four orders of society. They are based on their respective intrinsic qualities and the duties corresponding to them. I am the cause of this distinction. However, I am also not the cause.

Actions do not touch me. I have no desires seeking the fruits of actions. One, who understands me in that perspective also, does not stand bound by actions.

The noble ancients, seeking Mukthi (Liberation) had known this truth. Their actions were based on this truth. Arjuna! Let you also undertake actions accordingly.

What is Karma (Action)? What is Akarma (Inaction)? Even the learned (Vidwans) stumble in their correct perception. I shall teach you. Listen to me.

Karma has three dimensions. They are Karma, Akarma and Vikarma. They mean action, inaction and prohibited action respectively.

The philosophy of Karma is that one sees Karma in Akarma and Akarma in Karma. Action is seen in inaction and inaction is seen in action. It is to be meant that, while getting involved in action, to remain from attachment. Further, the realization, 'It is not I who does this action; this action has got me involved in it.' That sort of perception about action and inaction is possible for a Yogi.

One, whose actions, devoid of desire, attachment and inducement, are fired by the ignition called Gnanam, namely the realization that 'everything is god', is called a Panditha (Greatly Learned).

He will be deemed that he has cast aside the attachment towards the results of action, that he feels always fully contented, that he casts no desire towards objects and that even though he had undertaken action without aligning himself to it, he is not shackled by it and that he is firm in a state of inaction.

One who gives up desire, controls his body as also his vital senses, sacrifices his wealth and land and all his belongings, attends only to his duties, which he is expected to do physically, never suffers sins.

Deriving satisfaction over what has become his unexpectedly, standing beyond the pairs of opposites of joy-sorrow, victory -defeat, cold-warm, conquering over the vital senses and remaining free from jealousy, treating on par whatever is acquired and not acquired, if one carries out any action, he is left not bound by it.

One's Karma stands fully fulfilled, if he, free from attachment, getting rid of all sorts of constraints and keeping his mind firm in Gnana, performs his actions for the sake of Yagnas.

(Krishna talks about Yagna. His exposition on Yagna is similar to what we come across about Yaga dealt with in Vishnu Sahasranamam, (Yagna Bukh, Yagna Krith Yagni,... In Vishnu Sahasranamam Vishnu is identified with Yagna. He describes various types of Yagna. They all have been spelt out in Vedas.)

Krishna teaches Arjuna, thereafter,

Arjuna! Thus knowing about Yagnas, you get released from the bondage of action, through performing Yagnas.

Gnanam itself is Yagna. Sacrifice (Yagna) through Gnanam is superior to Yagna using material things. You should assimilate Gnanam of the highest order from seers. With humility and with affinity, learn by listening to them. With pure mind and with all your limbs prostrate to them, you serve them, listen and learn. Gnanis, who are enlightened, will impart Gnanam to you.

Even assuming that you have sinned more than what the worst sinner has done, you will, by using the boat called Gnanam cross all sins.

Arjuna! In the same way, a flame of fire reduces dry wood to ashes, the flame of fire called Gnanam extinguishes all actions to ashes. In the matter of purification, there is nothing in this world equal to Gnanam. In that man who has reached full and mature consummation by the practice of Yoga, Gnanam gets automatically identified.

He, who has controlled his senses, is industrious and is known to assimilate Gnanam, certainly gets Gnanam. Having attained that spectacular knowledge (Gnanam), he secures supreme peace in the form of god realization.

One, who is ignorant, lacks faith, is not interested to listen to good advices and is possessed of doubtful nature, gets lost. This world is not for those who are doubtful by nature and of vacillating mind. Nor does he get to the other world. He does not enjoy comforts. He enjoys no worldly happiness.

Arjuna! One, who sacrifices Karmas by Yoga, drives away his doubts by Gnanam and is blissful on account of complete mental peace, is not bound by Karmas.

Arjuna! Therefore, you cut away to pieces the doubts in your heart born out of ignorance by the sword called Knowledge (Gnanam) and establish Yoga. Fight.

18.5. Chapter Five

Arjuna asked, "You are telling that Karmas are to be renounced and you extoll Yogas of Knowledge. Please explain to me which of the two is certainly better."

Krishna said,

Renunciation and Karma are both good surely. However, Karma Yoga is superior to Sanyasa Yoga (Renunciation).

One, who neither hates nor desires, is a Sanyasi (Ascetic). It is because he is beyond the pairs of opposites, and is liberated from bondage. That is to say, joy-sorrow, gain-loss, victory-defeat, are equal to him and he releases himself from total attachment.

Those, who are not wise and are ignorant of Gnanam, speak of Karma Sanyasam (Saankya Yoga) and Karma Yoga as leading to divergent results. Gnanis (Wisemen) do not speak so. One, who undertakes either of the two, but with great determination and concentration, attains the fruits of both.

Saankya, those who sacrifice Karmas, reach that same supreme state, which Karma Yogis attain.

He, who sees Saankya (Sacrifice of Karmas) and Karma Yoga as the same, perceives the Truth.

Arjuna! Sanyasa (Renunciation-Asceticism) is not possible, without Yoga. In other words, without getting involved in actions, the state of renunciation cannot be reached). But, as Karma Yogi, one, who adopts Karma Yoga, with due concentration of mind by way of constant meditation reaches Brahmam (Supreme God) without delay.

One, who with absolute steadiness has realised the Truth, though he sees, hears, touches, smells, eats, walks, sleeps, breaths, talks, causes exits (Calls of nature), grasps, opens eyes, closes eyes, would believe that all these are the caused by the vital senses voluntarily and that he does nothing with his efforts.

He, who does acts offering them to Brahmam (Supreme God) without attachment, is not affected by sins, like the water over a lotus leaf.

Karma Yogis, with total detachment, only for purification of their mind, carry out actions, by their body, mind, brain and vital senses.

One, who adopts Karma Yoga, by forsaking the fruits of their actions, and due to the strict concentration of mind, attains durable peace. One, who does not accept Karma Yoga, in this manner, bowing to the effects of desires, is enticed by selfishness, by seeking the fruits of his actions, which have no value.

That one, who has kept under control his vital senses, keeping aside all his actions by the application of Gnanam, would be seen as himself doing nothing, as also not getting anything done by others; he rests happily in his own body consisting of nine openings, in a state of Yoga.

The inimitable God has neither created doers of actions (that is to say a sense of relief in a man that he is not the doer of actions), nor the doings themselves nor the benefits accruing from actions. God, who is immanent everywhere, has nothing to do with anyone's virtue or sin. As Gnanam (Wisdom) is covered by ignorance, all are left in delusion.

However, for that man whose ignorance gets destroyed by the mind rich in Gnanam, his Gnanam shines like Sun revealing Paramathma (Supreme God) in full splendor.

Those, who have kept their Bhuddi (Intellect) merged with Paramathma, have their Bhuddi identified with Paramathma and remaining there firmly established, also finally become one with Paramathma and have their sins totally wiped out by their Gnanam. They secure the privilege of no rebirth, attaining Supreme God.

The learned and highly modest men look with equanimity on all, whether he is a Brahmin or it is a cow or an elephant or a dog or a dog-eater, treating them all as Paramathma's creations.

Those, who have their minds equipoised firmly and have their belief of Paramathma fully stabilized will have their births and deaths won over even as they are alive. It is so because Brahmam (Paramathma) is free from any flaw. They are, therefore, firmly linked with Brahmam.

He, who has his Bhuddi (Intellect) solid and free from doubts, and is conscious of Brahmam, is firmly united with Brahmam, and does not rejoice while securing what is pleasing and does not regret when securing what is not pleasing.

Gnani, who shows no interest on extraneous matters, secures through meditation that happiness which is spiritualistic. He, with his identification with Brahmam through his unattached mind, concentrating by meditation, enjoys unmitigated happiness. He, who has purified mind of identifying himself with Paramathma, secures eternal grand bliss.

Arjuna! Those pleasures which are the products of the aspirations of the vital senses are the sources of grief. Those pleasures have their beginning and their end. A Gnani would not derive joy from them.

One, who has acquired in his life the ability to stand aloof from the urges of lust as well as anger, even moments before his death, is a Yogi and he alone is a happy man.

He, who sees happiness within himself and enjoys the delight of Athma (Soul) within himself, is illumined by the inner light of the Soul and such a Yogi is transformed as Brahmam, attains Brahmam and enjoys profuse peace, Brahmanandam.

Those seers, who have their sins purged, whose intellects are free from doubts, whose vital senses are under their full control, and who are bent to do good to all living beings, are those who have all the commendable requisites to get identified with Brahmam.

For that Yogi, who has eradicated desire and anger and has full control on his mind and has realised Brahmam, the abode of eternal peace is everywhere.

By blocking all external thoughts, fixing both the eyes between the eye brows, regulating the breaths of air, outgoing and incoming through the nostrils, controlling the five vital senses, Mind and Bhuddi, eradicating desires, fear and anger, with total contemplation on Mokasha as the ultimate refuge, one should meditate on Paramathma. Such a man realizes Supreme God.

He realizes me, who enjoys all Yogas (Sacrifices) and Tapas (Penances), who is the Supreme God for all the worlds and who has affinity towards all the living beings and he attains Peace.

That peace is Moksha.

18.6. Chapter Six

He, who carries out Karma (Duties) without expecting results, is a Sanyasi. He is Yogi.

He must possess that much mental strength as is needed to control his senses. He must dispel straying thoughts. He must have no attachment over worldly matters and Karmas.

He, with purified mind, must uplift himself. No inferior approach should degrade him. For one, his own self is his friend; his own self is his enemy too.

One, who conquers himself, is his own friend; one who fails to conquer himself, is his own enemy and is surrounded by hostility.

One should conquer himself, by treating equally the pairs of opposites, namely, cold- heat, joy-sorrow, honour-ignominy. He must search for peace. His intellect must be very clear, free from doubts. Their Gnanam will grow, acquiring light.

With the knowledge of the scriptures, with the benefit of healthy experiences, one's mind should reach fulfillment, not getting agitated by anything and he should keep senses under control. Such a man, who sees stones, sands, gold and other substances as equally the same, is a Yogi. Only he is spoken as a God-realised Soul.

One is spoken of Supreme, when he looks upon friend, foe, neutrals (Indifferent), contemptuous, relatives, virtuous and sinner with equanimity.

Yogi must live in an isolated place, remaining himself isolated, bringing under control mind and body, bereft of desire and belongings, thus not possessing anything, and he should be engaged in constant meditation. He must choose a seat which is neither high nor low, with the deer skin, dharba (Sacred Dry Grass) and cloth spread on it and his seat should remain firm free from vibrations and the seat must be placed in a spot free from dirt and impurities.

By keeping his mind in full concentration, controlling the functions of mind and senses, seated with no impurities around, he must undertake Yoga for self-purification.

Yogi, holding his trunk (Body), head and neck steady and straight, fixing his eyes on the tip of his nose and without getting distracted by the surroundings, with his mind kept under firm restraint, free from fear, observing the vow of strict celibacy (Brahmacharyam), remaining calm in mind, should sit with devoted contemplation by way of meditation on Me, holding the belief that I am the Supreme.

Such a Yogi attains eternal peace culminating in Moksha, abiding in me.

Arjuna! One, who eats too much, one who eats too little, one who sleeps long and the one who is awake all the time, they have no claim for Yoga.

Yoga removes sorrow of a man who eats the correct quantity, performs exercise, is industrious optimally, is disciplined in sleep as well as when awake.

When a man with controlled mind remains thoroughly concentrated on God and is free from desires towards unwanted matters, he is established in Yoga completely.

The flame of a lamp does not flicker in a place which is free from wind. Yogi is looked upon similar to that, when he remains with his mind controlled and desires eliminated.

The happiness which he derives by the application of brain power (Chitta) and by standing beyond the influences of senses and moving towards meditation on God, is limitless and he identifies himself with God.

That is Yoga, in which state nothing is deemed as nobler than what he has already secured, and remaining stable in that state, when no grief affects him. One should reach that state in Yoga, when he remains stable and is unperturbed by grief.

Mind, which is unstable and vacillating, must find out the cause and by suppressing that cause one must seek union with God.

For one, who sees me in everything and who sees everything in me, I am not lost by him and he is not lost by me.

I am in union with that Yogi, who believes that God is one and God is me, and worships me as one who dwells in all living beings, irrespective of his activities.

He, who by setting his own example, sees all as one and perceives with equanimity joy and sorrow, is considered as the highest of all.

Arjuna asked, "Mind is fickle. It agitates any one because of its nature. It is restless, turbulent, tenacious and powerful. It is as difficult to control Mind as it is to control wind. How then is Yoga possible?"

Krishna said

It is so no doubt! It is difficult to control mind. It vacillates. But, it is amenable to control by repeated practice and firm determination.

If there is no mind control, there is no Yoga. If one resorts to efficacious means, he can try to control Mind.

Arjuna asked, "For one, who does not endeavour and who hesitates to continue to resort to Yoga, though he believes in Yoga, and goes up to a stage, what happens to him?"

Krishna said,

One, who does good things, will not be exposed to misery.

One, who fails in Yoga, reaches that Loka which persons of good actions reach. After spending long there, he is reborn in a wealthy family.

Or he is reborn in a family of Yogis. But it is rare to obtain such a rebirth.

He continues to perform those measures with which he had endeavoured in his previous birth. He tries harder seeking Moksha. He is benefitted by his past efforts.

He, who tries assiduously, is absolved of his sins, gets purified, attains full maturity after many births and reaches Supreme State.

Yogi is superior to those who do penances, who have Gnanam and who are Karma Yogis. Arjuna! Let you become a Yogi.

Among all Yogis, that one who has superior faith in identifying himself with me with pure inner conscience, and with earnestness and devotion worships me, he is considered as the best Yogi.

18.7. Chapter Seven

Krishna said,

Having fixed your mind in me, and having surrendered to me, you, seeking Yoga, will, without doubt know about me completely. I shall tell you about it.

I shall impart to you that knowledge in which you will believe that there is nothing left to be known about me after learning from me what I am going to tell you.

Only one among thousands tries to have his mind ripe enough to know about me. Among those Siddas who have tried for that, only one succeeds in knowing about me completely.

Land, Water, Fire, Air, Ether, Mind, Bhuddi, Ego! (Ahamkaram) constitute my Prakrithi (Nature) and are thus divided in eight parts

But, the status of Prakrithi (Nature) thus divided into eight parts is of a lower category. You, therefore, understand that higher status of mine, sustaining the whole Universe which is different from the eight mentioned by me.

All Bhoothas (Living beings) are evolved from these two Prakrithis. I am the source of creation of the Universe. All worlds are born from me; they dissolve too in me.

There is nothing superior to me. These have been threaded in me like the gems in a string.

I am the basic taste in water; I am the glow for Moon and Sun; I am OHM (Pranava) for Vedas; I am the sound in Ether; I am the virility in men.

I am the pure odour inherent in Earth; I am the brightness in Fire; I am the life in all living beings; I am the austerity of ascetics.

Let you know that I am the eternal seed of all Bhoothas (Beings); I am the intelligence of the intelligent; I am the splendor of those having splendor.

I am the might of the mightiest free from attachment and desire; I am the desire in all beings but without conflict with Dharma (Righteousness).

All the entities, which are born with either Satwa Guna or Rajo Guna or Thamo Guna, are all evolved from me; but I am not in them; they are in me.

Deluded by the objects composed of these three Gunas of Prakrithi (Nature), the world fails to understand that I am immutable and distinct from them.

All the objects consisting of these three Gunas have their origin in me. They cannot be dispensed with because they are caused by my divine illusion. Those who surrender to me are able to cross them.

Those whose wisdom is obscured by my Maya are of demoniac nature. Such foolish and inferior people committing evil deeds do not reach me.

There are four types of men who worship me. They are men in distress; men who are desirous of knowing the Truth; men who seek worldly pleasures and those who are Gnanis (Men of wisdom).

Among these, one who is forever identifying himself with me and who has full concentration on me is the best. It is so because, I am extremely dear to that Gnani who knows me in reality and he is extremely dear to me.

All these four are indeed noble. But, Gnani is the most superior. I deem him as my very self. This is my view. That is because, that wise man has his intellect and mind established in me alone as the supreme god.

After completing many births, the Gnani surrenders to me realising that all this is Vasudeva. Such a Mahatma is very hard to find.

There are men who, carried away by desires, this and that, propelled by their own nature, worship other deities, adopting the norms relating to them.

Whichever divine form this devotee or that devotee chooses to worship with faith, I make his devotion to that form unflinching.

That devotee worships that deity with full faith. He secures through that deity, without doubt, his enjoyments prayed for, but as verily ordained by me.

The fruit accruing to those devotees of limited wisdom is for short duration and is perishable. Worshippers of gods attain their gods; My devotees, in whichever manner they worship Me, they come to Me and Me alone, eventually.

Those unwise men, who are ignorant of my supreme nature as immutable and peerless, regard me, who am the Supreme Spirit beyond the reach of mind and senses, and the embodiment of Truth, Knowledge and Bliss, to be in a finite form through birth as an ordinary human being.

Veiled by Yoga Maya (My Divine Potency), I am not manifest in all. Therefore, this deluded folk fail to recognize Me; they consider me as subject to birth and death.

I know all beings, past as well as present as also those that are yet to come. But, no one knows me.

By the delusion of pairs of opposites, arising from desire and aversion, all living beings in this world are falling a prey to delusion.

But, those men of virtuous deeds, whose sins have come to an end, being freed from delusion in the form of pairs of opposites born of attraction and repulsion, worship me with firm resolve in every way.

Those who having surrendered to me, strive for deliverance from old age and death, they realised Brahmam (The Supreme Soul), the whole Adyaathma (Totality of Jivans or embodied Souls), the entire field of Karma (Action), as well as My integral being comprising Adhibhutha (Pertaining to Elements, Worldly Objects), Adhidaiva (Pertaining to Gods, the sense Organs), and Adhiyajna (Pertaining to Sacrifice, all perceptions). They who possessed of steadfast mind, know them even at the hour of death, they too know me alone.

18.8. CHAPTER EIGHT

Arjuna asked,

What are Brahmam, Adyatma, Karma, and Adhibhuta? What is Adhidaiva?

How is Adhyatma in this body? How are you realised by one, who at the time of his death has his mind kept fully steadfast?

Krishna said,

Brahmam is imperishable. It is the most supreme. One's own soul is called Adyatma. The creative force of God which causes beings to exist is called Karma (Such as Yoga, Charity, and Homam).

Adhibhuta is perishable. Purusha (Indweller) is Adhidaiva. Adhiyajna is I, in this body.

(One that is imperishable, which is the most supreme of all those which are rare, is Brahmam.

The characteristics of that which never undergo any transformations are Adhyatma.

The deeds of creation of beings, making them stable and uplifting them, are Karma.

That which gets perished is Adhibhuta.

That leader in whom all beings ultimately dwell is Adhidaiva.

I am Yagna myself as all those offered in Yagna are all my creations.)

One, who even at the hour of his death is thinking of me alone, attains my State; there is no doubt about it.

One, who at the time of leaving his body at the time of his death, is thinking of an entity, whatever it is, he attains that and that alone, having absorbed that in his thought.

You should, therefore, be remembering me at all times, and fight in the war. You, by the dedication of your mind and intellect on me, will come to me alone, undoubtedly.

By engaging the mind properly in the constant meditation of that Supreme Purusha and by thinking of nothing else, you will come to me undoubtedly.

He, who with his mind disciplined through Yoga, in the form of practice of meditation of God and thinking of nothing else, and is constantly engaged in contemplation of God, attains the Supreme Divine Purusha.

One who meditates on me as the Omniscient, as the most ancient, as the ruler of the Universe, as subtler than the atom, as the supporter of all, as of the Inconceivable Form, effulgent like Sun, and far beyond the darkness of ignorance, and having the power of Yoga, holding the breath in the space between the two eyebrows, even at the time of death, with an unshaken mind, full of devotion, he reaches verily that Supreme Divine Purusha (God).

I shall tell you briefly about what knowers of Vedas speak as Imperishable, what into which enter the saints, who have given up desires and by practicing Brahmacharyam—that God I shall declare to you.

Having closed all the gates in the body (Controlled all Senses) and having firmly confined the mind in the heart, having fixed the life-breath in the head, and thus remaining steadfast in Yogic concentration on God,

Uttering the one-syllabled OHM, the symbol of Brahmam and remembering me, he who departs leaving the body, reaches the Supreme God.

For that steadfast Yogi, who constantly thinks of me daily and thinking on nothing else, I am easily attainable.

Having reached me, these great souls (Mahatmas) do not again take rebirth, which is the abode of sorrow and which is non-eternal, they having attained the highest perfection-Moksha.

All worlds from Brahma Loka downwards are subject to rebirth; but who reaches me, he has no rebirth.

Those wise men (Yogis) who know of one day of Brahma, which covers a thousand Yugas and his one night as extending to another one thousand Yugas, know the reality about Time.

All embodied beings (Manifest) emanate from the Unmanifest (Brahma's subtle body) at the coming of the 'day' (Cosmic Day); at the 'night' (Cosmic Night) they dissolve into the same subtle body of Brahma, known as the Unmanifest.

This multitude of beings, being born again and again are dissolved under the compulsion of their nature at the coming of the 'night' (Cosmic Night) and rise again at the commencement of the 'day' (Cosmic Day).

But, verily, there exists higher than that Unmanifest (Avyaktha), (Supreme Divine Purusha) another Unmanifest, which is eternal, which is not destroyed even though all beings are destroyed.

That which is called the Unmanifest and Imperishable, is also called The Supreme Goal. They, who reach it, never again return to this mortal world. That is My Supreme Abode.

That Highest Purusha is attainable only through unswerving devotion to Him alone, within whom all beings dwell, by whom all is pervaded.

(Paramapada is ever existent, eternal. It is not visible. Beings are perishable. Paramathma never perishes. Once attaining Paramathma, no being returns to this mortal world. Paramapada is my most supreme form. By knowing that Paramathma as the most Supreme Purusha, and by unwavering devotion, He is attainable. Those who show devotion to Paramathma should not seek attachment and allegiance to others. Only then rebirth can be prevented.)

Arjuna! I shall tell you that time (Path) when departing Yogis go, never to return, as also that time (path) to return.

Fire, Light, Day Time (The path in which are stationed Fire God and deities presiding over Day Time), the bright fortnight (Sukla Patcha), the six months of northern solstice (Utharayana), following this path, men who know Brahmam go to Brahmam.

Smoke, Night Time (The path wherein are stationed the deities presiding over Night Time), dark fortnight (Krishna Patcha), six months of southern solstice (Dakshinayana), the Yogis taking to this path on death is led by the above gods, one after another, and attaining by these to the Moon, the lunar light (and enjoying the fruit of his virtuous deeds in Heaven) returns to this mortal world.

These two paths, the bright and the dark are eternal. Proceeding on one, he reaches the supreme state, never returning; proceeding to the other, he returns to the mortal world, subject to births and rebirths.

Knowing these paths, no Yogi is deluded. Therefore, all times be steadfast in Yoga.

Realising this profound truth, the Yogi doubtless transcends all the rewards enumerated for the study of Veda as well as for the performance of sacrifices, austerities and charities, and attains the supreme and primal state.

(Yogi, knowing this, goes beyond what Vedas teach, and Yagna, Penance and Charities yield as rewards and attains the supreme and primal state.)

18.9. Chapter Nine

Krishna said,

Arjuna! By knowing Me, one will be free from undesirables and I shall now declare to you a great profound secret, without jealousy. That secret is the most profound knowledge combined with experience.

That Royal Secret, Royal Learning, is a supreme purifier, realizable by direct intuitive knowledge, the product of Dharma, very easy to perform and imperishable.

Those who do not have belief in this, failing to reach me, get caught in the circle of life and death.

My Form is not explicit. But, I am pervading the whole Universe. All beings dwell in me. But, I am not present in them.

My Self bears all; creates all. But, I am not present in them. Like air, which is spread all over, but ever remaining in ether, all beings who have originated from me, abide in me.

All beings enter Prakrithi (Me-Prime Cause) at the time of dissolution, one Kalpa. I create them again at the commencement of the next Kalpa.

I show no attachment to these acts. They do not bind me.

Under my implied supervision, moving and non-moving are created by Prakrithi (Nature). Due to this, the wheel of the world revolves.

Fools disregard me, who has taken this human form, not knowing of My Higher Stature as the Great Lord of all beings.

Of vain hopes, of vain actions, of vain knowledge, and senseless, they have adopted the delusive nature of Rakshasas and Asuras.

But, Mahatmas (Great Souls), who are imbued with my divine nature worship me constantly, with absolute and sole concentration on me, and not devoted to anything else, knowing me as the Imperishable Source of all beings.

Always glorifying me, striving, firm in vows, prostrating before me and always steadfast, they worship me with single-minded devotion.

Others, who by performing Gnana Yagna (Sacrifice through Wisdom) worship me, regarding me as One Absolute, as distinct, as manifest in all forms, faces everywhere.

I am the Vedic ritual (Krathu); I am the Sacrifice (Yagna); I am the offering to the departed(Swada); I am the medical herb and all plants (Aushadam); I am Mantra (Sacred Hymn); I am the clarified butter (Aajyam); I am the Sacred Fire(Agni); I am the oblation (Hutham).

I am the father (Pitha) of the world, mother (Matha), the supporter and the grandsire (Pithamaha), the one bound to be known, the Purifier, the syllable OHM and the three Vedas-RIK, SAMA and YAJUR.

I am the Supreme Goal (Gathi), Sustainer (Bhartha), Lord (Prabhu), Witness (Sakshi), Abode (Nivas), Refuge (Saranam), Friend (Suhrut), Origin (Prabhava), Dissolution (Pralaya), the Treasure holder to whom all beings return at the time of total destruction (Staanam Nidaanam), and Imperishable Seed (Bheejam Avyayam).

I give heat to Sun; I withhold and send forth rain; I am immortality as also death; both Existence and Non-existence.

The Knowers of the three Vedas, the drinkers of Soma, purified from sin, worshipping me through Sacrifices, pray for the path of Heaven; they reach the Holy Paradise and enjoy in Heaven, the Divine pleasures of the gods.

They, having enjoyed the extensive heaven- world, when their merits are exhausted, return to this world of mortals. Thus, abiding by the injunctions of the three (Vedas), seeking the worldly pleasures, they repeatedly come and go (return from heaven to this world, and this world to heaven).

To those men, who, thinking of no one else, worship me alone, to those even-minded in thought with me, I secure for them Yoga (That which is not possessed by them now but will be possessed by them later), and preserve for them Kshema (What they already possess).

(For those not going away from me, constantly thinking of me, holding me steadfastly in heart, performing virtuous deeds always, I secure for them everything, for the enjoyment of the present pleasures as also enjoyment of future pleasures.)

Even those devotees, who worship other gods, but endowed with faith, worship me alone, but by adopting the improper approach.

For, I am the enjoyer in (Bhoktha) as also the Lord (Prabhu) of all Sacrifices (Yagnas), but, they do not know me in reality as the Supreme Deity; they, therefore, return to life on Earth.

The worshippers of gods go to gods; worshippers of Pithrus (Manes) reach Pithrus; those who worship the spirits (Bhuthas) go the spirits; those who worship me come to me alone.

Whosoever offers me a leaf, a flower, a fruit, water, but with devotion, that I delightfully accept, offered by the pure-minded with love.

Whatever you do, whatever you eat, whatever you offer as oblation in Sacrifice, whatever you give in charity, whatever you do by way of penance, do that as an offering to me.

You shall thus be freed from the bondage of actions in the form of good and evil results, with your mind steadfast in Yoga of Renunciation (Offering all actions to me); thus liberated, you shall come to me.

I am disposed equally to all beings; there is none hateful to me, nor dear to me; but those who worship me with devotion are in me; I am also in them.

Even if the most sinful worships me, with devotion to no one else, he too should indeed be regarded as a sadhu (Noble man-saint), for he has rightly resolved so.

Very speedily, he becomes righteous and attains eternal peace. Arjuna! Know it for certain that my devotee is never destroyed.

Arjuna! Women, Vaishyas (Traders-third category), Sudras (Labourers-servants - Fourth category) whoever they may be, by taking refuge in me, they attain the Supreme God.

How much more, then, if they be Brahmanas and Royal Sages devoted to me! Therefore, having reached this impermanent and joyless world, do worship me with devotion.

Fix your mind on me; be devoted to me worship me; and make obeisance to me; thus having united yourself with me, taking me as the Supreme Goal, you shall come to me.

18.10. Chapter Ten

Neither gods (Devas) nor the great sages (Rishis) know of my origin, because I am the source of all gods as also of the great sages.

He, who knows me as birthless and without beginning and as the supreme lord of the worlds, he is undeluded and is liberated from all sins.

Buddhi (Intellect), wisdom, understanding free from confusion, forgiveness, truth, control over senses and mind, calmness, happiness, sorrow, birth and death, fear and fearlessness, non-violence, equanimity, contentment, austerity, charity, fame, infamy, these diverse traits of beings arise from me alone.

The seven great Rishis, the four ancients (Sanakas and others) and the Manus, possessed of powers like me, were born of my mind; all these creatures in the world have come into being from them.

He knowing truthfully these manifold manifestations of My being, and through Yoga power of mine, becomes established in unfaltering devotion (Yoga); there is no doubt about it.

I am the source of all creations; everything evolves from me; understanding this, the wise, endowed with loving consciousness worship me.

With their minds wholly fixed on me, with their lives surrendered to me, conversing and enlightening one another about my glories, they are satisfied and delighted.

To the ever-steadfast, worshipping me with love, I give Buddhi-Yoga by which they come to me.

In order to bestow my compassion on them, I, dwelling in their hearts, dispel their darkness born of ignorance by the illuminating lamp of Gnana (Knowledge).

Arjuna said,

"You are the Supreme Brahmam, the Supreme Abode, the Supreme Purifier, Eternal, Divine Purusha, God of all gods, unborn and Omnipresent.

All Rishis have spoken of you like wise, as also the celestial sage Narada, sages Asita, Devala and Vyasa; and you Yourself say so to me.

Oh Kesava! I believe as true all that you tell me. Bhagawan! Neither Devas (gods) nor Danavas (Demons) know your manifestations.

You Yourself know Yourself by Yourself! Oh Purushothama! Oh Source of Beings! Oh Lord of Beings! Oh God of Gods! Oh Ruler of the World!

You should indeed, without reserve, tell me of Your Divine glories by which you exist, pervading all the worlds.

How shall I, by constantly meditating, know you, Oh Yogin? And in what particular forms, Oh Lord, are you to be thought of by me?

Janardhana! Tell me again in detail, of Your Yoga Power and Your Immanent glory; for I know no satiety in hearing your nectar-like words."

Bhagawan (Krishna) said,

Arjuna! Now I shall declare to you my Divine glories, immanent, in their prominence; there is no end to the details of My manifestations.

Arjuna! I am the Self seated in the hearts of all beings; I am the Beginning, the Middle and also the End of all beings.

I am,

Vishnu among Adityas.

Radiant Sun among the luminaries.

Marichi among the Maruts.

Moon among the Stars (Asterisms).

Sama Veda among Vedas.

Indra among the gods (Devas).

Mind (Manas) among Indriyas, the Senses.

Intelligence among the living beings.

Sankara among Rudras.

Lord of Wealth, Kubera among Yakshas and Rakshasas.

Agni among Vasus.

Meru among mountains.

Brahaspathi, the chief among the priests.

Skanda among the army generals.

Ocean among the reservoirs of water.

Brighu among Maharishis.

Single syllable OHM.

Japa Yagna among Yagnas (Sacrifices).

Himalayas among the immovable.

Aswatha among the trees.

Narada among the celestial sages.

Chitra Ratha among Gandarvas.

Kapila among Siddas (Perfect Ones).

Uchchaishravas, born of Amrutha (In Ocean of Milk) among the horses.

Airavatha among the lordly elephants.

King among men.

Vajrayutha (Thunder bolt of Indra) among the weapons.

Kamadhuk (Kamadhenu) among the cows.

Kandarpa (Manmatha) the cause for off-springs.

Vasuki among serpents.

Anantha among Nagas.

Varuna among water deities.

Aryama among ancestors (Pithrus).

Yama among controllers.

Prahlada among Daithyas.

Kala (Time) among the reckoners.

Lion (Lord of the beasts) among the animals.

Vainatheya (Garuda) among the birds.

Wind among the purifiers.

Rama among the wielders of arms.

Makara (Shark) among fishes.

Ganga among the rivers.

Beginning, Middle, as also the End among creations.

Knowledge of Self, of all knowledge.

Logic in all arguments.

First Letter 'A' among all letters.

Copulative compound among different types of compounds (Dual coordinates-Samasi

among compounds (Dwanda).

Inexhaustible Time (Everlasting Time).

Sustainer of all, having many faces in all directions.

All-devouring Death.

Prosperity of those who are to be prosperous.

Fame, Prosperity, Speech, Memory, Intelligence, Firmness and Forgiveness among feminine

qualities.

Brihat Samam among Samams (Hymns).

Gayathri among Chandas (Metres).

Meergaseersha month among months.

Vasantha Ruthu (Spring Season) among seasons.

Gambling among the fraudulents.

Glory of the glorious.

Victory, Industry (Remaining always brisk), goodness of the good.

Vasudeva among Vrishnis.

Dhananjayan (Arjuna) among Pandavas.

Vyasa among Munis(Sages).

Usana (Sukracharya) among poets.

Sceptor (Symbol of Power to Punish) among punishers.
Neethi (Justice- Statesmanship) among those who seek to conquer.

Silence (Mounam) among secrets.

Gnanam (Knowledge) among Gnanis (Gnanis).

Arjuna! And whatever is the seed of all beings, that also am I. There is no being, whether moving or non-moving that can exist without me.

There is no end to my divine glories. This is but a brief statement by me of the particulars of my glories.

Whatever it is that is glorious, prosperous or powerful in any being, know that to be a manifestation of a part of my splendor.

But, of what avail to you is the knowledge of all these details. I exist supporting this whole world by one part of myself.

18.11. Chapter Eleven

Arjuna asked Krishna,

"I desire to see your real divine form."

Krishna replied,

"Arjuna! See my divine form, by hundreds and thousands of different sorts, of various colours and shapes.

See in my body, the whole universe centers in One, including the moving and non-moving and whatever else you desire to see.

You cannot see me with your present eyes. I shall bestow you with divine eyes. See my divine Yoga."

Having spoken like this, the great Lord of Yoga, Lord Sri Hari, showed to Arjuna his supreme form, as the Lord of the Universe.

With numerous faces, eyes, mouths, with numerous wonderful sights, with numerous divine ornaments, with numerous weapons, He showed such a form. Wearing divine garlands, necklaces and garments, anointed with divine fragrances, the All-wonderful, Resplendent, Endless, facing all sides, He showed His Viswa Roopam.

If the splendor of one thousand Suns was to blaze all at once, simultaneously, in the sky, that would be like the splendor of that Mighty Being.

There, in the body of the God of gods, Arjuna saw the whole universe, resting in one, with all its infinite parts.

Then, Arjuna filled with wonder, with his hairs standing on end, bowed down his head to the God and spoke with joined palms.

"Oh God! I see all gods in your body, and hosts of various classes of beings, Brahma, Lord of Creation, seated in the Lotus (Padma Asana), all Rishis and celestial serpents.

I see you of boundless form on every side, with manifold arms, stomachs, mouths and eyes; neither the end, nor the middle nor the beginning do I see. Oh Lord of Universe (Visweswara! Oh Cosmic Form (Viswa Roopam)!

I see you with Crown, Mace, and Discus, a mass of radiance shining everywhere, very hard to look at, all around blazing like burning fire and Sun; incomprehensible.

You are the Imperishable; the supreme being worthy to be known; You are the great Treasure House of this universe. You are the imperishable, Protector of the Eternal Dharma. In my opinion, you are the ancient Purusha.

I see you without beginning, middle or end, infinite in power, of endless arms, Sun and Moon being your eyes, the burning fire (Agni) is your mouth, heating the whole universe with your radiance.

The space between earth and heavens and all the quarters is filled by you alone. Having seen this, your wonderful and terrible form, the three worlds are trembling with fear, Oh Great-souled Being!

You indeed enter these hosts of Devas; some praise you in fear with joined palms; Rishis and Siddhas greet you saying, 'May it be well,' and praise you with sublime hymns.

Rudras, Adityas, Vasus, Sadhyas, Viswe Devas, the Twin Aswins, Maruts, Ushampas, and hosts of Gandarvas,

Yakshas, asuras and Siddhas, they are all looking at you quite astonished.

Having seen Your Immeasurable Form, with many mouths and eyes, Oh Mighty Armed, with many arms, thighs and feet, with many stomachs and fearsome with many teeth, the worlds are terrified and so too am I.

On seeing you with your form touching the sky, flaming in many colours, with mouths wide open, with large fiery eyes, I am terrified at heart and I find neither courage nor peace, Oh Vishnu!

Having seen of your mouths fearsome with teeth, blazing like Pralaya fires, I know not the four quarters, nor do I find peace; be gracious, Oh Lord of Devas, Oh abode of the Univese!

All the sons of Dritharashtra with hosts of kings of the earth, Bhishma, Drona and Karna with the warrior chiefs of ours, enter hurriedly into your mouth, with terrible teeth and fearful to behold. Some are found sticking in the gaps between the teeth with their heads crushing into pulp.

These heroes of the human world enter into your flaming mouths, like many torrents of rivers flow towards the ocean.

All moths rush hurriedly into a blazing fire for their own destruction; in the same manner, these creatures hastily rush into your mouths of destruction.

Devouring all worlds on every side with your flaming mouths, you are licking in enjoyment. Your fiery rays filling the whole world with radiance are burning, Oh Vishnu!

Tell me who you are, so fierce in form. Salutations to you, Oh God Supreme! Have mercy. I desire to know you, the Original Being. I do not know your purpose."

Krishna said,

I am the mighty world-destroying Time (Kala), now engaged in destroying the worlds. Even without you, none of the warriors arrayed in hostile armies shall live.

Therefore, stand up. Secure fame. Conquer the enemies and enjoy the flourishing kingdom. By Myself, they have indeed already been killed. You be a mere instrument, Oh Arjuna!

Drona, Bhishma, Jayadratha, Karna and other brave warriors of war have already been killed by me. You do kill. Do not be distressed with fear. Fight. You shall conquer your enemies in war.

Arjuna, after hearing Kesava's (Krishna's) speech, was trembling with fear and with joined palms bowing, prostrating to Krishna, in a choked voice, said," Krishna! The world rejoices and delights in praising you; Rakshasas run away in fear into all the directions, whereas hosts of Siddhas bow to you.

As you are Great-souled and the prime cause even for Brahma, how could those Siddhas not bow to you, greater them all? Oh Devesa! Oh Abode of the Universe! You are the Imperishable, that which is beyond both the Manifest and the Unmanifest.

You are the Prime God, the Ancient Purusha, and the Supreme Refuge for all in the universe. You are the Knower, the Knowable, and the Supreme Abode. You pervade the entire Universe, Oh Diety of Many Forms!

You are Vayu (Wind), Agni (Fire), Varuna (Water) Chandra (Moon), Prajapathi (Brahma), and Prapithamaha (Grand Great Father). I bow to you. I bow to you again and again, thousand times.

Salutations to you, before and behind! Salutations to you from every side! You are infinite in power, infinite in prowess, and you pervade all and you are all.

Not knowing about your Viswa Roopam and your all greatness, I might have uttered words out of indifference or kindness or curtly, on account of my friendship with you.

I might have made fun of you causing you disrespect, in play, in bed, in assembly, in eating house, or in solitude or in the presence of friends. I request you to pardon me.

You are the father for this world of moving and non-moving beings. You are indeed fit to be worshipped and you are the paramount Guru. There is no one comparable to you. You have unparalleled glories. There is no one greater than you in the three worlds.

Therefore, I shall prostrate with my body to you, worshipping you, who is to be worshipped and who governs everything, offering my salutations to you and praying earnestly for your pardon. You should show mercy to me, like a father to his son, a friend to another friend and a lover to his beloved.

I am delighted over seeing you now, what I have not seen before. My mind is still struck with fear. You please show me your previous worldly form. Have mercy on me.

I desire to see you as before, with your Crown, Mace, Discus, in your former form only, having four arms, Oh Thousand Armed! Oh Universal Form!"

Bhagawan (Krishna) said,

My Supreme Form was shown to you by my Yoga power, full of splendor, All Embracing, Limitless, Primeval, Infinite. This Universal Form has never been seen by anyone other than yourself.

Neither by the study of Vedas, nor by Yagnas (Sacrifices), nor by gifts, nor by rituals, nor by severe austerities (Penances), can I be seen in this form in the world of men by anyone other than you.

Do not be afraid or bewildered on seeing me in such a terrible form; with your fear dispelled and with gladdened heart, now behold again this form of mine.

After speaking to Arjuna, Krishna again showed his own form and he consoled Arjuna who was terrified.

Arjuna said,

Having seen now your gentle human form, I am now composed and restored to my own nature.

Krishna said,

It is very hard to see this form of mine, which you have seen. Even the gods are longing for ever to see me in this form. Neither by Vedas nor by austerities nor by gifts nor by sacrifices can I be seen in this form as you have seen me.

But, by single-minded devotion, can I, of this form, be known and seen in reality, and also entered into. Oh Arjuna! Do all for me. Look upon me as the Supreme. Be devoted to me. Be free from attachments. Do not bear enmity towards anyone. A devotee full of devotion to me, surrendering to me reaches me. I accept that purified devotee.

18.12. Chapter Twelve

Arjuna said,

There are devotees, who with concentrated devotion worship you; there are others who worship the Imperishable, Unmanifest. Of these, who realise Yoga better?

Krishna said,

Those who divert their minds on me, with great belief, and with concentration, worship me, they are best in Yoga.

Others, who have strict control on senses, always with equanimity are keen for the welfare of all the living beings, worship as their own self the unthinkable, the unmanifest and the changeless, they also reach me really.

For those who are set on the Unmanifest, the strain is greater because the goal, the Unmanifest is very hard for one to reach.

But, who by dedicating all actions to me, regarding me as the Supreme, meditating on me with undiverted devotion, worship me, I become before long the Savior, to those whose minds are thus pivoted on me by pulling them out of the ocean of finite experiences, Samsara.

Fix your mind on me only. Place your intellect in me. Then, you shall live in me alone, without doubt.

If you are unable to fix your mind steadily on me, then by Yoga of Constant Practice (Abyasa Yoga), seek to reach me.

If you are unable to practice Abyasa Yoga, you be intent on performing actions for my sake. By so carrying out actions for my sake, you shall attain perfection.

Intellect is superior to Abyasa. Meditation is superior to Intellect. To remain unattached towards the fruits of actions is superior to meditation. Renunciation is the beginning of peace.

One, who shows no hostility against any being, is friendly to all, is merciful, has given up ego, is never arrogant, treats happiness as well as sorrow as equal, is tolerant, remains satisfied fully always, possesses a subdued nature, has firm conviction, places as Yogi his mind and Bhuddi on me, is dear to me.

He, about whom the world is not annoyed, who is not annoyed with the world, who is free from joy or avarice or fear or anxiety, is dear to me.

He, who is free from wants, is pure, alert, unconcerned, untroubled, renouncing all sense of ownership, is dear to me.

He, who never rejoices nor hates nor grieves nor desires and who forsakes good and evil actions, and is full of devotion to me, is dear to me.

He, who remains impartial towards friend or foe, is unconcerned whether honour or dishonor, unperturbed whether heat or cold or in pleasure or pain, who is free from attachment, to whom censure or praise is equal, who is silent, content with anything, not caring being homeless, steady minded, full of devotion to me, is dear to me.

They who follow this immortal Dharma, thus devoted to me, endowed with faith, regarding me as their Supreme Goal, such devotees are extremely dear to me.

18.13. Chapter Thirteen

Krishna said,

This body is called Kshetra. He, who knows it, is called Kshetrajna.

You know me as the Kshetrajna in all Kshetras. Kshetra and Kshetrajna are two different. One has to realise this by Gnana (Knowledge). Kshetra has relationship with the mind. Kshetrajna is associated with me. This has to be understood through Gnanam (Knowledge).

I shall tell you in detail. What is Kshetra? What is its nature? What are the changes taking place in it? What is it from? Who is it? What are his great attributes?

Moola Prakruthi (Nature's Origin) is the mother of all. The five elements (Land, Water, Fire, Air and Ether), the Ego, The Intellect, The Unmanifest (Primordial Matter), the ten organs of perception and action, the Mind, and the five objects of sense (Sound, Touch, Colour, Taste and Smell),

Also, desire, avarice, aversion, pleasure, pain, the physical body, consciousness, firmness: this is Kshetra with its evolutes, stating briefly.

Humility, unpretentiousness, non-violence, forgiveness, service to the teacher, purity, steadfastness, self-control, indifference to the objects of senses and also absence of egoism, perception of the evils, death, old age, sickness and pain, non-attachment, non- identification of self with son, wife, home and the rest, and constant even-mindedness on the attainment of desirable and the undesirable, unswerving devotion to Me by Yoga of non-separation resorting to solitary places, distaste for the society of men, constancy in self-knowledge, perception of the end of true knowledge, this is declared to be Knowledge, and what is opposed to is ignorance

I shall pronounce that which is to be known, knowing which one attains Immortality. That Supreme Brahman who has no beginning is neither called Sat (being), nor ASAT (non-being).

He exists in the world, enveloping all, with hands, and feet everywhere, with eyes, heads and mouths everywhere, with ears everywhere, shining by the activities of all senses, yet without the senses; unattached, yet supporting it; devoid of qualities, yet their experiences, within and without all beings, the unmoving as also the moving; because of subtle nature, it is both near and yet far away.

(Far and Near are of three types. Place, Time and Matter are three. Para Brahmam is stated to be far yet very near. Past, Present, Future are three segments of Time. Para Brahmam exists in all these three. Matters have three phases; Birth, Growth and Death. Para Brahmam is associated with all these three. He was there before birth; He is with growth; He is there after death. Creation, Preservation and Destruction are done by Para Brahmam).

Undivided, yet He exists as if divided in beings. That is to be known as the Supporter of Beings; He devours and He generates.

Para Brahmam is the light of lights; it is beyond darkness; it is knowledge; the concept of knowledge, seated in the hearts of all, to be reached by knowledge.

Thus Kshetra, Knowledge, and the Knowable have been stated. Knowing this, My devotee enters into My Being. He has a sense of consciousness that he has become one with Me.

You now know that Matter (Prakrithi) and Spirit (Purusha) are both without beginning; and you also know that all the modifications (Vikaras) and qualities (Gunas) are born of Prakrithi.

In the production of the effect and cause, Prakrithi is the cause; in the experience of pleasure and pain, Purusha is the cause.

Purusha seated in Prakrithi experiences the qualities born of Prakrithi; attachment to the qualities is the cause of his birth in good and evil wombs.

The Supreme Purusha in this body is called the Spectator (Who sees), the Permitter (Who permits), The Supporter (Who supports), The Enjoyer (Who enjoys), the Great Lord (Easwara) and the Supreme Self (Paramathma).

He, who knows the Purusha together with the qualities, in whatever condition he may be, he is not born again.

Some, by meditation, behold the Self in the Self by the Self; others by Saankya Yoga (Yoga of Knowledge), and some others by Karma Yoga.

Others also, not knowing this, worship having heard of it from some others; they too cross beyond death, if they would regard what they have heard as their Supreme Refuge.

Whenever any being is born, the non-moving or the moving, you know, Oh Arjuna, that is from the union between the Kshetra and Kshetrajna.

He, who sees the Supreme Lord (Paramathma) existing equally in all beings, sees the unperishing within the perishing.

He, who sees the same Lord everywhere, equally dwelling, destroys not the Self by the Self (Birth and Death do not occur to him); therefore he goes to the Highest Goal. (Parama Gathi).

He, who sees that all actions are performed by Prakrithi alone and that the Self is actionless, he alone verily sees.

When he sees the whole variety of beings, as resting to the One, and spreading forth from That (One), he then becomes Brahmam.

(There are thus two important aspects to be known. One is to know about the association with Paramathma. The other is to know about the dissociation with Prakrithi. Paramathma observes equanimity in this world, full of ups and downs. Though matters may perish, He is not perishable. He possesses the most supreme power; one who realises this is a Gnani. Gnani realises that he carries within himself the power of Paramathma. Because of his union with Paramathma who provides everything, he does not identify himself with the body which is perishable. Gnani's body may perish. But, he will not recognize that he has perished. He identifies himself with Paramathma.)

Being without beginning, and being devoid of qualities, the Supreme Self, the Imperishable, though dwelling in the body, neither acts nor is tainted.

As the all - pervading ether is not tainted because of its subtlety, so too the Self, seated everywhere in the body, is not tainted.

Just as one Sun illumines the whole world, so also the Paramathma illumines the whole Kshetra. But, He never makes Himself as part of him. He offers brightness.

They, who, with their eyes of wisdom come to know of the distinction between Kshetra and Kshetrajna, and of the liberation from Prakrithi of the being, go to the Supreme (Param).

(All actions emanate from Prakrithi. This is the truth. If this truth is realised, one will be conscious that he is not the cause of any action. Once that consciousness is acquired, that all the individual characteristics of beings and their body, form and acts are all generated by Prakrithi, he reaches Brahmam at that stage. His association with Prakrithi will cease.)

Paramathma, the prime source of all, is without beginning. He is without origin. He is unperishable. He is free from attachments. Though he is the occupant of the body, he is not bound by its actions. The doer and enjoyer is not Paramathma.)

18.14. Chapter Fourteen

Krishna said,

I shall again declare to you that Supreme Knowledge, the best of all knowledges, knowing which all the sages have attained Siddi (Supreme Perfection) after this life.

Taking refuge in this knowledge, they have attained to My Being and are neither born at the time of creation nor are they disturbed at the time of dissolution.

My womb is the great Brahmam (Moola Brahmam). I place my germ in that from which all beings are born.

For all forms, whichever are produced in all wombs, the Great Brahmam (Moola Prakrithi) is their womb. I am the Father giving the seed.

Satwam, Rajas and Tamas are the three qualities (Gunas) born of Prakrithi and they bind the Indestructible Embodied one fast in the body.

Satwa Guna is immaculate; it is illuminating, flawless. It binds through attachment to happiness and knowledge.

Quality of Rajas, which is of the nature of passion, is born of desire and attachment. It binds fast the embodied one by attachment to action.

Quality of Tamas is born of ignorance, deluding all embodied beings; it binds fast by heedlessness, indolence and sleep.

Satwam attaches to happiness, Rajas to actions while Tamas clouds knowledge, attaches to heedlessness.

Satwam rises, suppressing Rajas and Tamas; Rajas suppressing Satwam and Tamas; Tamas suppressing Satwam and Rajas.

When, through every opening in this body the light of intelligence shines, that means Satwa is dominant.

When Rajas dominates, greed, activity, involvement in actions, restlessness and longing arises.

Darkness, inertness, heedlessness and delusion arise when Tamas is predominant.

The embodied one, when meeting with death in Satwa, with quality predominant, he reaches the spotless higher worlds.

One meeting with death of Rajas quality is born among those attached in action.

Dying in Tamas, he is born in the midst of the senseless (Such as animals, birds etc).

In the same way, the quality of a man tends to shape him and charts his course; his activities are also based on them.

For Satwic, the fruit of good action, accrues, which is pure; Rajas leads to pain and Tamas to ignorance.

Knowledge and wisdom arise from Satwa, greed and avarice from Rajas and heedlessness, delusion, ignorance, bad habits and shortcomings arise from Tamas.

Satwic people go upwards (Holy Heaven), Rajasic dwell in the middle (reborn as men) and Tamasic, abiding in the lowest Guna go downwards (Hell, full of misery).

When embodied one reaches the stage higher than the three Gunas, he attains My Being, liberated from birth, death, old age and miseries and becomes immortal.

Arjuna asked,

What are the marks of identity of one, who has crossed these Gunas? What is his conduct? How does he cross these three Gunas?

Krishna said,

Satwa Guna is illuminative; Rajas Guna propels one for action; Tamas Guna leads one to desire and delusion. The person with bliss crosses all these Gunas. He never gets perturbed and remains unswerving.

One, who is seated like one unconcerned, is not moved by the Gunas, who knowing that the Gunas operate, is still self-centered and does not swerve.

Light, activity and delusion when present in him, he does not hate nor longs for them when absent,

Alike in pleasure and pain, who dwells in the Self, to whom a clod of earth, a precious stone and gold are alike, to whom the dear and the not-dear are the same; firm, the same in censure and self-praise, the same in honour and dishonor, the same to friend and foe, absorbing all undertakings, he is said to have crossed beyond the three Gunas.

And he, serving Me with unswerving devotion and crossing beyond the Gunas is fit to become Brahman. I am that Brahmam.

18.15. Chapter Fifteen

Wise people speak of the indestructible Aswaththa tree. It has roots above, branches below. Its leaves are Vedas. One knowing it alone is a knower of Vedas.

Its branches are spread below and above. It is nourished by Gunas. Sense objects are its buds; below in the world of men, the roots are stretched forth, originating in action.

Its form is not perceived here as such, neither its end nor its origin nor its foundation nor its resting place. Having cut this firm-rooted Aswaththa tree with the strong axe of non-attachment,

That God should be sought after, where having gone, none returns again. Refuge is to be sought in that primeval Purusha from which all activities stream forth from time immemorial.

Free from pride and delusion, victorious over the evil of attachment, dwelling constantly in the Self, their desires having completely vanished, freed from the pairs of opposites such as pleasure and pain, the undeluded reach that Eternal God (Parama Avyayam).

Sun does not shine there, nor Moon nor fire. To which one having gone does not return, That is My Supreme Abode.

An eternal portion of Myself (My Amsam) has become living souls in the world of life, abiding in Prakrithi, draws to itself the five senses, with Mind for the sixth.

When the Lord obtains a body, and when He leaves it, He takes these and goes with them as the wind takes the scents from the flowers.

It is while dwelling in the senses of hearing (Ear), sight (Eye), touch, taste, and smell, as well as in the Mind, He enjoys the objects of senses.

The ignorant does not see Him departing from, or dwelling in the body or enjoying the objects of senses, even when it is connected with the three Gunas. Only those endowed with the eyes of wisdom are able to realise it.

The seekers (Yogis) striving from Perfection behold Him dwelling in the Self; but the unrefined and the unintelligent, even though striving do not see Him.

Know that the Light which is residing in Sun and which illumines the whole world, that which is in Moon and fire, it is Me. It is I who spreads that Great Light.

Permeating the Earth, I support all beings, by My energy. Becoming the 'juicy' Moon, I nourish all herbs.

Becoming Vaishraanara, I abide in the body of beings, and associated with Prana and Apana digest the four- fold food. (Biting, Swallowing, Tasting and Sucking).

I am the heart seated in the hearts of all; from Me are Memory, Knowledge as well as their absence. I am that which has to be known in all the Vedas. I am the author of Vedantha, and I am the knower of Vedas.

There are two Purushas in the world, the Perishable (Kshara) and Imperishable (Akshara). All beings are perishable; the embodied soul (Koothasthah) is called Imperishable.

Supreme Paramathma, the Highest Self, The indestructible Lord is distinct, pervading the three worlds, sustaining them.

As I transcend the perishable and as I am even higher than the imperishable, I am called as Purushothama (The Noblest Purusha) in the world and in the Vedas.

He, who undeluded, thus knows Me, the Supreme Purusha (Purushothama), he, all knowing, worships Me, with his whole being.

Arjuna! Thus the most secret teaching (Saastra) has been imparted by me. On knowing this, one becomes wise and all his duties are accomplished.

18.16. Chapter Sixteen

Fearlessness, Purity of Mind, Remaining focused on Yoga of Gnanam (Knowledge), Generosity, Modesty, Good Deeds, Study of Sastras, Penance, Integrity, Non-violence, Truth, Not prone to anger, Renunciation, Peace, Avoidance of back-biting, Mercy towards living beings, Free from ambition, Softness, Bashfulness, Non-vacillation, Brightness, Patience, Completeness, Cleanliness, Not being deceitful, non-arrogant, these good qualities adorn one who is born out of divine grace.

Vanity, Pride, Self-indulgence, Anger, absence of wisdom are the bad qualities associated with one born in demoniac influence.

Divine attributes facilitate the removal of bonds of birth and demoniac characteristics lead towards entanglements in the mode of living and to bind one in the circle of birth and death. Arjuna! You are born by the divine grace.

In this world, there are two categories of men one due to the divine grace and the other demoniac. The divine tendencies of a man have already been dealt with. You now listen to me about the demoniac tendencies.

Those with demoniac tendencies are ignorant of Dharma (Righteousness) and Adharma (Unrighteousness). Purity, Discipline and Truth are absent in them.

'This world is not real. It has no origin and no support. There is no God. The world has come into being due to the sexual union between one with another.'

They propagate this theory and disgraceful souls turn into cruel enemies of society destroying the world.

They submit themselves to unfulfilled ambitions, acquiring the bad qualities of vanity, pride and arrogance, because of their evil activities. (Such as worshipping small deities in burial grounds, consuming intoxicants, indulging in prostitution etc.)

They are sure to end in pitiable death and they seek immeasurable worries and distress, and for them sensual lust is supreme.

Binding themselves with hundred ropes of ambition and seeking refuge in sensual lust and anger, they are hunting for treasures for the sake of sensual pleasure.

Their assertions are,

'All these have been acquired by me now. I shall fulfill this ambition of mine now. I have this in my home. Very soon, all wealth will be mine.

This enemy was killed by me. I shall, hereafter, kill all others too. I believe only in getting. I am an enjoyer. I have acquired all. I am strong. I am full of happiness.

I possess wealth and I belong to a high race. Is there one comparable to me? I shall perform Yaga. I shall be charitable. I shall enjoy.'

With such boasts, there are persons with demoniac qualities, who are deluded because of their ignorance.

Getting deluded by many such thoughts and intentions, they are blinded by ignoble pursuits and get immersed in sensual pleasures and ultimately even enter into the loathsome hell.

Thus involved in self-acclaim, full of vanity, showing arrogance because of wealth and out of hypocrisy they carry out Yagas just for name's sake, not in accordance with the prescribed procedures, but for the sake of false propaganda.

They possess egoism, brute force, arrogance, lust and anger. They despise Me, dwelling in their own bodies as in those of others.

I cast again and again into demoniacal wombs in this world those haters, sinners, cruel and vilest among men.

Not reaching Me, these stupid men are born life after life in demoniac wombs and then sink down to still lower plane.

Desire, anger and greed, these triple gates of hell, cause the downfall of the soul. One should, therefore throw away all these three.

Freed from those three gates of hell, man works for his own salvation and thereby attains the supreme goal, God.

Discarding the prescriptions of the scriptures, he, who acts to the contrary way, submitting to his own sweet will, such a person neither attains perfection (Siddi) nor the supreme goal nor even happiness. There is no scope at all for attaining the supreme goal.

Therefore, the scripture alone is your guide in determining what should be done and what should not be done. Knowing this, you ought to perform any such action as is ordained by the scriptures. You should reject what is rejected by the scriptures and what is not approved in them.

18.17. Chapter Seventeen

Arjuna said,

Men, without knowing the prescriptions contained in the scriptures, but with devotion and faith, worship you. What is their status, Satwam or Rajas or Tamas?

Krishna said,

That faith appearing in a man's nature is of three types. They are Satwa, Rajas and Tamas.

The faith shown by a man depends on his basic nature. Satwic men worship gods, Rajasic men worship Yakshas and Rakshasas and Tamasic men worship the spirits of the dead and ghosts.

Those men who practice terrible austerities, not prescribed in the scriptures, given to hypocrisy and egoism, impelled by the force of lust and attachment,

Senselessly torturing all the elements in the body and Me also, who dwells within the body, you may know these to be of demoniac nature.

The food which is dear to one, as also Yagnas (Sacrifice), Penance and Charity are of three categories.

The foods which augment life span, purity, strength, health, joy, appetite, which are tasty and made of ghee, which is substantial and agreeable are dear to Satwic.

The foods which are bitter, sour, saline, excessively hot, pungent, dry and burning are liked by Rajasic. They are productive of pain, grief and disease.

That which is stale, tasteless, putrid and rotten, refuse and impure, is the food liked by Tamasic.

That Yagna (Sacrifice) which is performed by men without the desire for fruit and as prescribed by ordinance, with a firm faith that Yagna is a duty is Satwic.

That Yagna (Sacrifice) which is performed by men seeking fruit and for ostentation is a Rajasic Yagna.

That Yagna (Sacrifice) which is performed contrary to the ordinances, in which no food is distributed, and which is devoid of hymns (Mantras) and gifts, and which is devoid of faith is Tamasic.

Worship of the gods, Brahmins (Twice Born), the teacher (Guru) and the learned (Praajna), with purity, straight-forwardness, celibacy (Brahmacharyam) and non-injury (Ahimsa) are called the austerity of the body. (Sarira Tapas).

Speech which causes no controversies, and is truthful, pleasant and beneficial, and the practice of the study of Vedas, those constitute austerity of speech (Vaangmayam Tapas).

Serenity of Mind, noble–heartedness, silence, self-control, purity of nature, these together are called mental austerity (Manasa Tapas).

This three-fold austerity practiced by steadfast men with the utmost faith, desiring no fruit is Satwic.

The austerity which is practiced with the object of gaining good reception, honour and worship and with hypocrisy is Rajasic. It is unstable and transitory.

The austerity which is practiced with self-torture, out of some foolish action, for the purpose of destroying another is Tamasic.

That act of charity (Dhaanam) which is done, knowing it to be a duty, in a fit time and place, to a worthy person, from whom nothing is expected in return, is Satwic.

That gift which is given with a view to receiving in return or looking for fruit again or reluctantly, is Rajasic.

That gift which is given at a wrong place and time, to unworthy person, without respect or with insult, is Tamasic.

OM, TAT, SAT have been declared to be the triple destination of Brahmam. By that were created formerly the Brahmanas, Vedas and Yagnas.

Therefore, with the utterance of OM are begun the acts of Yagna (Sacrifice), Dhaanam (Gifts) and Tapas (Austerity), and the various acts of gift performed by the seekers of liberation.

The word SAT is used in the sense of Reality and of Goodness; and also, the word SAT is used in the sense of an auspicious act (Mangalakaram).

Steadfastness in sacrifice, austerity and gift is also called SAT and also, action in connection with these, for the sake of the Supreme is called SAT.

Whatever is sacrificed, given or performed and whatever austerity is practiced without faith, it is called A-SAT; it is not for here (as one lives now) or hereafter (Death).

18.18. Chapter Eighteen

Arjuna said,

Krishna! Sanyaasam (Renunciation) and Sacrifice (Abandonment)—I want to know their truth.

Krishna said,

Sages understand Sanyaasam to be the renunciation of works with desire. The wise declare that the abandonment of the fruits of all actions as Tyaga.

Some learned men say that all actions should be abandoned as evil; some others say that acts of sacrifice (Yagna), gift (Dhaanam) and austerity (Penance) should not be given up.

You hear from me the truth about Tyaga (Abandonment). Tyaga is of three kinds.

Yagnas (Acts of Sacrifice), Dhaanam (Charity) and Tapas (Austerity) should not be abandoned. They should be performed, because worship, charity and also austerity are the purifiers of even the noble.

But, these acts should be performed leaving aside attachment and the fruits. This is my certain and supreme belief.

Renunciation of obligatory actions is not proper; the abandonment of these due to delusion is Tamasic.

He, who due to fear of bodily trouble, abandons action because it is painful, is a Rajasic. By such Rajasic abandonment, he does not obtain the fruit of abandonment.

Whatever obligatory action is done, merely because it ought to be done, abandoning attachment and also fruit, that abandonment is Satwic.

He, who abandons, with purity, being intelligent, with all his doubts thrown away, does not hate a disagreeable action, nor is he attached to an agreeable action, is intelligent and is man of true renunciation.

It is not possible for an embodied being to abandon actions entirely, but he who relinquishes the fruits of actions is called a Thyagi (Relinquisher).

The three-fold fruit of action, evil, good and mix of both, accrues, after death, only to those who have no spirit of abandonment, never to total relinquishers.

Arjuna! Learn from me, these five causes for the accomplishment of all actions, as declared in the Saankya system, which is the end of all actions.

The seat (Body), the doer, (Ego), the various organs of perception, the different functions of various organs of action and also the presiding deity as the fifth,

These five are the causes for whatever action a man performs by his body, speech and mind, whether right or the reverse.

Such being the case, he who, owing to his untrained understanding, looks upon his Self alone, as the doer, that man of perverted intelligence does not view alright.

He who claims that it is self which performs all actions, is of perverted intelligence. He does not know the truth. He does not see alright.

He, who is free from the egoistic notion that 'I do everything', whose intelligence is not tainted, though he slays these people, he does not slay, nor is he bound by the action.

(He, who is not interested in the fruits of action, who never endeavours to enjoy the fruits of action, does not get entangled in their bond, whatever action he undertook).

Knowledge, the Known, and the Knower are of the three-fold impulse to action; the organs, the action, the agent form the three –fold basis of action.

Knowledge, action and actor are declared in the science of temperaments (Guna) to be of three kinds only, according to the differences of temperaments. Hear them also.

That by which one sees the one indestructible reality in all beings, undivided in the divided, know that knowledge as Satvic.

But, that knowledge which sees in all beings various entities of different kinds and are different from one another, know that knowledge as Rajasic.

But, that knowledge which clings to one single effect, as if it were the whole, without reason, without foundation in truth and narrow, that is declared to be Tamasic; that is to hold to the theory that the body, which is prone to birth and death, is alone the Atma (Soul).

An action which is performed free from attachment, done without love or hatred, with no desire for fruit, that action is Satvic.

That action which is done by one, longing for desire or gain, done with egoism, or with much effort, is Rajasic.

That action which is undertaken from delusion, with no regard for the consequence, loss, injury and ability is Tamasic.

A doer, free from attachment, non-egoist, endowed with firmness and enthusiasm, unaffected by success or failure is Satvic.

A doer who is passionate, desiring to gain the fruits of action, greedy, harmful, impure, full of delight and grief is Rajasic.

A doer who is unsteady, vulgar, unbending, cheating, malicious, lazy, despondent and procrastinating is Tamasic.

Arjuna! I shall tell you about the three-fold divisions of Understanding (Buddhi) and Fortitude (Druthi).

That which knows the paths of work (Pravurthi) and renunciation (Nivrurrthi), what ought to be done and what ought not to be done, fear and fearlessness, bondage and liberation, that 'Understanding' is Satvic.

That by which one wrongly understands Dharma and Adharma and also what ought to be done and what ought not to be done, that 'Understanding' is Rajasic.

That which enveloped in darkness, sees Adharma as Dharma and all things as perverted (Such as bad as good, evil as noble), that 'Understanding' is Tamasic.

The unswerving fortitude by which through Yoga, the functions of the mind, the Prana and the senses are restrained, that 'Fortitude' is Satvic.

That fortitude by which one holds to duty, pleasure and wealth, one of attachment and craving for the fruits of actions, that 'Fortitude' is Rajasic.

The constancy because of which a stupid man does not abandon sleep, fear, grief, depression and also arrogance, that 'Fortitude' is Tamasic.

Arjuna! Now hear from me, of the three fold pleasure in which one rejoices by practice and surely comes to the end of pain.

That which is like poison at first, but in the end like nectar, that 'Pleasure' is Satvic, born of purity of one's own mind, due to self-realization.

That 'Pleasure' which arises from the contact of the sense organs with the objects, which is at first like nectar but is in the end like poison, that is Rajasic.

That 'Pleasure', which at first and in the sequel deludes the Self, arising from sleep, indolence and heedlessness is Tamasic.

There is nothing on earth or again in heaven among the Devas (Heavenly Beings) who is totally liberated from the three qualities, born of Prakrithi (Matter).

For Brahmanas, Kshatriyas, Vaishyas and Sudras, the duties are distributed according to the qualities born of their own nature.

Serenity, self-restraint, austerity, purity, forgiveness and also uprightness, knowledge, realization, belief in God are the duties of Brahmanas, born of their own nature.

Prowess, splendor, firmness, dexterity and also not fleeing from battle, generosity, lordliness, these are the duties of Kshatriyas, born of their own nature.

Agriculture, cattle-rearing and trade are the duties of the Vaishyas, born of their own nature.

Service is the duty of Sudras born of their own nature.

Devoted each to his own duty, man attains Perfection (Siddi)

A man attains Perfection (Siddi) by worshipping with his own duty Him, from Whom beings arise and by Whom all this is pervaded.

A man should carry out the duties which are his because of his birth and by nature for him to attain Perfection. Worlds and living beings have sprung from Paramathma. Paramathma is pervading in them all. By carrying out one's own duties, as expected of him, he worships Paramathma in that way. He attains Perfection. He reaches Paramathma.

One's own duty is better, though it may be devoid of merits, than the duty of another well performed. He, who does his duty ordained by his own nature, does not incur sin.

One should not abandon the duty to which one is born, though faulty; because all undertakings are enveloped by evil as fire is by smoke.

He, whose intellect is unattached everywhere, who has subdued the self, from whom desire has fled, he, through renunciation, attains the Supreme State of Freedom from action.

You learn from Me that Supreme Knowledge of one, who has attained perfection, reaches Brahmam.

Endowed with a pure intellect, controlling the self by firmness, relinquishing sound and other objects, and abandoning attraction and hatred, dwelling in solitude, eating just little, speech, body and mind subdued, always engaged in meditation and concentration taking refuge in dispassion, having abandoned egoism, power, arrogance, desire, anger and aggrandizement and freed from the notion of mine and therefore peaceful, he is fit to become Brahmam.

Becoming Brahmam, serene in the Self, he neither grieves nor desires for anything; as he is the same to all beings, he obtains a supreme devotion towards Me.

By devotion, he knows Me in Essence, what and who I am. Then having known Me in My Essence, he forthwith enters into the Supreme.

Doing all actions, always taking refuge in Me, by My grace, he obtains the Eternal, Indestructible State (Saaswatham Padam Avyayam) or Abode.

Mentally renouncing all actions in Me, having Me as the Highest Goal, resorting to the Yoga of discrimination, always fix your mind in Me.

Fixing your mind upon Me, you shall, by My grace, overcome all obstacles, but, if, from egoism, you will not hear me, you shall perish.

Filled with egoism, if you think, 'I will not fight', your resolve is vain, because nature will compel you to fight.

Arjuna! If through delusion you do not wish to do anything (fight), even that you shall do perforce, bound by your Karma, born of your nature.

The Lord (Eswara) dwells in the hearts of all beings, causing all beings, by His power of illusion, to revolve as if mounted on a machine.

Arjuna! Rush to Him for refuge with all your being; by His grace you shall obtain Supreme Peace (Param Shanthi) and Eternal Abode (Saaswatham).

Thus, the Wisdom which is a greater secret than all secrets has been declared to you by Me; having reflected upon it fully, you now act as you choose.

Hear again My supreme word, most secret of all; because you are My dear beloved. Therefore, I will tell you what is good for you.

Fix your mind upon Me; be devoted to me; sacrifice for me; bow down to me. You shall come, surely then, to Me alone, I promise to you truly, because you are dear to me.

Completely abandoning all Dharmas take refuge in Me alone, I will liberate you from all sins; do not worry.

This is never to be spoken by you to one who is devoid of austerities or devotion nor to one who does not render service nor to one who does not desire to listen nor to one who criticizes me.

He, who, with supreme devotion to Me, will teach this Supreme Secret to My devotees, shall come to me without doubt.

There is none among men who does dearer service to Me, and there shall none on earth dearer to me than he.

And he who will study this secret dialogue of ours, by him I shall have been worshipped by the 'sacrifice of wisdom.' (Gnana Yagnam); such is my conviction.

That man also who hears this, full of faith and free from malice, he too liberated shall attain to the happy worlds of those righteous deeds.

Arjuna! Have you heard this with single-pointed mind? Has the distraction caused by your ignorance been dispelled?

Arjuna said,

My delusion is destroyed as I have now gained my memory through you. Oh Achyutha! I am firm. My doubts are gone. I shall do according to your word.

Conclusion:

"Wherever is Krishna, the Lord of Yoga, wherever is Arjuna, the archer, there are prosperity, victory, happiness and firm policy. This is my conviction."

18.19. Charamasloka

Sarva Dharmaan Prithyajya Maamekam Saranam Vraja

Aham Thvaam Sarva Papebyo Mokshyishyami Maa Sucha.

Krishna tells Arjuna these very significant words, "You completely abandon all Dharmas; Surrender to me alone; I shall liberate you from all sins; do not worry."

This verse is considered as the epitome of Srimad Bhagwad Gita.

This was imparted to Arjuna by Gitacharya Lord Krishna. Gita ends almost with this verse. The teaching is not meant for Arjuna alone. It is for the entire humanity.

Krishna's preaching is, "You surrender to me alone." He adds, "I shall liberate you from all sins. (You shall attain Moksha)".

In the eighteen chapters of Gita, Krishna has expatiated on the various paths, by adopting which Moksha is to be attained. But, in this particular verse, Krishna makes it clear that any such path would be redundant. 'You may not pursue them. There is yet another path. That is a very easy path. You adopt that easy path only. You surrender to me alone. I shall accept you. Do not worry.' This is Krishna's teaching.

Yes! It is necessary to surrender to Krishna, the Supreme Lord (Paramathma). It is important that the surrender should be to Him. It is equally important that the surrender should be to Him alone. 'Alone' makes all the difference.

Surrender has to take place, with total faith in Him. It can be accomplished just in a moment.

The principles to be followed which are absolutely essential, are

- To favour Him, before approaching Him.
- To avoid opposition to Him, that is not to show lack of faith before approaching Him.
- To hold faith that He will protect.
- To plead to Him seeking protection.
- To show humility that there is no other path available.

Krishna's teaching underlines the essential requirement of seeking absolute surrender. He also states that all Dharmas are to be given up completely.

To stand clarified on this statement, let the message be analysed further. In His earlier teachings, He has elaborated on the other paths for attaining Him and on the essential requirements (Dharmas) for resorting to those paths. (Karma Yoga, Gnana Yoga and so on). But, it is possible that those paths and Dharmas qualifying them are not conducive for quick results. They may even be strenuous for adoption. Gnanam (Knowledge) may also be required for the purpose. Krishna now says that they may all be abandoned completely. He utters, 'Thyajya', nay 'Parithyajya'. Thyajya means abandonment. Parithyajya means complete abandonment. Krishna thus stresses on the 'complete abandonment' factor, followed by the 'alone' factor of faith in Him. The implication of this message is, one should not say, 'I surrender to you. But, I shall seek other paths also'.

That approach will mean that there is no unswerving faith in Him alone, contradicting one of the essential principles mentioned above. Krishna would not accept that lackadaisical surrender, a wavering surrender, an unwilling surrender, an attempt for looking out for alternatives. Krishna would not accept such a qualifying surrender. That is the reason why Krishna wants not only the surrender of a devotee, but very importantly the surrender to Him alone.

Krishna's reference to 'abandoning all Dharmas' also needs to be analysed.

There are four categories of people. A Brahmin has to perform his daily rituals such as Sandya Vandanam. A Kshatriya may be called upon to fight in war. A Vaishya cannot abandon his basic duty of agriculture, cultivation, trading etc. and the fourth category cannot abandon service. Bhagawan does not ask for the abandonment of these basic inevitable duties. Krishna has called upon Arjuna to fight in the war.

Bhagawan's message is that the daily duties expected of one are to carried out. But, that should be free from attachment. These daily duties have no link to the principle of surrender. His teaching is that the other paths are not necessary.

The implication is that if one still entertains the desire to seek other paths, and if they are to prove unsuccessful, the path of 'surrender' will also be found to be infructuous due to lack of 'full faith' on it. That is the reason why Krishna lays emphasis on 'complete abandonment of all Dharmas.'

Let us again take up for analyzing the words, 'Me Alone.' That is to say that surrender to Bhagawan alone is the path. The aim is to attain Bhagawan. Here Krishna touches upon the dual aspect of 'Krishna is the path' and 'Attainment of Krishna is the fruit.' The path is 'He' and the fruit is 'He'. He is thus the combination of both. Bhagawan grants the fruit easily, what Dharmas confer belatedly and after very strenuous efforts.

Let us now look into the significance of the word 'I'. He says, "I shall liberate you from all sins." His clear and categorical message is, "I alone have the power to liberate you from all the sins."

The scripture says, "Sriman Narayanan is the ultimate refuge for granting liberation." ('Mukthanam Paramaa Gathi').

The implied message is, 'You might have committed guilts. You might have incurred sins. I shall protect you. No one else has the power to protect you thus.'

Now, let us take up the word, 'You'

What sort of 'you'? "It is you who have abandoned completely all other paths. It is you who have surrendered to Me Alone." He stresses that there should be no other exploration of other means for obtaining the 'fruits.'

Now, coming to the words, "All Sins", the implication is that one, surrendering to Him might have incurred many sins, before the surrender. Bhagawan liberates him from all such prior sins. How about the sins which he may incur after the surrender? Sins may be incurred due to ignorance. Sins may be with his explicit knowledge also. Bhagawan absolves him of the sins incurred due to ignorance. There is a strong possibility that one surrendering to him will not commit sins after surrender. If unfortunately he incurs sins, Bhagawan will bless him to realise his mistakes, seek atonement and surrender again. Bhagawan will let him off awarding milder punishment and thus liberate him from all such sins too.

Krishna concludes by saying, "Do not worry." These are his words of consolation. That is to mean that one should cease to worry once he has sought Krishna's mercy. There should be no vacillation on that faith. The implied message contained in Krishna's words is, "If you are left unprotected once you surrender to me, the guilt is mine."

SRIMAN NARAYANA IS ALWAYS FREE FROM GUILT.

Bhagawan tells, in essence, to the mankind,

"You have limited wisdom. You possess limited power. Your life span is limited. You may not be in a position to bear the burden of righteous pursuits (Dharma based actions). You need not have to resort to those paths, which are not familiar or known to you, which are incapable of being carried out by you, and which are likely to yield the fruits belatedly. I am available. I am easily accessible. I am protecting all the worlds. I have the capacity to protect you. By choosing to have Me alone as your path, you surrender to Me. You are dear to Me. I am merciful. I am independent. When you seek to attain Me because of your resolve, I shall remove all the impediments preventing you and offer to you all privileges in equal measure as they are available to

Me, at all times and at all places, and give opportunities for you to be at My service and you will experience the full Brahmanandam (Heavenly Blisss) in Moksha. Do not worry.